The Heart of Achilles

The Heart of Achilles

Characterization and
Personal Ethics in the *Iliad*

Graham Zanker

Ann Arbor

THE UNIVERSITY OF MICHIGAN PRESS

First paperback edition 1996
Copyright © by the University of Michigan 1994
All rights reserved
Published in the United States of America by
The University of Michigan Press
Manufactured in the United States of America
⊛ Printed on acid-free paper

1997   1996   4   3   2   1

A CIP catalogue record for this book is available from the British Library.

Library of Congress Cataloging-in-Publication Data

Zanker, G. (Graham), 1947–
   The heart of Achilles : characterization and personal ethics in the
Iliad / Graham Zanker.
       p.   cm.
   ISBN 0-472-10514-0 (alk. paper)
   1. Homer. Iliad. 2. Homer—Characters—Achilles. 3. Achilles
(Greek mythology) in literature. 4. Characters and characteristics
in literature. 5. Ethics, Greek, in literature. 6. Trojan War in
literature.   I. Title.
PA4037.Z185   1994
883'.01—dc20
                                                            93-43677
                                                                 CIP

ISBN 0-472-08400-3 (pbk : alk. paper)

For my parents

Acknowledgments

This book is in certain important ways a by-product of my teaching of the *Iliad* in translation to senior undergraduates. Their alertness and gratifying desire to understand what they perceive to be an outstanding poem have imposed on me the agreeably challenging task of addressing questions that seem to interest them especially. In particular, how can we hope to judge the words and deeds of the heroes of the *Iliad* without forming a coherent picture of the ethical thought-world presented by the poem? How, in turn, can we presume to appreciate character and characterization on the *Iliad*'s own terms? How, if at all, does the text manipulate our responses to its characters? Are our responses utterly different from what we can glean of those of the *Iliad*'s original audiences? Is there continuity, or does the epic somehow present us with both continuity and discontinuity? It has been a pleasure to delve into these Homeric questions (among others) with such engaged and inquiring classes.

I have benefited from discussion of my ideas by participants at seminars delivered at Tübingen, Cambridge, and Stanford. I have enjoyed convivial and instructive informal discussions of the project with Katherine Adshead, James Altham, Charles Brink, Simon Goldhill, Richard Kannicht, Arnd Kerkhecker, David Konstan, M.M. Mackenzie, David Midgley, Peter Parsons, Michael Reeve, Malcolm Schofield, Michael Silk, Oliver Taplin, Peter Toohey, and Martin West. I gratefully acknowledge debts of an even greater magnitude to Rick Benitez, John Casey, Paul Crittenden, Pat Easterling, Mark Edwards, Neil Hopkinson, Harold Tarrant, and John Vallance, who, at exceptionally busy times even for them, generously took the time to read earlier drafts of the whole book, challenging it on all fronts, from methodology to argument and specific detail. The University of Michigan Press' anonymous readers have constructively stimulated me to yet further reconsideration of several important issues. The kind friends whose names appear on this long support list cannot be blamed, either individually or collectively, for my own waywardness or for any consequent blemishes that remain.

The University of Canterbury has supported me generously by giving me a nine-month leave in 1991 and several research grants. The Deutscher Akademischer Austauschdienst enabled a two-month stay at Tübingen in 1989, at a crucial stage in the direction that the book was to take. My Cambridge College, Gonville and Caius, provided me with ideal conditions in which to complete the bulk of the manuscript, during a most congenial and productive five-month stay in Cambridge in 1991. I happily record here my thanks to all these institutions.

My wife, Ruth, with a full-time tertiary teaching and research position of her own, has once again lovingly supported my work on a book in many practical ways, not least by means of her unerring nose for self-indulgence. My sons, Thomas and Hugo, have consistently contrived to bring me back down to earth, reminding me that on the whole, it, too, is quite a nice place to be. And my parents, to whom this book is dedicated, have fostered their grateful son's progress in Classics from the moment they presented him, in his eleventh year, with reputable translations of the *Iliad* and the *Odyssey*.

Contents

1

Motives for Cooperation in the *Iliad*

Beginn
immer von neuem die nie zu erreichende Preisung;
denk: es erhält sich der Held, selbst der Untergang war ihm
nur ein Vorwand zu sein: seine letzte Geburt.
—R.M. Rilke, *Duineser Elegien*

A Question of Values

This book sets out to examine why the heroes of the *Iliad* cooperate with one another and to analyze the nature and range of their cooperation, seeking especially for moments when the heroes go beyond formal or conventionalized cooperation, to conduct that is more spontaneously generous. We cannot fully understand the way the epic characterizes its people in general and Achilles in particular, a second preoccupation of this study, unless we have a cogent picture, on the one hand, of the value-system by which they are presented as living—what is admired in human conduct and what is deplored—and, on the other, of the multiplicity of motives that prompt behavior. This entails a definition of the dominant value-system in the *Iliad*, in particular where it impinges on the issue of cooperation, and of the motivations guiding the heroes' responses to it. We must be especially careful here to distinguish the ethical standards displayed by the characters and those held by the narrator: he may construct his characters to convey a background ethical scenario against which he may oppose his own. This, I argue, is precisely the strategy employed in the *Iliad*. To take some uncontroversial examples: the narrator has an obvious liking for Menelaos and Patroklos, and he shows a distaste for killing in battle in his "obituaries" which contrasts with his picture of the triumphant vaunting of the killers themselves. In this chapter, I am principally concerned with eliciting the ethical values by which the epic's characters are presented as living.

Defining these values here really means redefining them, because although the older models have much to teach us still, they are, I suggest, either insufficiently comprehensive or require modification, particularly because they fail to account for the full range of the motivations and emotions that the text shows as operative. Even the word *cooperation*, in its specific application to the *Iliad*, demands definition. A.W.H. Adkins gave it currency in the study of Greek values, putting it in an antithetical relationship with *competition*.[1] But the dichotomy is not necessarily a true one, because it is easy to find moments in the *Iliad* where warriors vie with one another in battle to achieve the common goal of victory.[2] I take cooperation to mean, within the context of the *Iliad*, behavior that will forward a joint endeavor, but also behavior adopted to further the welfare of another, especially in friendship. Furthermore, I take it that the specifically Iliadic motives for cooperation are predominantly materialistic, whereby one party cooperates out of a desire for gifts, for example; individualistic, whereby the aim is often honor or the avoidance of shame (frequently gifts are at stake here, too); justice-based, whereby a hero may feel constrained by a sense of fair play, however defined; or affective, in which case an emotion like pity feeds into and conditions a degree of altruism, though we shall find that the *Iliad* does not make the hard-and-fast distinction between the emotion of pity and the moral quality that modern thinking standardly draws. I submit that all four of these promptings can be identified as heroic and commendable.[3] Just how they hang together will, I hope, be explained in the course of this study. If, then, such motivations and emotions are observably at work, a model of Iliadic values must be found that will accommodate them.

The model proposed by Adkins, which analyzes the *Iliad*'s value-

---

1. Adkins 1960b, 6f.

2. It is interesting, moreover, that at *Protagoras* 348c Plato makes Sokrates acknowledge Diomedes' words to Nestor at *Il.* 10.224–26 as the forerunner of his dialectic method. Diomedes says that he is keen to enter the enemy's camp, but he requests a companion, because when two embark on a venture, one of the two notices before the other where an advantage lies. Thus Sokrates is presented as viewing the competitive element in dialectic as supportive. See Benitez 1992, 237.

3. For a general analysis of cooperation in the modern context, see Argyle 1991, 3–5, who does not, however, appear to find much room for the sense of fair play in cooperation.

system almost exclusively in terms of honor and the ability of the *agathos* to maintain his competitive preeminence, is very familiar.[4] Against it, critics like A.A. Long have argued that Adkins fails to take proper account of what Long sees as a morality based on appropriateness[5] (though Adkins could always reply that "appropriateness" is determined by appropriateness to social standing, or one's esteem in one's community). H. Lloyd-Jones, though agreeing that shame, with honor at the opposite end of the same stick, does "the main work of morality,"[6] argues that Adkins' approach pays insufficient attention to the justice that Lloyd-Jones sees Zeus dispensing, particularly in book 24, the evidence of which Adkins tends to ignore. C.J. Rowe and D.L. Cairns have argued persuasively that the heroic code includes disapproval of excessive self-assertion.[7]

Do the approaches adopted by Adkins and his critics do justice to the variety of motivations on the basis of which the gods and humans of the *Iliad* act and react? Most of Adkins' critics seem to agree that his approach has a lot going for it—this book is no exception. But if the behavior of the protagonists is construed mainly against a single standard of the competitive—the pursuit of honor—and if, given the results orientation of ethical thought in the *Iliad*, intentions are as negligible as Adkins implies, we may wonder where there is room for real conflict in the poem, and whether its narrative should not be more mechanical and predictable than it seems to be. For example, if the dispute between Achilles and Agamemnon in book 1 can be reduced to one over quotas of honor, what is there to stop the process? We may wonder what has happened to the sense of fairness to

---

4. See esp. Adkins 1960a, 1960b, 1963, 1971, 1987.

5. Long 1970.

6. Lloyd-Jones 1983, 15. On shame, see esp. von Erffa 1937, 4–43; Hooker 1987b (though see Zanker 1990, n.14 and below, p. 120, n. 13) and now Cairns 1993, 48–146 and Williams 1993, 75–102, 219–23.

7. Rowe (1983), supported and amplified by Cairns (1993, 5–14, 95–103), who locates the inhibitory impulse in "shame," *aidôs*. See further the reactions to Adkins by esp. Dover 1983, Gagarin 1987, Lloyd-Jones 1987a, Lloyd-Jones 1987b, Williams 1993, 4–6, 41, 64, 75f., 81, 100. Cairns (1993, 71–79) makes an important qualification to the model drawn by Adkins (1960b, 46–57) of the results-centeredness of Iliadic society, arguing, for example, that in *Il.* 6 Hektor reproves Paris not for bad results but because of the discrepancy between his own ability and motivation and others' expectation that he will take a full part in the fighting.

which Achilles and the venerable Nestor seem to give expression, or to the emotional relations between Agamemnon and Achilles, which Agamemnon makes clear have been smoldering for some time. And how well does Adkins' model cope with book 24, where Achilles seems to respond to Priam's supplication not only because of Priam's gifts, though these are a necessary part of the transaction, but because of what seems like a sense of fellow suffering and a feeling that it is right to return Hektor's corpse, and where Achilles is largely unconcerned with Priam's gifts and the fact that he cannot hope for the future benefits of reciprocity to which his new guest-friendship with Priam would in normal circumstances entitle him?

Adkins did not regard himself as examining one type of motive (the competitive) and ignoring others. He thought that he was offering an integrated study of the value-system (and, more broadly, of the thought-world) of the mode of human life presented in the Homeric poems. He also thought that the status-based concerns of what he characterized as a "shame-culture" or a "results-culture" inform Homeric thinking about what we see as "justice," "cooperation," and "friendship," and about the psychological models associated with this thinking. However, Adkins neglected to consider the Achilles of book 24, which effectively debarred him from presenting a comprehensive coverage of his chosen field.

Does the sense of justice that people like Lloyd-Jones see in the poem play the role that Lloyd-Jones believes? How can we reconcile the justice of Zeus in book 24 with the god who hung Hera from heaven with two anvils tied to her ankles, as an assertive response to her encroachment on his honor when she maltreated his favorite, Herakles (15.18–33)? Zeus often seems far more concerned with his honor than with the rights and wrongs of his relations with gods and men.

Let us try to open out the debate by considering a brief interaction in the poem that concerns the cooperative relationship that normally obtains between two brothers.

Menelaos' victory over Paris in the single combat narrated in book 3 of the *Iliad* is rendered inconclusive when Aphrodite spirits Paris away from the battlefield (3.380–82). In book 4 Hera insists that Zeus send Athene to find a way to get the Trojans to break the oaths of truce that they had sworn with the Achaians (4.64–67). After the notoriously hard bargaining in which Zeus trades off his beloved

Troy against Argos, Sparta, and Mykenai, Zeus ultimately yields to Hera's wishes. Athene, disguised as the Trojan Laodokos, persuades Pandaros to break the truce by shooting an arrow at Menelaos. The arrow strikes home, the blood runs down Menelaos' legs, and nobody knows that Athene has deflected the arrow's flight and that Menelaos' tunic has actually arrested it. What thoughts does the text present as running through Agamemnon's mind while he holds his brother's hand, convinced that he is going to die?

The brotherly sense of loss is certainly present in Agamemnon's speech (4.155–82). If Menelaos dies, Agamemnon says, it will cause him terrible grief (169). His emotional response is moreover tinged with self-recrimination, as we can see when he says that the treaty he struck with the Trojans has meant death for his brother (155). Merging with both reactions is the feeling that Menelaos has been the innocent victim of the Trojans' perfidy in breaking the treaty (157). Agamemnon is undeniably concerned here with justice. Later in the speech, there are further glimmerings of grief as the king pictures his brother's bones rotting in the earth (174) and a Trojan boasting that, among other things, Agamemnon left his own brother behind (181). But honor and shame are also major considerations. In the second half of his speech, Agamemnon is obsessed with the thought that he will forfeit his reputation as a warrior able to assert his wishes if Menelaos dies (171–82). His army will immediately want to return to Achaia (172), and on his arrival, he will be a target for shaming rebukes (171); he will have left Helen behind, with the result that she will be something for the Trojans to boast over (173); and Menelaos will lie rotting in Trojan territory, his mission unaccomplished (175). Agamemnon imagines what the Trojans will say as they dance on Menelaos' grave: they will express the gloating and insulting wish that Agamemnon's wrath will be directed with equal futility against everyone else—equal, that is, to the ineffectuality of his expedition (179), from which he will have had to return home with empty ships and without his brother (180f.). The king hopes that the earth will swallow him when people say such things about him (182). Finally, when he sends Talthybios to fetch a doctor, he remarks that whoever hit Menelaos with the arrow will have fame, and that the Achaians will have grief (197, repeated by Talthybios at 207). The logic of this formulation is that the anonymous archer will have fame and joy, and that the Achaians will have grief and the reverse of glory and fame, dishonor.

As the text presents it, Agamemnon's fraternal solidarity with Menelaos, both in their joint mission and in what Agamemnon takes to be a crisis in their relationship, involves a sense of outraged justice and anticipatory sorrow, but it is shot through with external considerations of honor and what men will say. Agamemnon's expressions of affection and even his powerful statement of his belief in Zeus' punishment of the injustice that he thinks has brought his brother to his death must vie with an intense concern with his honor, or the loss of it. The speech vividly characterizes the manic-depressive ruler, as is borne out by Menelaos' rather impatient command to cheer up, his prudential advice not to unnerve the soldiery, and his practical description of the nonfatal wound (184–87); Menelaos realizes that his life is not in danger before Agamemnon begins his lament (151f.). This may be the only time in the *Iliad* that Agamemnon is not entirely self-centered. Even he is capable of some concern for another. This concern may be uncharacteristic and unsustained, but if Agamemnon can be generous to any degree, generosity is possible for anyone in the *Iliad*. That said, however, if Agamemnon's striking reaction of shame is in any way typical of warriors who are brothers, we may wonder about the general nature of solidarity, loyalty, and cooperation between fellow warriors in an army where ties of blood are not present.

Agamemnon's speech tells us important things about the human views of the gods' reactions to adverse circumstances. Agamemnon refers in the earlier section of his speech to the absolute effectiveness of oaths: "By no means is our oath in vain . . . " (158f.). This effectiveness, Agamemnon continues, is guaranteed by Zeus, who sooner or later will make the Trojans pay dearly (161) with their lives and those of their women and children.[8] Zeus will shake his aegis in anger at this case of deception (168). Zeus is pictured in his role as Zeus Horkios, Zeus of Oaths. Oaths are part of his province, and infringements of them are an affront to his honor. The word used to describe the Trojans' "paying" for their breach of the treaty, *apotînô*, is philologically related to *tîmê*, and entails the restoration of honor to the

---

8. On the idea of Zeus' ultimate vengeance here and in other Greek literature, see West 1978, on *Works and Days* 218; Kirk 1985, on *Il.* 4.160–62.

aggrieved parties,[9] here to Zeus Horkios and the Achaians. So we have an affective component (seen as operative in Zeus' anger), the ultimate moral element (for why else should Zeus become angry in the first place?), and the honor-aspect, couched in terms of results. Again the affective and moral drives seem to be weaker, more remote factors: to judge from Agamemnon's speech, they apparently stand in need of the honor-constraint as a buttress. (In Agamemnon's case concern with honor merely swamps his emotional and moral reactions for the moment, but Zeus' anticipated angry assertion of his honor is presented as nothing less than the simultaneous assertion of a moral principle, here in the form of the punishment of oath-breakers.) But Agamemnon's view of Zeus' justice is notoriously out of kilter with the god's real attitude at this juncture, for he is ambivalent and aloof, at least as far as the oath is concerned. He makes no attempt to conceal his love of Troy (17–19, 31–36, 46–49), but after suggesting that the choice lies between stirring up the war again or creating friendship between the Trojans and the Achaians (14–16), he tells Hera literally to do as she wishes (37–38). Only in book 24 does the disjunction disappear.

Among both mortals and immortals (at least in the mortals' view of them), three types of motivation can be discerned in attitudes to relationships: the results-oriented, the emotional, and the moral. But does the combination, dominated by the honor-factor, remain unchangeable throughout the *Iliad*? When Achilles mourns Patroklos in front of his mother at 18.79–93, he complains of the loss of his armor, which the gods gave to Peleus on the day of his marriage to Thetis. The loss of armor would among normal heroes be considered a loss of honor,[10] but Achilles makes no mention of honor in this connection, instead lamenting the loss of his friend, as the dominant theme of his speech, and denying that Zeus' restoration of his honor gives

---

9. So Heubeck 1949, 252–54 (= *Kl. Schr.* 1984, 125–27); Adkins 1960b, 23, 27f.; Adkins 1972, 14f. Note, for instance, the formula "to render up [*apotînô*] the honor [*tîmê*] which is appropriate" (τιμὴν ἀποτινέμεν ἥν τιν' ἔοικεν), at, e.g., 3.286, 289f., 459.

10. Quite apart from the undesirability of honor in any form going elsewhere, as Agamemnon claims happens to him when Chryseis, his prize for valor, is taken from him (1.120), there is the thought that stripped of your armor you can be killed dishonorably, "naked, like a woman" (so Hektor at 22.124f.), or that without your armor your corpse can be treated shamefully.

him any pleasure now that Patroklos is dead (80f.). Honor still plays a part: Achilles says he "honored" Patroklos above all others (81); his own life, he says, is undesirable if Hektor "does not render up the honor for" killing Patroklos (*apotînô*, 93); and a little later we find him accepting that his death is imminent, but wanting to win "noble glory" (*kleos esthlon*, 121). Even here, however, the standard-looking phraseology is belied by Achilles' statement of personal, internal motivations for revenge: "Nor does my spirit bid me live . . . , unless Hektor . . . " (90f.). Agamemnon would never have understood the compelling power of personal affection voiced here, let alone the comparative neglect of honor.

This change in emphasis and in the way in which the different elements of motivation are brought together is a principal concern of the present book. By examining this change, we shall explore some of the complexity and ambiguity of the *Iliad*'s ethical system and concept of heroism[11]—more specifically, the multiplicity of the drives behind the heroes' moments of cooperation and, beyond cooperation, generosity.

The Yardstick of the Past

There is a further dimension to this complexity that scholars have tended to miss. The *Iliad* is careful to describe certain key events that occurred in the course of the war against Troy prior to the dispute between Achilles and Agamemnon. Chief among these is Achilles' generous treatment of King Eëtion, recounted by his daughter Andromache to Hektor in book 6 (414–28). When Achilles sacked Thebe, he killed Eëtion, but because he felt respect for the king (*sebazomai*, 417), he did not strip him of his armor, and he erected a tomb and a memorial for him. As an aggrieved enemy, Andromache can still

---

11. A chief target will, therefore, be Finley's hugely influential analysis of Homeric heroism at Finley 1978, 108–41, esp. 113f., where he makes the famous statement that "The heroic code was complete and unambiguous . . . ," a view that has already been refuted from a different perspective by Schofield (1986), who rightly stresses the importance in the *Iliad* of excellence in counsel, whereby conflicting claims of honor may indeed be debated, if not resolved. See further below, p. 42.

acknowledge Achilles' generous respect, and the *Iliad* makes reference to the occasion at strategic moments: for instance, when the ambassadors come across him playing the lyre that he took from Thebe (his generosity to Eëtion and his earlier efforts on the Achaians' behalf contrast with his rejection of the embassy's supplication; 9.185–89); when Andromache throws from her head the veil Aphrodite gave her on the day of her wedding to Hektor, doing so at the very moment that Achilles is mutilating Eëtion's son-in-law (22.468–72); and when pieces of plunder from the expedition are mentioned in the Funeral Games, at which point the plunder, given as prizes, signifies Achilles' return to his normal generous disposition (23.826–27). All these backward glances throw Achilles' present attitudes into deeper relief and show Achilles behaving as he used to do. Otherwise, Achilles claims to Lykaon, who had successfully supplicated him for his life in an earlier encounter, that before Patroklos' death, it was "more dear" (more *philos*) to him to spare defeated enemies (21.100–102), but that now Lykaon's plea will be savagely rejected; Achilles' past normal behavior shows that there was room for respect, kindness, and pity.

Adkins' model in particular fails to take account of the change in moral temper between Achilles before and after the conflict with Agamemnon and the death of Patroklos, so it is methodologically dangerous to take Achilles' behavior in the main narrative of the *Iliad* as typical of the other warriors of the poem. When we see Achilles behaving as befits him, we see, for example, that his own protection of Kalchas in the assembly (1.85–91), Patroklos' kindly behavior toward Briseis (19.287–300), and Hektor's toward Helen (24.767–72) can be seen as appropriate to people of superior social status, *agathoi* who know how to behave. Such qualities as kindness, pity, loyalty, and chivalry—and, we may add, rationality, or "excellent counsel"[12]—are not alien to the "code" formulated by Adkins but included in it, and talk of the value-system is in danger of cutting out what the *Iliad* has to say if we ignore the range of motives that the value-system seems to imply in the more "normal" circumstances than the events narrated in the *Iliad*'s main narrative.

---

12. On *euboulia*, see Schofield 1986.

The Basis of Cooperation

Honor, Shame, Guilt, and Fame; Friendship, Pity, and Fairness

Even in the main narrative of the epic, people assume that friendship, pity, and so forth should be exercised, however little expression the thought may receive in practice. Aias takes it as a matter of censure that Achilles is unmoved by the Achaians' friendship for him (9.630f.). Phoinix urges that Achilles should not have a pitiless heart (9.496f.) and later claims that up until the Achaians' supplication, Achilles' wrath has not been a cause for righteous indignation, not at all *nemessêton* (523),[13] which implies that Achilles' continuing lack of pity and cooperation will be deplored. The narrator's view of the episode and Achilles' behavior is very different, as chapter 3 will make clear, but at least we see the characters conveying the opinion that commendable, cooperative conduct is not prompted by self-assertive motives alone, though that is the impression left by Adkins' analysis. By the dramatic date of the *Iliad*, the gentler motivations have tended to become overwhelmed by the self-interested ones. I hope to demonstrate here how the gentler promptings cohere with the more "persuasive" drives.

We normally associate generosity with acting beyond the requirements of right relations and cooperative behavior. We might therefore conclude that Agamemnon's expression of concern for his brother in book 4, for example, is not particularly generous. In any case, before we can identify moments in the *Iliad* where generosity is exercised (however we may ultimately decide to define it), we must ask what kind of behavior the warriors of the poem would agree to call cooperative and what sanctions they can invoke to encourage it.

We have already had occasion to question how solidarity between brothers compares with that between warriors unrelated by blood

---

13. On the relationship of *aidôs* to *nemesis*, where "*Aidôs* . . . foresees and seeks to forestall *nemesis*," see Cairns 1993, 51–54, 83–87; Cairns also furnishes detail that supports an analysis of *nemesis* as indignation at conduct unbecoming, though I do not think that the importance of this for viewing *nemesis* as part of the appropriateness-standard is as fully appreciated as it should be, e.g., in Menelaos' appeal to save Patroklos' corpse at 17.254f.

but bound together in some common cause. The assumption behind the comparison is that the bond between brothers is the stronger case. This thinking is Iliadic as well as modern. In his emotionally charged appeal to Achilles to accept the Achaian embassy, Aias explicitly uses fraternal ties as an a fortiori argument (9.632–38). If a man's brother or son is murdered, Aias urges, he checks his anger when the murderer "pays compensation" (*apotînô*, 634), and the murderer can stay in the same community; Achilles is behaving unreasonably, therefore, because the Achaians have robbed him of a mere girl and are prepared to return her together with lavish additional compensation. Aias tacitly assumes that receipt of the "value" of a brother or son will assuage the brother or father's sense of loss or desire for retribution. In other words, "worthy" compensation, a concept that integrally involves *tîmê*,[14] can persuade a man to override the impulses that family relationships might demand in such circumstances, and even to live in an at least formally peaceable manner with the man who has wronged him.

Precisely what is this "honor," this *tîmê*, that is evidently so central to the heroic life? In brief, *tîmê* is the preserve of warriors high on the social scale, who maintain their standing in society through the exercise of their prowess, or *aretê*, in battle, sport, or the council.[15] It is necessarily expressed in the honor-gifts, *gera*, with which the warrior is "honored" at the division of spoils, as, for example, when the Achaians allot Briseis to Achilles, when he takes the armor of an opponent as a trophy,[16] when he is offered gifts by a suppliant like Agamemnon in book 9, or when a penalty is paid to him.[17] Constantly tried and proven, *tîmê* wins *kûdos*, "the property of having

---

14. The element of *tîmê* in "legal" compensation is often ignored; see, e.g., Gagarin 1986, 11, 104 n. 12. But if a notion of *tîmê* is not present, the parallel with Agamemnon's gifts of honor breaks down, and Aias' argument is irrelevant.

15. Hoffmann 1914, 71–95, 97f.; Adkins 1960b, 31–36; Redfield 1975, 33f.; Riedinger 1976, on whom see n. 83 below; Finley 1978, 28, 108–10, 113–22, 133. On "excellent counsel," see esp. Schofield 1986.

16. This act will win the hero *kleos*, as Diomedes says at the prospect of capturing Aineias' noble chariot-horses (5.273), or as Hektor says about Patroklos' armor (17.229–32; cf. 130f.).

17. Note the term for "worthy penalty" at 3.286f., etc., quoted in n. 9 above.

success and going forth as victor," "the 'glory' of success, prestige, authority, dignity, high rank,"[18] and can result in *kleos*, "fair fame," which will be public, and which will provide the only form of immortality to which the Iliadic hero can aspire.[19] *Tîmê* is instrumental to fame, which is the overriding general aim of the heroic life and "code." And in the *Iliad*, fame can be won by other means than the acquisition of *tîmê*. When Helen tells Hektor that Zeus has decreed an evil doom for her and Alexandros so that the two of them will become subjects of song for future generations (6.356–58), she shows that even a noncombatant can be assigned a part in the "famous deeds of the heroes," *klea andrôn*. Because of his physical beauty, moreover, a Ganymedes achieved Olympian immortality, which passed into heroic song (5.265f., 20.231–35), and Odysseus disdained mere immortality (*Od.* 5.206–20). In both cases, this kind of perpetuation of one's name is located in the sole power of the inscrutable gods, for the greater pathos of mortality. But when Zeus tells Thetis that he is stopping the gods from stealing Hektor's body from Achilles' possession and is granting this *kûdos* to Achilles as a reward to him for right and proper behavior (24.110), he shows that fame can be won by good moral action. Thus the heroic code is not exclusively coterminous with the successful pursuit of *tîmê* but comprehends other qualities as well.

The reverse of such fame, anonymity, is what the hero fears most. This is clearly seen, for example, when Achilles, terrified at the prospect of being drowned by the River Skamandros, expresses the wish that he had died at the hands of Hektor, the Trojans' "most excellent man" (*aristos*), because then an *agathos* would have been killed by an *agathos*, but instead he will be swept away like a young swineherd lad whom a stream sweeps away as he crosses it in a storm (21.275–83). The similes depicting the world of anonymous herdsmen, woodcutters, craftsmen, and widows often seem designed to create a contrast based on the same thinking.[20] In short, take away a hero's *tîmê*, and

---

18. Fränkel 1975, 80.

19. The classic expression of the thought is Glaukos' comment on the "generation of men" at 6.145–51. For a recent discussion of fame's compensation for death, see Lynn-George 1988, 121f., 153–59, 191, 198–200, 213–15, 256–58, 266, 271f.

20. See Lynn-George (1988, 198–200, 263–65) who argues that the shield of Achilles has this function as well (174–200).

you take his raison d'être as a warrior, as Achilles argues to the embassy in book 9, because it deprives him of a potent source of fame.[21]

All this is background to the argument that is the linchpin of Aias' speech in the Embassy and that is particularly informative for our inquiry. Aias claims that Achilles "does not remember the 'friendship' [*philotês*] with which his comrades honored him above all others beside the ships": οὐδὲ μετατρέπεται φιλότητος ἑταίρων / τῆς ᾗ μιν παρὰ νηυσὶν ἐτίομεν ἔξοχον ἄλλων (630f.). The appeal to *philotês* looks like an appeal to pure, affective ties, to a loyalty, as some would translate it,[22] based on friendship. But precisely what does this "friendship" consist of?

For a lexicographer like Cunliffe, *philotês* means simply "Love, affection, favor, regard."[23] E. Benveniste argues that though the original reference of the word was communal and institutional, "the ancient relationship of favour from host to guest, from god to man, from master to his inferiors, from the head of the home to the members of his family . . . is a close tie which is established between persons and which subsequently turns this 'friendship' into something personal."[24] J.T. Hooker has more recently drawn attention to the evidence of Linear B, which yields compounds like *pi-ro-pa-ta-ra*, the feminine equivalent of Philopatôr, "Father-Loving One," which suggests "that, as far as its meaning can be ascertained, the Greek stem had the sense of 'affection'." He further argues, following H. Fränkel, that the "affectionate" sense is basic but also denotes " 'connection' or 'association'," the latter never completely supplanting the former: "Hence it is wrong to suppose that all human relationships alluded to by Homer are explicable in institutional forms."[25] This is a direct

---

21. The heroic position is challenged by Hesiod in the *Works and Days,* which champions the possibility that a peasant farmer might achieve *aretê,* in the sense of a superior position in the peasant community; see Zanker 1986.

22. Lloyd-Jones 1983, 17; Thornton 1984, 146 n. 17.

23. Cunliffe [1924] 1963, s.v.

24. Benveniste 1973, 281. Benveniste is followed by, e.g., Taillardat (1982), who uses the institutional interpretation to propose an etymology of *philos,* etc., based on the root for the Greek words for (originally contractual) "trust," *peithomai,* and the like.

25. Hooker 1987a, 46f.

attack on Benveniste, and also on Adkins, who argues that what is *philos* to the *agathos* need mean nothing at all to him on an emotional level, because it merely entails what is advantageous to the *agathos* in his hostile, competitive world.[26] Hooker's line of argument has now been convincingly modified and extended by D. Robinson, who demonstrates that Homeric *philos* is in fact always affectionate, never possessive: even one's heart, mind, hands, knees, and limbs are one's "friends," especially when they are under threat, though they remain one's "sympathetic friends" on other occasions as well.[27] The "heart," *thûmos*, actually gives an interesting insight into the workings of affection in the *Iliad*: not only is it "a friend" of its owner, but it can be observed conveying the emotions of love between man and woman, sexual love, longing for absent dear ones, and grief for them;[28] thus it plays a passive and an active role in human affection. For his part, however, Hooker rounds off his attack by pointing out that Achilles' relationship with Patroklos, an example that particularly concerns us, "cannot be accounted for solely according to the conventions of Homeric society, and individual predilection must be allowed to play a large part."[29] Hooker did not live to fulfill his intention to enlarge on this statement at a later juncture, but let us consider its implications for our inquiry.

Evidence of affection is forthcoming in abundance. It is present at the beginning of book 16, the first real moment—and the last—in which we see Achilles and Patroklos actually engaged in an extensive discussion. Achilles, we are told, "pities" the weeping Patroklos (*oiktîrô*, 5), but the actual tone of his address to Patroklos is more complex. Is his extended simile comparing Patroklos to a little girl clutching at her mother's skirts to be read purely at its face value, as a further expression of pity for a friend who is clearly distressed? Or is it a case of chaffing sarcasm? It is more probably to be read as the latter. After suggesting and discounting various hypothetical reasons why Patroklos might have cause to grieve, Achilles finally turns to the most likely scenario, that Patroklos is touched by the plight of the

---

26. Adkins 1960b, 30–37; see also Adkins 1963, where Adkins champions the possessive origin of *philos* to support his view of Homeric society.

27. Robinson 1990, followed by Cairns 1993, 87 n. 126.

28. Caswell 1990, 35–44, 50, 65–73.

29. Hooker 1987a, 63f.

Achaians dying beside their ships "on account of their transgression" (18), an elliptic way of referring to their failure to support Achilles against Agamemnon.[30] On this point Achilles is in deadly earnest, and the conclusion must be that Achilles' "pity" is tinged with a sense of menace, which the simile is partly designed to defuse, by what is most convincingly taken as mockingly ironical badinage.[31]

This is a deft characterization of the relationship in one of its comparatively more relaxed moments. Affection is the clear basis of the association, and other interactions play a natural part. In moments of greater tension, however, the affective element becomes overwhelming. When Patroklos' ghost appears to the sleeping Achilles and requests immediate burial, he asks Achilles to give him his hand, because once he is in Hades, there will be no return, and gone are the moments when the two will sit apart from their friends and take counsel (23.69–92). His request for a common grave, which will be in accord with their youth together in Peleus' house, effectively puts their relationship in a context of kinship.[32] Achilles suggests that Patroklos' desires would have been fulfilled anyway as a matter of course, and he urgently begs Patroklos to stay and allow one last, brief embrace to indulge their sorrow in lamentation (94–98). Poignantly, the embrace desired by both friends cannot take place. Once Achilles has given Patroklos the lock of hair he vowed to give River Spercheios on his return to Phthia, signaling the unity of their death (and hence their life), and once the cremation is over, a simile directs the reader's view of the emotional realities of the situation. Achilles collects Patroklos' bones "as a father grieves as he burns the bones of his son, unmarried, whose death causes grief and misery to his parents" (222–23). At such junctures we would normally expect a simile denoting grief in the animal world, and this strategy is employed of Achilles and Patroklos in book 18, when Achilles is said to mourn Patroklos like a lioness whose cubs have been taken by a hunter (318–22). Similes from the animal world involve a parent's emotion for his or (more generally) her offspring, pure of additional

---

30. Sophokles' *Aias* also condemns the whole Achaian army for their supine obsequiousness.

31. For Taplin (1992, 177) the simile reinforces the "intimate and emotional atmosphere"; no reasons are given.

32. Halperin 1990, 85.

considerations like shame and other emotions that infiltrate a Homeric human relationship.[33] Here, however, the same rationale can be observed in a human relationship; the substitution of a human for an animal parent intensifies the sense of pure, emotional loss that Achilles feels.

A final example that illustrates Achilles' emotion for Patroklos is the way Priam and Achilles break off the formal aspect of their supplication encounter to grieve for their lost loved ones. Achilles grieves at one moment for Peleus, whom he knows he will never see again, and at the next for Patroklos (24.507–12). Again the friendship is placed on the same footing as the ties of kinship, here between a father and son. The emotional component is quite manifest in both cases.

But in line with Hooker's model of Homer's friendship, there is an institutional aspect in the relationship between Achilles and Patroklos. When Achilles agrees to send Patroklos into battle in his armor, he explicitly says that Patroklos will win him great *tîmê* and *kûdos* in the eyes of all the Achaians, so that they will return Briseis and give glorious gifts (16.83–86). But Patroklos is to restrict his offensive to driving the Trojans back from the ships; if he were to go further, he would make Achilles less honored, more "without honour" (*atîmos*, 89–90), because he would eclipse Achilles in the Achaians' esteem. Patroklos' fatal mission is thus conceived as a means of winning *tîmê* for Achilles. That act is, as it were, Patroklos' institutional obligation to Achilles.

Achilles grows only too aware of his institutional obligations to Patroklos, quite apart from the emotional side of the friendship. There are two occasions on which this is expressed unambiguously. The first is when Iris reminds him of his duty to stop Patroklos' body from being mutilated by Hektor: "May shame [*sebas*] come upon your heart that Patroklos should become a plaything for the Trojan dogs, for it would be a disgrace if the corpse were to come home shamefully

---

33. See further 4.433–35, 9.323–24, 11.113–19, 12.167–70, 17.4–5, 133–36, with the response of the mother bird in the portent at Aulis at 2.315. See Moulton 1977, 101–6 for further discussion of the parent animal similes and the motif of selflessness, particularly in relation to Achilles and Patroklos. The motif of horses mourning their dead drivers is also pertinent: 11.161f., 17.426–40, 19.408ff. For similes featuring human mothers protecting their children, see 4.130f., 8.271, 12.433–35, 16.7–11.

disfigured" (18.178–80). Iris' words command Achilles' assent, and Achilles has a duty to his friend's corpse that is based on the incentive of shame. The second passage to consider in this connection is the moment in book 24 when Achilles, having lifted Hektor's corpse onto a bier and then carried it onto Priam's wagon, addresses Patroklos and begs him not to be angry about Achilles' kind treatment of Hektor's corpse, because Priam has given honorable ransom-gifts, and Achilles will give Patroklos an appropriate share of them (592–95). Achilles here construes Patroklos as having a right to compensation for Achilles' return of Hektor's corpse, and this is couched in terms of the appropriate portion of honor. The emotional and institutional aspects of the friendship are well brought out when Achilles tells Thetis that he takes no pleasure in Zeus' fulfillment of his promise: "Why should I have any pleasure in all that when my dear comrade has died, Patroklos, whom I honored above all my other comrades, as much as my own life?" (80–82).

There is another layer to Achilles' desire to avenge Patroklos' death. The key texts are his statement that he has no desire to continue living unless Hektor is killed by his spear and "pays the penalty" (*apotînô*) for stripping Patroklos' corpse for its spoils (18.90–95); his wish to die because he failed to defend his comrade from his death (98–100); and his lament that despite his martial prowess, he has been sitting idle, "a useless weight on the ground," not defending Patroklos and his other companions—a lament that causes him to curse human strife and conflict like that which set the whole train of events in motion (101–13). These passages are an indication that Achilles senses that he has not fulfilled an obligation, and they suggest the operation of guilt on Achilles' mind: he indirectly expresses feelings of guilt when he acknowledges that his quarrel with Agamemnon made him a "useless weight" when he could have been effective in Patroklos' and the Achaians' defense. We have clearly gone beyond a mere sense of shame. Yet the shame and honor incentive is soon reinstated when he concludes his speech to Thetis by saying that now he will win "noble glory" (*kleos esthlon*) by making the Trojan women realize how long he has been away from the battle as they tear their cheeks over the menfolk that he will kill (121–25). Thetis agrees with this formulation when she says in answer that "it is truly no base thing to ward off sheer disaster from one's exhausted comrades" (128–29).

A sense of guilt is one reason why Achilles wants to avenge Patroklos. It appears as a more remote drive than the sense of shame that Achilles feels, but the operation of guilt in decision making in the *Iliad* should not be denied, as some scholars suggest it should.[34] It seems that guilt and shame coexist in the thinking of the epic's characters. On this analysis, guilt is, like the promptings of the affections and the sense of fair play, an "ultimate" drive that receives practical expression through the agency of the proximate sanctions of facing the shame of what people will say and of pursuing honor. The whole exchange between Thetis and Achilles is an exemplary demonstration of the two tiers of guilt and shame in the matter of friendship: the guilt-motive, though less clearly articulated, is clearly discernible, and it is actuated by the incentives of shame and its complement, honor, which are given a far more direct expression as the more compelling reasons for action.

The final major component of friendship as presented in the *Iliad* is inextricably interwoven with the others and concerns the desire to do the "right thing" by one's friend. The conversation between Achilles and Thetis shows that Achilles realizes he has not employed fair play in his dealings with Patroklos and with the Achaians. Therefore he feels guilt. Therefore, as a creature of the *Iliad*, he also feels shame and wants to counterbalance it—negatively, by his wish to "die immediately," and positively, by his desire to win noble glory by returning to his comrades' defense.

Such is the range of emotions involved in the Iliadic concept of *philotês*. Acts done within the framework of friendship may be kindly, but the degree of the kind of generosity that involves at least some recognition of responsibility for others may not be high. Even if we are not Kantians or Christians, we tend to feel that generosity is the more admirable when expectations of reciprocity and reward are more or less waived, that is, when the kind behavior is more or less disinterested and other-regarding. The *Iliad*'s standard conception of

---

34. So, classically, Dodds 1951, 1–63; cf. Lloyd-Jones 1983, esp. 1f., 26, 70f.; Lloyd-Jones 1987a. The idea that shame and guilt are at all necessarily exclusive and the distinction between shame- and guilt-cultures have recently been subjected to a trenchant and convincing challenge by Cairns 1993, 14–47 (with lit.) and also by Williams 1993, chap. 4, esp. 92 ("We can feel both guilt and shame towards the same action").

philotês integrally involves affection, reciprocity, and notions of honor and shame. The only situation in which general Iliadic *philotês* could be converted into other-regarding generosity is one in which the reciprocity sanctioned by the honor- and shame-incentives plays a less prominent role, and in which affection and the desire to do the right thing by a person predominate as motives, ideally over guilt as well, because kindly action prompted by a sense of guilt can be said to bring the reward of assuaging feelings of guilt. Therefore, if the *Iliad* presents a recognizable case of disinterested concern and generosity in any form, it presents something significant indeed.

Interesting in this connection are the cases where the possibility is raised that enemies might become joined in *philotês*. Benveniste quotes 3.94, 7.302, and 22.261–66 as proof that "The behaviour expressed by *philein* always has an obligatory character and always implies reciprocity."[35] But each of these examples only follows the pattern that obtains in *philotês* among people on the same side. When Hektor says at 3.93f. that the winner of the single combat will be entitled to Helen and all her possessions and that the rest can seal friendship and trustworthy oaths, he only offers the complete cessation of hostilities between Trojans and Achaians, and there will be no remarkable aspect to their future friendship at all; at least that is how the two sides take it, "rejoicing" at the prospect of the end of the war (111–12). One example, surprisingly not quoted by Benveniste, sets the pattern for the other passages he mentions. This is the moment when Diomedes realizes that he and Glaukos are ancestral guest-friends, so that they are "dear guest-friends" to one another in their homelands (6.224). Diomedes has an emotional response: he "rejoices" (212). Then follows the agreement not to fight one another, which would be an affront to the institution of guest-friendship, and the abnormally unequal exchange of armor, remarked on as such by the narrator (226–36),[36] which shows equality in such negotiations to be the expected thing. A more typically equal exchange of armor in *philotês* takes place when Hektor suggests that he and Aias call it a day in their duel (7.288–302); he has been worsted, and although at lines 273–82 the heralds have made the duel inconclusive by stop-

---

35. Benveniste 1973, 280, attacked by Hooker 1987a, 57f.
36. See most recently Kirk 1990 on 6.234–36, for the difficulties involved in this passage, and Donlan 1989 for an attractive solution to them.

ping it, Aias seems to gloat over the victory (312).[37] In this instance, however, we are only told that the people who will show joy are their respective communities (294–98, 307f.), and Hektor makes it clear that they will have an opportunity to fight again (290–92), because no institutional taboo prevents a return bout.

The case of Achilles' refusal in book 22 to accept Hektor's suggestion that they treat one another's corpses respectfully is rather different and serves a different aesthetic purpose. At line 265 Achilles claims that it is as impossible for Hektor and him "to be friends" as it is for lions and men or wolves and sheep to make "trustworthy oaths" (261–64). Here, given the pitch of implacability that has been reached in Achilles' attitude toward Hektor, the idea of "being friends" is absurdly inapposite and underlines the impossibility of the *philotês* on which the other combatants had been able to agree. Hektor similarly shows that *philotês* is unlikely at this stage when he cuts short his meditation on whether to renew the offer to return Helen and her possessions. He says that there is no way in which he can "whisper a lover's sweet nothings" to Achilles (127), the absurdity of which is even more patent. Raising the possibility of an accord, both times on the basis of some reciprocal negotiation, and then merely rejecting it is a means of contrasting the relations between Achilles and Hektor with those between whom such a negatively charged emotional relationship does not exist. Yet the basic machinery must be the same if the horror of the reversal of normal attitudes is to be felt. Therefore, reciprocity is normally an essential component of *philotês*, even between enemies, just as it is with the friendship between parties on the same side. Truly interesting for our inquiry would be a case where an enemy entered into *philotês* with another enemy without hope of reciprocation or without real interest in the reciprocation offered. Will not Achilles call Priam "old man, my friend" (*geron phile*, 24.650)? What is his attitude to the ransom-gifts that the king brings for Hektor's corpse?

In Aias' appeal to Achilles in the Embassy, Aias plainly has in mind a notion of comradely concern and can therefore call Achilles'

---

37. Edwards (1991, 4), following de Jong (1987a, 101f.), convincingly takes "rejoicing in his victory" (312) as implicitly presenting Aias' point of view; cf. Kirk (1990) on 311–12, who argues that "Aias is . . . rejoicing in the victory that was his by rights."

heart "wild" and "proud" (9.629), "unrelenting" and "base" (636), and the hero "cruel" (630) and "pitiless" (632). But Aias is operating on two levels: he appeals to *philotês*, an emotional tie with which he claims that the Achaians have honored Achilles preeminently, a tie expressed in terms of *tîmê* and strengthened by it.[38] This kind of thinking is illustrated further in Aias' a fortiori case, in which affective considerations are subordinated to honor even in the relationship between two brothers on the one hand and a father and his son on the other. So when Aias concludes his plea for Achilles' mercy with his powerful statement that the ambassadors are, of all the Achaians, the "most closely associated with" (*kêdistoi*) and the "dearest," most *philoi*, toward Achilles (641f.), he is appealing to the claim of affection. But it is the weaker, more remote claim, and it requires the reinforcement of the stronger, proximate incentive, which Aias has been at pains to underscore; this is true even of his reference to the ambassadors' status as Achilles' guests (640f.).

This analysis of loyalty suggests that the motives for loyal cooperation are more complex than scholars have thought. Adkins contends that heroic society in the *Iliad* operates by the results-oriented, *tîmê*-based, competitive code, including the moments when the heroes cooperate.[39] Against this, Lloyd-Jones argues that a notion of loyalty, if not a word for it, is clearly present in the poem as a whole and is based on a sense of justice.[40] Adkins has to some extent laid himself open to attack by his tendency to equate the cooperative virtues with corporate activity and by assuming that "the only basis for co-operation is fairness."[41] As a consequence, Long is able to object that "The fact that some co-operative activities are seen in terms of *tîmê* may be relevant to Homer's neglect of intentions, but it does not rob them

---

38. The same nexus exists in a god's love for a mortal, as we can see from Agamemnon's statement at 9.116–18: "Worth many warriors is the man whom Zeus loves in his heart, as now he has honored this man [Achilles], by conquering the army of the Achaians." On the role of *aidôs* in *philotês*, see Cairns 1993, 89–95; Cairns however, seems to me to undervalue the function of affective pulls in his discussion of Aias' words and of other passages, such as Hekabe's appeal to Hektor at 22.82–84.

39. Adkins 1960b, 30–60, esp. 51f.

40. Lloyd-Jones 1983, 15, 17, 26f.

41. Adkins 1960b, 6f.

of the right to be called 'co-operative'."[42] A distinction can be drawn between the type of cooperation in which people pursue a common goal from motives that may be very different from "fairness," and the "quieter," "cooperative" virtues that are based on "fairness," justice, and so forth. If the distinction is drawn, Adkins' categories can be saved, as far as they go, but they take insufficient account of the claims of affection on which Aias places considerable weight.[43]

At the same time, it is clear from Aias' speech that emotional ties are in themselves a weak bargaining point for the characters of the *Iliad* (though we shall find the poem's narrator presenting a very different view), and even a brother's *philotês* plays a lesser part in a murder settlement than "worthy" compensation. In a heroic society, that weakness is perhaps not unexpected. But affection and a sense of fairness must be the ultimate motivation. Why else would one bother with things like peaceful settlements and friendly cooperation in the first place? Competitive honor is presented as the more compelling proximate motive for cooperation. Aias' speech brings out this distinction as orthodox thinking among the *Iliad's* heroes, and it is significant that the appeal to the ultimate motive of friendship occurs in a speech that causes Achilles to make a major concession and drop the idea of leaving for home; it is essential to understanding the reasons why the heroes of the *Iliad* can be persuaded to cooperate, show loyalty, and behave generously toward one another.

---

42. Long 1970, 125.

43. One last approach may be noted here. Gagarin (1987, 300) doubts that loyalty is a moral virtue, replacing it as such with pity, "which indicates concern for another person simply for his own sake." He argues (287–303) that Homeric ethics can be divided into "legal" and "religious" areas, which are "nonmoral," and the "moral" (i.e., not self-interested) area—the "legal" area covering relations among regular members of a society, the "religious" guiding the behavior of mortals toward gods, and the "moral" covering dealings with "unprotected persons," like suppliants, beggars, and guests. In his reply, Lloyd-Jones (1987b, 309) points out among other things that the argument collapses "when there is talk of the pity Achilles ought to feel for his fellow-soldiers," who belong to Gagarin's group of members of a society bound together by some form of legal bond. Adkins (1987, esp. 314–17) makes the same point in a fuller discussion and argues that Gagarin's broadest example of disinterested concern, a commander's for his army, is explained "in terms of [*aretê*], [*tîmê*], and [*philotês*] . . . and is presumably 'legal.'" For further discussion see Zanker 1990, 211–13.

Similar things can be said about the workings of another affective pressure, pity. The importance of pity for cooperative behavior in the *Iliad* is illustrated by Aias when he criticizes Achilles for lacking it. The meaning, associations, and functioning of pity can be briefly outlined in this context. Some modern English critics tend to view pity purely as an emotion,[44] partly because of the apprehension that pity can lead to immorality—for example, if someone were to murder a driver out of anger generated by pity for a child whom he had run over accidentally.[45] But the history of the meaning of pity in English should caution us not to assume that its modern English usage is necessarily a guide to pity in a foreign work of art like the *Iliad*. In Middle English "both *pite* and *piete* are found first in the sense 'compassion,' subsequently both are found also in the sense 'piety'; the differentiation of forms and senses was here scarcely completed by 1600."[46] Compassion was seen as integrally associated with respect for the Christian god and was a matter of Christian morality. I suggest that the Middle English usage is more of a guide to the Iliadic concept of pity than the modern, because in the *Iliad* pity and morality are by no means divorced, and pity is consistently seen in a positive light.

The people of the *Iliad* can experience pity on a purely emotional level, as is shown when the egregiously gentle Patroklos pities (*oiktîrô*) the wounded Eurypylos and interrupts his errand for Achilles to treat his comrade's wound (11.814–48).[47] Even in more institutionalized contexts like supplication, people can talk purely in terms of the emotional element in pity. This is abundantly clear in Priam's supplication to Hektor to avoid single combat with Achilles and fight from inside Troy: Priam implores his son to have pity (*eleêson*) on him on the grounds of his old age and the suffering that his family will have to face after Troy's destruction, and especially in view of the

---

44. See, e.g., Lloyd-Jones 1987b, 309, against Gagarin 1987, 300: "Pity is not 'a moral quality,' as Gagarin calls it, but an emotion."

45. See further Adkins 1987, 312, 315. For Nietzsche's repudiation of pity as a specifically moral quality, see Crittenden 1990, 23f.

46. *Oxford English Dictionary*, 2d ed. (1989) s.v.

47. See also, e.g., Hektor and Andromache at 6.407f., 431, 484, and assorted warriors pitying their comrades in battle at, e.g., 5.561, 610; 17.346, 352.

most pitiful (most *oiktos*) death to which he himself will come (22.38–76). To pity is a morally right response, and not to pity is wrong. The plainest proof of this is found in Apollo's disapproval of Achilles' loss of pity (*eleos*): Achilles is "murderous," his mind is not just, he is unbending, and as savage as a lion, his behavior no longer befits a man of his rank and status, and he is in danger of incurring the indignation (*nemesis*) of the gods at his self-assertion beyond his station (24.39–54). In the words of W. Burkert, "[*eleos*] and related fields of response form a group of specifically human values in the Homeric world." Burkert demonstrates that pity is an essential part of human nature, and that, without it, a human becomes "das tote Ding," as Patroklos shows when he compares the pitiless Achilles with a creation of the sea and rocks (16.33–35).[48] At no point in the *Iliad* does pity lead to immoral behavior.

Yet, just as with *philotês*, the affective and moral elements in pity are standardly buttressed by appeals to *aidôs* ("shame" or "respect")[49] and honor. At least part of Apollo's complaint about Achilles is based on the fact that, as he puts it, Achilles has no *aidôs* (24.44) and is not living up to his position in society. Suppliants regularly make appeals for pity and respect, as we find with Lykaon addressing Achilles (21.74), Hekabe pleading with Hektor (22.82f.), and Priam entreating Achilles (24.503).[50] Lykaon's plea to Achilles to have respect and pity is particularly illuminating, because Achilles rejects it with his statement that it was "dearer" to him to spare the Trojans (21.101f.) before Patroklos' death, a statement that explicitly exposes the affective aspect of pity and sparing. Significantly, however, all the ambassadors to Achilles in book 9 couch their appeals for Achilles' pity in terms of honor, *tîmê*. Odysseus begs Achilles to pity (*eleairô*) the Achaians in their distress on the grounds that "they will honor" him like a god, because he would win great *kûdos* for them (9.301–3). Phoinix

---

48. Burkert 1955, 129, 69–75; Burkert adduces pity as a personal, human act as proof of a Homeric concept of individual personality (113). Moral censure is clearly present in Patroklos' words on Achilles' aenaretic pitilessness at 16.33 and in Achilles' report at 16.203–6 of what the Myrmidons have been saying about him.

49. On *aidôs*, see the studies detailed in n. 6 above.

50. See also 22.123f., 419, and 24.207f., 309. At 24.309 Priam prays to Zeus that he will find Achilles "friendly" (*philos*) and "ready to pity" (*eleeinos*), thus bringing out the affective aspect of pity as well.

seems to refer to Achilles' pity both as a moral obligation—when he says, "You should in no way have a pitiless heart"—and as a matter of excellence, honor, and might—in his remark that even the gods can be swayed, despite their superiority in all these respects (496–98).[51] Phoinix' address as a whole demonstrates how easily the characters of the epic are to be viewed as letting the emotional, moral, and honor-related components of pity merge into one another.[52] Finally, when Aias calls Achilles pitiless, the description is a rider to the proposition that Achilles should remember the friendship with which the Achaians honored him, which demonstrates what Aias considers to be his main point of leverage. For reasons that we shall see, the ambassadors' confidence in honor as an incentive for Achilles' pity, or compliance in general, could not have been more misplaced at this point in the hero's thinking. In the *Iliad*, pity is an emotion and a virtue that requires the support of the shame and honor constraints, especially in the case of supplication, which we shall examine more closely below. It will be obvious that here I part company with Adkins, especially in my layering of the proximate and ultimate motives for commendable behavior.

A passage that demonstrates the centrality of honor and the other side of the same coin, shame, to the *Iliad*'s idea of loyalty is Agamemnon's "inspection" of the Achaian army, the Epipolesis (4.223–421).[53] This passage has been neglected by students of Homeric notions of loyalty. The neglect is hard to account for, because an episode in which a king rallies his men might reasonably be expected to yield conclusive evidence for the sort of arguments that have a persuasive claim on the Iliadic warrior's loyalty and cooperation.

Agamemnon counts on the effectiveness of the appeal to shame and honor, apportioning the one or the other as he considers appropriate. An important factor here is the shame-based, public "rebuke"

---

51. See further below, p. 34–36, on the Prayers. Burkert (1955, 129) concludes from Phoinix' words, "gerade dadurch wird ἐλεεῖν von den Göttern her als gültiger Wert sanktioniert."

52. N.B. Phoinix' negativity about Meleagros' pity without gifts, and his commendation to Achilles to comply with the Achaians and accept their gifts (9.597–605).

53. Much of what follows in this section is adapted from my remarks at Zanker 1990. For the operation of honor and shame on loyalty, see now also Cairns 1993, 83–87.

(*neikos*). In his general address to the Achaians, he rebukes them
(241), calling them "reproaches" and asking them, "Are you not
ashamed?" (242). He compares them with fawns who have no
strength (245). Here the king calculates that a firm rebuke will shame
the Achaians into cooperation.[54] More complex is his rebuke of Mnes-
theus and Odysseus (336): they would hang back, he says, even if the
battalions of the Achaians were fighting it out before their very eyes,
but when it comes to feasting they are always among the foremost
(338–48). (In fact, they have not heard the war cry and are waiting
for another battalion to start the battle; 331–35.) The public nature of
honor and shame is well brought out when Odysseus asserts in retali-
ation that Agamemnon will see him mixing it with the front fighters
of the Trojans (350–55). When Agamemnon smiles at seeing that
Odysseus is nettled, it is because he has judged Odysseus accurately
and has correctly calculated that the appeal to shame would work,
so he now takes back the rebuke (359). His rebuke of Diomedes and
Sthenelos (368) involves a damaging comparison between Diomedes
and his father, Tydeus: Tydeus did not cower, but fought for his
friends, and killed fifty Kadmeian youths who ambushed him, bring-
ing an "unseemly," "shameful" death on them (396), only to father a
son who was worse than he in battle, "though better in council."[55]
Diomedes is stunned into silence, "out of respect for the rebuke of
his revered king" (402). The word for "respect" here, *aidestheis*, is

---

54. This is even more clear in the words of Hera as Stentor at *Il.* 5.787:
"For shame, Argives, vile bringers of reproach, admirable in looks alone."
In the Recall, Agamemnon also appeals to the Achaians' sense of shame and
honor (2.115, 119ff., 137ff.) in his test of their morale. Why then is the test
such a failure? First, the Achaians' morale is at a low ebb. Second, their king
is now apparently accepting the dishonor of defeat at the hands of a numeri-
cally inferior enemy. Third, he undermines the sanction of Zeus' promise
(111ff.); see Kirk 1985, on σχέτλιος at line 112 describing Zeus as "consistently
wicked." Finally, as Taplin (1992, 92) points out, it is all too true that Aga-
memnon has "lost many of his people" (2.115) and that the Trojan allies are
giving the Trojans great help (2.130–33). Agamemnon has pushed his act too
far. Once Odysseus reveals that the king is merely testing the army's morale
(193), the soldiers can be brought to heel again on the shame- and honor-
appeal (196f., 284ff., 325, 339, 356).

55. Here sarcastic, as with Odysseus to Thersites at *Il.* 2.246 (note "im-
moderate of speech," 212), though otherwise commendatory, as of Nestor
at 1.248 (note "sweet in speech"; cf. 19.82). See Kirk 1985, on 2.246, 4.400.

shame-based, though it is clear that "respect" is the appropriate rendering at this point from Diomedes' words at lines 412–18, where he says that glory will follow Agamemnon (415).[56] Sthenelos is restrained by no such chivalry and concludes from arguments based on their performance at Thebes, which he claims was superior to that of their fathers, that Agamemnon should not place their fathers on the same level of competitive honor as him and Diomedes (410).[57] In the case of other warriors, the king appeals to the fact that he especially honors them. This happens when he addresses Idomeneus, whom he honors above all the other Achaians (257), whether on the battlefield, at any other task, or at feasts, where Agamemnon claims that he never allows Idomeneus' cup to go unfilled with wine, though ordinary guests have a limited share (259–63). Similarly, Agamemnon can see that the two Aiantes are ready and eager for action, so he forgoes giving them orders, which would be "inappropriate" (*ou . . . eoik̑*, 286).

The Sanction of Institutions: The Kingship, Oaths, Guest-Friendship, and Supplication

The Epipolesis, together with Agamemnon's premature lament for Menelaos and Aias' appeal to Achilles, provides strong support for

---

56. Kirk (1985, on 401–2) also points to "revered" (αἰδοίοιο) at 402 as supporting this interpretation. Taplin (1992, 97, 135f.) sees Diomedes' respect as based on the confidence that "We came with god on our side" (9.49), which he takes to be a reference to the portent at Aulis.

57. With 410 compare Achilles' words at 9.319: "We are all in the same *tîmê*, the base with the noble" (ἐν δὲ ἰῇ τιμῇ ἠμὲν κακὸς ἠδὲ καὶ ἐσθλός). Achilles now seems to regard *tîmê*-competition as meaningless in view of Agamemnon's treatment of him and in view of human mortality; see further below, pp. 65–76. On the role of shame and honor in the interchange between Agamemnon, Sthenelos, and Diomedes, see also the valuable remarks in Cairns 1993, 95–103. This passage in the Epipolesis illustrates a fundamental difference between the general moral climates of the *Iliad* and the *Odyssey*. At 409 Sthenelos claims that Tydeos and Kapaneus perished "by their own recklessness," *atasthaliai*; their "recklessness," as with Hektor's at 22.104, is nonmoral, but it involves the assertion of human will when the portents of the gods have directed otherwise (this is true of Hektor and Poulydamas: see 12.195–250). Contrast the use of the word *atasthaliai* to describe actual offenses against the gods at *Od.* 1.7, 34; 12.300; 21.146; and 22.416, where the word carries a moral connotation.

the view that the ethical profile of the society of the *Iliad* is predominantly one of a shame-culture, and it makes it quite evident that public shame or honor is a sufficient incentive for loyalty among the Iliadic warriors. Moreover, shame and honor are essential to the only other sanctions of loyalty in the poem, the institutions of kingship, the oath (*horkos*), the tie between hosts and guests (*xeniê*), and supplication (*hiketeia*). Within the results-oriented framework of Homeric society,[58] these sanctions are competitive in significant ways, and to this extent I agree with the Adkinsian analysis. Here again the Epipolesis furnishes valuable testimony. We must, however, remember to be wary of overtidy distinctions. The more remote, underlying rationale for appropriate behavior toward unprivileged persons like suppliants, for example, seems to be based on considerations of fairness and emotions like pity: the similes featuring parent animals' selfless care for their young suggest that something more than simply the promptings of shame and honor are at work.[59] Such motivation requires the support of the more persuasive factors of honor and shame. However, we would be wrong to discount the possibility that the mechanism can work the other way: *tîmê* can be softened by the other motives, as we see with Achilles and Eëtion and with Achilles and Priam.

The institutions involve *tîmê*, whether one views them from the perspective of the gods or from that of mortals. The competitive incentive of honor operates among the gods. We have, for example, Poseidon's claim that he is of equal honor (*homotîmos*) with Zeus because they and Hades received equal *tîmê* at the original allotment (15.185–99). He is angered by Zeus' command that he leave the battlefield, which Zeus substantiates by his claim that he is "much superior in might and senior in age" (165f., 181f.). Poseidon argues that Zeus should be content with his *tîmê*—the sky (194f.)—and let the other gods do what they will over common territory—the land and Olympos (193): his children are who he should rebuke (197–99). He may be persuaded by Iris when she picks up his point about seniority (201–4), but his compliance is grudging, because he says he is angered when Zeus reproves (210) a god who is an equal in

---

58. Adkins 1960b, 34–37; Adkins 1963, 34–37; Adkins 1971, 4f.; Finley 1978, 117–23.

59. See above, p. 15f.

allotted sphere of influence (209). Poseidon is determined to defend and assert his prestige, his *tîmê*. The gods of the *Iliad* are driven by honor and shame just as much as the mortals. Important, too, is Poseidon's phraseology when talking about the allocation of the different "provinces," *tîmai*. A province is more than just a sphere of influence: it is the physical embodiment of a god's prestige.[60]

The same is true of kingship, the *horkos*, *xeniê*, and *hiketeia*. These institutions are under the chief patronage of Zeus as the origin of the king's *tîmê*, as Zeus Horkios, Xeinios, and Hikesios.[61] They are, like the sky, his *tîmê*. Infringements of them are affronts to his *tîmê* which he will not tolerate, and against which he must reassert his *tîmê*. Why should these institutions have been included in his sphere of concern and so become his *tîmê* in the first place? There does not seem to be

---

60. This is the picture of Olympian *tîmê* in Hesiod's *Theogony*; see Zanker 1988, 73–75. At 8.208–11 Poseidon's acceptance of Zeus as a deity "of much greater sway" whose supremacy should not be challenged is contrastingly automatic. The difference may be that here he is not directly active in altering the course of the battle; he thus does not feel that his autonomy or prestige is under threat of curtailment by Zeus, and hence he has no need to assert his *tîmê*.

61. It will be seen from what follows that I agree with Dodds' insistence that we distinguish "the punishment of perjury as an offence against the divine [*tîmê*] (4.158ff.), and the punishment of offences against hospitality by Zeus Xeinios (13.623ff.)" from "a concern for justice as such" (Dodds 1951, 52 n. 18; cf. Lloyd-Jones 1983, 5); but I see "a concern for justice as such" as the ultimate, if weaker consideration, and the concern for *tîmê* as the proximate and more potent factor in the gods' enforcement of correct behavior. I disagree with the thesis of Gagarin (1987, 292–97, 302f.) that the gods' punishment of infringements of rules governing behavior toward "unprotected persons" like guests and suppliants, which Gagarin calls "moral rules," is "only indirect," while "violations of religious rules bring severe punishment" because the gods' *tîmê* is involved. Both *xeniê* and *hiketeia*, Gagarin's "moral considerations," directly involve the gods', and especially Zeus' *tîmê*, which on Gagarin's reasoning makes them "religious rules." Consequently, the categories are false; suppliants "cite the protection of Zeus as a reason for their supplication to be granted" (Gagarin 1987, 294). See Phoinix at 9.502–14 and Odysseus at *Od.* 9.269–71. See further Adkins 1987, 317–19. Neglect of the Prayers passage (on which see below, p. 34–36) also permits Gould (1973, 80 n. 38, following von Wilamowitz-Moellendorff [1928] 1962, on Hesiod *Works and Days* 327, and Dodds, loc. cit.) to assert that the *Iliad* has no reference to Zeus as protector of suppliants, though his analysis of *hiketeia* is standard.

a competitive rationale for giving unprivileged persons protection, for example, but it is easy to see how this might be explained in cooperative or affective terms, in terms of pity, for instance, and that a cooperative sense that protecting them is proper needs the buttressing it receives from the Zeus-connection. On this view, the more remote motivation is based on cooperative values, and the Zeus-connection provides it with a shame/honor-sanction, as a device to ensure that what is seen to be proper in principle is realized in practice. Consider in this context Zeus' speech to Thetis at *Iliad* 24.104–19. There Zeus paves the way for Priam's supplication of Achilles (117–19) by asking Thetis to report to her son, on the one hand, that the gods, himself in particular, are angry with him for his treatment of Hektor's corpse and for not ransoming it (113–16),[62] and, on the other, that Achilles will win pleasing gifts (119) while Zeus personally protects his *kûdos* (110); he has already emphasized the importance of *tîmê* while talking of Hektor at lines 65–79. Zeus shows clearly here that he has a sense of what is good or bad, independently of the competitive incentives, which provokes his affective response; but he also supports his command by recourse to the honor-based, competitive criterion.[63]

Nestor makes Iliadic thought on the kingship quite clear when he urges Achilles to remain loyal to his king in book 1. The naked reason why Achilles should act loyally is that Agamemnon is "stronger, since he rules over more men" (1.281). The legitimation of Agamemnon's position is his superior *tîmê* as a king to whom Zeus has given *kûdos* (278f.). This is also the thinking of Odysseus as he recalls the Achaians from their headlong flight after Agamemnon's disastrous test of their morale. To the leaders, he asserts that kings are protected by Zeus, that their *tîmê* comes from him, and that the god loves them (2.196f.); to the troops, he insists on the necessity for one king alone,

---

62. This especially picks up the affective and moral element in Apollo's complaint at line 44f.: "Thus Achilles has lost ⟨or has destroyed⟩ *eleos*, nor does he have any *aidôs*."

63. Adkins first observed that a society in which competitive virtues are predominant could never entirely devalue the "quieter" virtues (Adkins 1960b, 61; 1971, 14), though he offers a different analysis of shame/guilt motivation from the one I am presenting here and does not make the distinction between ultimate and proximate motives that I do. See further below, p. 59–64.

one to whom Zeus has given authority (205f.). For Zeus at least, the relationship with his protégés involves both affection and concern for them as incarnations of his *tîmê*. Men, too, can regard their king with affection and act loyally to him out of the feeling that such behavior is right. Achilles claims that he followed Agamemnon and Menelaos to win honor for them for their pleasure, despite the fact that he had no personal grievance with the Trojans (1.152–60). He later stresses this selfless loyalty when he compares himself with a mother bird tirelessly feeding her chicks, a simile that brings out very clearly the existence of some affective component in Achilles' earlier relationship with his lords (9.323–27). But the stronger claim on loyalty is again the *tîmê* involved in the relationship between the king and his subject, in this context the king's superior worth and social position, based, as they are, on his superior strength. This is again demonstrated by Achilles, precisely when he rejects Agamemnon's ambassadors in book 9: once he has come to doubt the value of *tîmê* as a whole, he can see no reason to cooperate with Agamemnon at all, even though the king has offered full compensation for the slight to Achilles' honor. Affection and the sense of fair play, which is implicit in Phoinix' statement that until this point Achilles' behavior has not been a matter of *nemesis*, that is, others' indignation at self-assertion beyond a person's station, are thus weaker reasons for loyalty to one's king and require the strength that *tîmê* normally provides in Iliadic society. This is the basis of Agamemnon's claim on his men's cooperation, though the instability of the arrangement is most clearly expressed in Achilles' complaint that Agamemnon, because of his higher status and sway (*kratos*, 16.54),[64] has robbed him, though an equal (16.53), and is thus presuming to treat his equal as his subject.

The situation regarding oaths is put quite clearly by Agamemnon in his words to the stricken Menelaos after the Trojans break the treaty and just before the Epipolesis (4.155–68). We have seen how the king expresses his confident belief that the sacrificial blood that sealed the treaty oaths has not been shed in vain because sooner or later Zeus Horkios will intervene and the Trojans will pay (*apotînô*, 161) with their lives and those of their families, thus giving back the

---

64. See Janko 1992, on 16.52–55.

tîmê to Zeus and the Achaians. The notion of Zeus Horkios' absolute
efficacy is twice repeated in the Epipolesis, when, for instance, Aga-
memnon in his general address states that Father Zeus does not help
men "on the strength of falsehoods," and that as a result the warriors
may be certain that Troy will fall (4.234–39; cf. 269–71). In the *Iliad*
cooperative activity based on the sanction of the oath is, in terms of
its instrumentation, predominantly a matter of *tîmê* as far as both
Zeus Horkios and the mortals involved are concerned, and it is there-
fore a matter of competition, not necessarily the direct and primary
result of any notion of justice, whether on the part of gods or men.[65]
That is not to say, however, that the gods are not ultimately
prompted by feelings of outrage and by some conviction about the
independent value of protecting things like oaths, although such pro-
tection is proximately ensured by the *tîmê*-criterion.

In the *Iliad* two major oaths bind the Achaian force together. The
story recorded by the pseudo-Hesiodic *Catalog of Women* of how
Tyndareos extracted oaths from Helen's suitors to help her husband
recover her if she were ever abducted,[66] a knowledge of which the
narrative seems to assume on the part of its audience, must lie be-
hind the *Iliad*, because there would otherwise have been no compel-
ling reason for the Achaian host to follow Agamemnon.[67] The story
is probably referred to in the Epipolesis, when Idomeneus assures
Agamemnon that he will be a trustworthy comrade "just as I prom-
ised and agreed in the first place" (4.267). The *Catalog* tells us that
Idomeneus was one of Helen's suitors.[68] His reference to the original
oath comes soon after Agamemnon's general statement to the

---

65. By a peculiar quirk of Homeric thought, *tîmê* is also central when
people refuse to fulfill an oath to cooperate. We see this happening when
Odysseus says to Agamemnon in the Recall that the Achaians want to make
the king a reproach, *elenchistos*, among all men by not (οὐδέ; for the paratactic
sequence see Kirk 1985, ad loc.) fulfilling the oath they made on leaving
Argos (2.284–88). The implicit logic here is that the Achaians want to shame
Agamemnon by demonstrating his lack of power to exact their fealty to him.
In a competitive, results-oriented society, the allocation or removal of *tîmê* is
a matter of who can enforce his will; when a king cannot do so, the sanction
of Zeus Horkios will move elsewhere.

66. Frr. 196–204 Merkelbach-West 1967.

67. So e.g. Kirk 1985, on 4.267. Cf. e.g. Taplin 1992, 57.

68. Fr. 204.56 Merkelbach-West 1967.

Achaians that Zeus will punish the Trojans because he will not be an ally to them "on the strength of falsehoods" (234–39); moreover, Idomeneus agrees with Agamemnon's doctrine in the words immediately after his assurance of continuing loyalty (268–71). Idomeneus must abide by his oath for the same reasons that the Trojans should have and because he would otherwise lose *tîmê:* note how Agamemnon needles him into action by commanding him to go forth into battle "like the man you claim that you used to be in the past" (264), thus appealing to the hero's sense of shame.[69] Apart from the oath to Tyndareos, there is a general oath of allegiance, sworn as the army leaves Argos, that they will not return home until they have sacked Troy (2.284–88, 339). Both these oaths, motivated primarily by shame and *tîmê*, are competitive, even though they command loyalty and corporate activity.

The matter becomes even more clearly pointed in the case of guest-friendship and supplication.[70] Odysseus' words to Polyphemos in the *Odyssey* are commonly and rightly quoted as valid for the *Iliad* as well: "Zeus is the agent who confers *tîmê* upon suppliants and guests, Zeus the god of hospitality [*xeinios*], who accompanies revered guests," so Polyphemos should "have shame before the gods," or "respect," for Odysseus is his suppliant (*Od.* 9.269–71).[71] Zeus will give *tîmê* to the suppliant, who disclaims any right to *tîmê* to gain his supplication, and to the guest-friend, who claims *tîmê* equal to that of his host.[72] The *Iliad* talks just as explicitly about guest-friendship.

---

69. Cf. Lloyd-Jones 1987a, 5.

70. On *xeniê* and *hiketeia*, see in general Gould 1973; Stagakis 1975, 94–112 (which however chooses not to discuss the *Iliad* [95 n. 7] and ignores the distinction between *xeinos* and *hiketês*); Schlunck 1976; Finley 1978, 99–103, 123; Pedrick 1982; Mueller 1984, 28–76; Thornton 1984, 113–24; Herman 1987; Lynn-George 1988, 200–209; Goldhill 1990. On the "institutionalizing" of the rituals, which naturally merge into one another, and the *tîmê* involved in them, see Adkins 1960a, 24f.; Gould 1973, 90–94; Herman 1987, passim, esp. 34–40. Adkins (1963, 34–37) emphasizes the competitiveness and reciprocity inherent in the *philotês* entailed when a suppliant becomes a guest-friend. On the shame-element, see Gould 1973, 87–90; Cairns 1993, 105–19. Lloyd-Jones (1983, 5, 49, 176; 1987a, 4, 5f., 7) overplays the role of justice in these institutions.

71. Cf. Eumaios at *Od.* 14.56–58; see further Adkins 1960a, 25f., followed by Gould 1973, 94 n. 101.

72. Gould 1973, 90–94, esp. 93f.

Defending the ships, Menelaos shouts at the Trojans that they are
full of shame, for they committed an outrage against him when they
stole Helen and many of his possessions, and they had no fear of the
wrath of Zeus Xeinios, who will sack Troy (13.622–25). Menelaos
goes on to express his surprise that Zeus should favor the Trojans,
who are such insolent offenders (631–34).[73] In book 9 Aias' reminder
to Achilles that the ambassadors have been accepted under the roof
of his hut is another instance of the same thinking: because Achilles
has received them, he is under the obligation of hospitality to fulfill
his guests' request and to relent, and the obligation is expressed in
terms of Achilles' respecting his dwelling (640). If there is no inde-
pendent value in protecting people like suppliants, guests, and
strangers, why does Zeus think it right for them to be given protec-
tion?

Though the *Iliad* speaks of guest-friendship and the obligations of
the host to the guest, as in the passages just considered, or when, for
example, Nestor tells how Achilles welcomed him and Odysseus
with "the gifts of hospitality [*xeinia*], which it is proper that guests
should have" (*Il.* 11.779),[74] supplication is by far the more important
of the two institutions in the poem. The essential statement on it in
the *Iliad* is given by Phoinix in the passage on the Litai, the personifi-
cations of prayers (9.502–605). Phoinix' picture of the Litai and his
supporting exemplum, the story of Meleagros, have been seen as a
late addition to the poem because of an alleged affinity with the
Justice passage in Hesiod's *Works and Days* (220–47).[75] But it has been
argued that the "obvious affinities" substantiate the thesis that the

---

73. Herman 1987, 125. On Menelaos' speech, see Taplin 1992, 169f., 192;
and see 103–9 on the guilt of Troy, passed on to the whole community by
association.

74. Significantly, the narrator invokes Zeus as the doubled motivation of
Glaukos' false calculation of reciprocity in his exchange of gifts with Di-
omedes (6.234f.). Only the activity of the patron god of *xeniê* and *hiketeia* can
be postulated when irregularities like this occur.

75. Dodds (1951) and Gould (1973) ignore it (see n. 61 above); Page (1959),
269–315 argues for book 9's late authorship (on the Prayers passage see esp.
300f.). Cf. Lesky, *R.E.* Suppl. 11, 1968, s.v. "Homeros," coll. 726, 790f., and
Kirk 1962, 214f., followed by Lloyd-Jones 1983, 6, 16–18. The integrity of
book 9 and the placing of Phoinix' speech is also defended by Reinhardt
(1961, 212–42) and Motzkus (1964, 37–46).

Iliad's concepts of Zeus Horkios, Xeinios, and Hikesios "are not easily separated from" Hesiod's explicit presentation of Zeus as the protector of justice.[76]

Phoinix' words demand closer scrutiny. Phoinix states by way of prelude that even gods can be made to change their minds, even though they are greater than mortals in point of their *aretê*, *tîmê*, and strength (*biê*, 9.497–98), that is, in point of their competitive excellences. Mankind should a fortiori yield to people who supplicate them (*lissomenoi*, 501).[77] The sanction of supplication is the highest: Zeus. He is the father of the Prayers (502). These reward men who respect them (508) but "supplicate" Zeus (511) to send Blind Folly (Atê) to the noncompliant, so that they may forfeit their claim to *tîmê* and "be punished" (*apotînô*, 512). Therefore, Phoinix concludes, Achilles should grant that honor be accorded the daughters of Zeus, for such *tîmê* changes the mind of others, however noble their degree (*esthloi*) may be (514). He goes on to add that if Agamemnon were not offering gifts, he would not attempt to make Achilles relent, but the king is offering many (515–19); moreover, he has sent Achilles' dearest friends to "supplicate" him, and it would not be right for him to "put a reproach upon" their words or their mission (520–23). We have observed the connection between honor and "friendship" (*philotês*) from Aias' words later in book 9 (630–31); and Achilles is literally honor-bound to help those "dearest friends." In the story of Meleagros, Phoinix refers to the successive supplications of the Aitolian elders (574), his father Oineus (581, 583), and his wife (591), and he makes special play of the promise of gifts by the elders (576). When Meleagros relents, the Aitolians renege on the gifts, but the hero staves off destruction all the same (597–99). It would be worse if Achilles were to step in when the ships were already ablaze, Phoinix continues (600–602); if he were to enter the war "without gifts," that is, like Meleagros, at the last moment before total destruction by the enemy, he would not, even if he fended off the war, enjoy the same *tîmê* as he would if he responded immediately to the offer of

---

76. Lloyd-Jones 1983, 18.

77. Here, just as clearly as at 1.502 (Thetis' supplication of Zeus "in entreaty," *lissomenê*), the verb *lissomai* denotes supplication, though Gould (1973, 76 n. 12) reminds us that the contexts in which the verb occurs in Homer cannot all "unequivocally be classed as acts of supplication."

the gifts (602f.), in which case the Achaians would "honor" him like a god (603).

Nothing here is alien to the ethical concepts or phraseology of the rest of the *Iliad*.[78] Throughout, the appeal is to competitive prestige (*tîmê*), whether the prospect of it held before Achilles, the obligation that it be conferred on the Litai, or Zeus' punishment of those who do not have shame before or honor them. Zeus punishes or removes the *tîmê* from men who do not yield to supplication in precisely the same way that he reasserts his *tîmê* against men who disrespect those other great provinces of his: kingship, the oath, and guest-friendship. The sending of Blind Folly here is only a more purposeful deployment of the goddess than Agamemnon's invocation of her in book 19 (91–94), and presumably critics like Dodds would not athetize the Apology. And the doctrine of the Prayers paradigm is not so obviously similar to the moral behind Hesiod's Justice passage in the *Works and Days*. There the sanction for cooperation is principally and explicitly "justice," or "righteousness,"[79] and there is no reference to *tîmê*. Here Zeus' protection of suppliants may ultimately be conditioned by affective motives or by the sense of fairness, but the actual constraint to act cooperatively remains competitive shame and honor.

Supplication can secure loyalty in the main narrative of the *Iliad*, just as we see happening in the story of Meleagros. Sarpedon advises Hektor to be continuously careful to keep his allies constant by supplicating them (5.491). This constitutes an indefeasible claim on compliance, by virtue of Zeus' concern with his *tîmê* as Zeus Hikesios. When Agamemnon in the Epipolesis tells how the people of Mykenai refused the supplication (4.379) of Tydeus and Polyneikes as they gathered allies (377) for their attack on Thebes, he justifies his people's refusal on the grounds that they had received signs from Zeus himself (379–81); only thus can he fully exonerate them before their suppliants and the god. Nestor similarly recalls how he and Odys-

---

78. See Rosner 1976 (with lit.). If, as, e.g., Pedrick (1982, 132 n. 29) argues, the idea of Zeus' sending of Blind Folly is "alien to both epics, and suits Phoenix' arguments rather than any theology," Phoinix' arguments, so out of kilter with general belief in the *Iliad*, would be weak indeed. Anyway, what has happened to Agamemnon's statement that Zeus, Moira, and Erinys visited him with Blind Folly in the assembly (19.87–88)?

79. So Dickie 1978, followed by Verdenius 1985, on *Works and Days* 9, δίκη, against, e.g., Gagarin 1973, 81–94. Cf. Schmidt 1986, 125–35.

seus had gone around Achaia gathering allies (11.770; cf. 781). The scene when they reach Peleus' house is a paradigmatic illustration of *xeniê*, and the naturalness with which the act of supplication follows demonstrates how parallel the two institutions were thought to be.[80] Peleus and Menoitios oblige by sending Achilles and Patroklos (782–83). The acceptance of such an entreaty increases your honor, as Phoinix' speech makes strikingly clear. On the other hand, as I shall argue, in book 24 Achilles can accept a supplication for reasons that transcend *tîmê*—his pity for the fellow sufferer who reminds him of his own shattered relationship with his father. Here, at the climax of the whole poem, an affective response, in which a sense of fair play is also active, eclipses the honor- and shame-motives. Once a man has gained a supplication, he is obliged to render *charis*, "gratitude," to his new allies. When Sarpedon is killed, Glaukos castigates Hektor for abandoning Sarpedon's corpse to Aias and the other Achaians, because Sarpedon was his *xeinos* and comrade. Glaukos argues that the Lykian contingent will not fight on Troy's behalf now that Hektor has offered no *charis*,[81] and moreover, he asks how lesser men will be able to count on defense from Hektor when he leaves a hero like Sarpedon as spoil for the Achaians. If only Patroklos' corpse were captured, he continues, the Lykians and Trojans would have a bargaining point in their efforts to recover Sarpedon's body (17.142–68). Glaukos' charge is answered by Hektor in his exhortation to Glaukos and others to capture Patroklos' corpse: he claims that he is actually exhausting his own people by demands for gifts and food for the allies (225f.), and he offers rewards to the man who takes the corpse of Patroklos from Aias (220–32). In another important example, the lack of *charis* for services rendered is something Achilles particularly laments in his complaint about Agamemnon's treatment of him (9.315–17).

Even where a supplication is not made, *tîmê* is an incentive for loyalty or pity. At *Iliad* 5.252–73 Diomedes refuses to vacate the field

---

80. Gould 1973, 90–94.

81. See further Herman 1987, 123f. On "recruitment," Taplin (1992, 55–66) emphasizes the need for the "summoner" to render *tîmê* and *charis*, discusses the breakdowns occasioned when the summoner reneges on these, and discusses the moments when other claims override those of the summoner, as with Diomedes and Glaukos.

despite Sthenelos' advice, because it would not be "befitting a noble" (*gennaion*, 253), and because there is a fair prospect of winning *kûdos* (260) and *kleos esthlon* (273). In book 11 Odysseus debates whether to stay on and fight alone now that the Achaians have fled, but he checks himself with the reflection that only "inferior men" (*kakoi*) quit the field and that the man preeminent in battle ("whoever is *aristos*") stays his ground (401–10). Again the competitive excellences, this time that of *aretê*, are the persuasive factor,[82] and courageous, lone opposition supports the corporate interests. The potency of shame (*aidôs*) is underlined in words of Agamemnon's in book 5; respect one another, he says, for when men do so there is greater safety, but there is no *kleos* or defense (*alkê*) when men flee (528–32). Again loyalty and the success of a corporate venture are presented in terms of shame and honor,[83] though again the parent animal simi-

---

82. So Dickie 1978, 94; on Hektor's motives at 6.441–46, Dickie's other main example, and 22.99–130, see below, pp. 55f., 60f. For Odysseus' monologue as a "Paradefall" of a human reaching a decision without the intervention of a god, see Lesky 1961, 13.

83. In a rare authorial judgment, the narrator presents successful mutual defense in purely prudential terms. At 17.364–65 the Achaians are said to have fallen in far fewer numbers than the Trojans in the fighting over Patroklos, "for they were always mindful to ward off sheer destruction from one another throughout the throng" (cf. the bare reportage of 3.9). Elsewhere, as in Agamemnon's exhortation (which Aias repeats at 15.561–64), the value of competitiveness in tactical cooperation is emphasized, and it is expressed in speeches; see, e.g., 2.362–68; 12.267–72; 13.236–38, 275–94; 15.295–99.

That cooperation in corporate ventures and loyalty to the group can legitimately be viewed as a matter of competitiveness is a grave obstacle to the argument of Long 1970, 122–35 that there are examples in Homer where Adkins' competitive excellences, which are based on *tîmê*, are "used to commend quiet excellence and to condemn certain breaches of it," as for instance when one warrior upbraids another for holding back from the fray. Long's replacement for Adkins' schema, the "standard of appropriateness," is in any case not essentially very different from Adkins' *agathos*-criterion, whereby the man who has achieved "excellence" by virtue of birth, wealth, and the physical and military prowess to defend his superior position in society stands for and is used as an example to commend the values of his class. Long (135, citing with approval Adkins 1960b, 20f.) writes that "'Appropriateness' is closely, if not logically, related to social status and the behaviour this demands in a wide range of circumstances." Small wonder that Adkins (1971, 12–14) found himself in broad agreement with Long on the matter.

les point to motives behind these values, however much they may need to be underpinned by them.

The case of Achilles is interesting here. His coming to Troy in the first place was the result of Nestor and Odysseus' supplication of Peleus, but he did not swear an oath to Tyndareos, and he came to Troy, as he puts it, without any grievance against the Trojans, just to restore the *tîmê* of the Atreidai (1.152–60), loyally and selflessly suffering on their behalf (9.321–27), though simultaneously, following Peleus' parting words, aiming for the title of *aristos* (11.783f.). There is undoubtedly an element in Achilles' loyalty that is based at least in part on an affective component in his relationship with Agamemnon, and he stresses it more than any other hero. But a threat against his *tîmê* is enough to nullify this aspect of his motivation, so he now ignores Peleus' other piece of parting advice, that "friendly cooperation [*philophrosûnê*] is better" (9.256). Even that perspective is honor-based, because Peleus goes on to instruct Achilles to stay clear of wrangling so that the Achaians "might honor him the more"

Riedinger (1976) would locate cooperation in *tîmê*. He sees *tîmê* and *philotês* as equivalents and argues that the "dear friends" of the hero confer *tîmê* on him for services rendered to the community, so that there is no room for heroic individualism (244–54). But the equation of *tîmê* and *philotês* (precarious enough in any case, especially as soon as one accepts the affective element in *philotês*) involves, on Riedinger's construction, a tautology that makes, e.g., Aias' words about honoring Achilles with friendship meaningless; and Riedinger ignores the question of the hero's pursuit of *kleos* (fatal in the case of Hektor, both for himself and his community) and the hero's personal sense of shame/dishonor when he fails to meet his objectives (again as with Hektor), which means that the community is not the only donor or stripper of *tîmê*. To say that the "rules of the game" of *tîmê* are "acceptés et utilisés sans discussion, sans la moindre trace de réflexion critique" (254–62) ignores the doubts entertained by Achilles in *Il.* 9 (see further Schofield 1986). Finally, Riedinger argues that conferring *tîmê* implies generosity, not any calculation of advantage, which, he says, explains why Chryses and Thetis can make requests of a deity that otherwise look "exorbitant" (262–64). But there is nothing exorbitant about these requests, and both petitioners are basing their request to be honored on services rendered (*Il.* 1.39–42, 394–412).

The analysis of loyalty in the *Iliad* by Roisman (1984, 5–46) is vitiated by its failure to appreciate the role of *tîmê* as a driving force in securing loyalty; most glaringly, perhaps, Roisman (14–17) ignores the importance of *tîmê* in the *philotês* with which Aias says the Achaians honored Achilles at 9.630f.

(257f.). The proximate idea of competitive *tîmê* in Peleus' farewell advice is made even clearer in Nestor's reportage of it, according to which Peleus advised Achilles "always to be the most excellent [*aristeuein*] and to stand out from the rest" (11.784), in the standard phraseology.[84] All this is further demonstration of the presence of cooperative motives and the overriding persuasiveness of *tîmê* in the standard thinking of the heroes of the epic, though book 24 shows affective and cooperative responses existing independently of *tîmê* and transcending its constraint.

The overriding cogency of the honor-incentive is now quite apparent. Yet there are exceptional cases where people cooperate without reference to the claims of honor at all. Positive emotions and a sense of fairness can activate kind or loyal behavior by themselves. These affective drives are more in evidence among the Trojans, because they are fighting for their community, and their women and children are actually present.[85] In her lament for Hektor, Helen tells how Hektor never once insulted or rebuked her, and how with kindliness and gentle words (24.772), he restrained any of her in-laws who recriminated her; he was the only one apart from Priam who was gentle (*êpios*, 770, 775) and affectionate (*philos*, 775) to her. Hektor's chivalry may have been motivated by the noble treatment that the honor-constraint in the heroic code expected the warrior to extend to his dependents, but in the case of Hektor especially, we may entertain the probability that personal feelings, whether pity or affection, and thoughts of fair play are even more influential in directing his behavior toward his sister-in-law, which seems to have the support of her own choice of words.

Among the Achaians, Patroklos is particularly commended for his gentleness. When Zeus sees Hektor stripping Achilles' armor off Patroklos' body and putting it on, he comments that Hektor should not have killed the "gentle and mighty" friend of Achilles (17.204). Mene-

---

84. Cf. 6.208. This poses a problem for Lloyd-Jones' conclusion (1983, 16; 1987a, 5) that "Peleus . . . was able to appreciate some at least of the 'quieter virtues.'" The competitive spirit of the words is noted by Lloyd-Jones himself (1983, 183). The selective reports by Odysseus and Nestor's interview with Peleus are usefully discussed from a narratological point of view by de Jong (1987a, 173–75).

85. See, e.g., 8.55f.; cf. the situation of the allies, described by Dolon at 10.420–22.

laos urges Meriones and the two Aiantes to save Patroklos' corpse by reminding them of his "gentleness," for while he was alive he was "kindly" to all (17.669–72). Briseis, too, singles out the quality in her lament over him, calling him "kindly" and recalling his promise to make her Achilles' wife on their arrival back in Phthia (19.287–300). In a vain attempt to encourage Achilles to kindness and to accept his plea for his life, Lykaon mentions the gentleness of Patroklos (21.96). Patroklos displays a concern for his comrades that is not at all prompted by considerations of honor when he spontaneously pities the wounded Eurypylos (11.814) and treats his wound (828–36, 842–48), when he pities the Achaians as the Trojans sweep upon the wall around the encampment (15.395–404), when he chides Achilles for being pitiless (16.30–35), and when he makes the suggestion that he go into battle dressed in Achilles' armor to give the Achaians some respite (16.36–45). His response is a pity borne of his affection for his comrades, not at all by the sorts of incentive mentioned by Lykaon in his plea for pity, in which he stands on his honor-sanctioned rights as a suppliant, offering appropriate gifts (21.74–96). Achilles' pity for Priam, given without any real influence from the honor-constraint, is conditioned by a very different set of experiences, and it even differs from the kind of mercy he showed to Eëtion, whose city, Thebe, he sacked, and whom he did not strip of his armor after he had killed him, but "respected" and gave full burial honors (6.414–20). Moreover, a contrast is often drawn between a warrior's gentleness toward his group and his harshness toward outsiders or enemies. We have just seen Helen's appreciation for Hektor's gentleness toward her,[86] and earlier in the scene of lamentation, Andromache speaks of his concern for his city and his mercilessness in battle (24.725–45). In the cooperation that Achilles extends toward an enemy and without reference to the honor-sanction, we are surely justified in talking in terms of generosity.

The model that I propose here of the sort of factors that may impel the Iliadic hero to cooperative or generous behavior seems to me at least to have the merit of opening up the possibilities for recovering motivations and intentions: not only shame or guilt, but shame *and* guilt; not only honor or justice, but honor *and* justice, and other

---

86. On the similarities between the threnodies of Briseis for Patroklos and Helen for Hektor, see Taplin 1992, 205.

emotions and motives besides, including some measure of concern
for others. The model offers disjunction and conjunction. Neither in
life nor in letters is one motive necessarily exclusive. In this way we
may hope to avoid the minimalism and reductivity of Adkins' ap-
proach. And ours need not be a "pick-and-mix" procedure, provided
we analyze behavior with a strict eye to the appropriateness of our
analysis within the referends we have set up.

To conclude this section of our inquiry, we may ask whether
friendship, pity, and justice are part of the heroic code. Here at last
we must confront Moses Finley's claim that prowess "is the hero's
essential attribute," that honor is "his essential aim," and that the
heroic code "was complete and unambiguous," basic social values
being "given, predetermined," "not subject to analysis or debate."[87]
Friendship, pity, and justice are perceived as factors that may legiti-
mately impinge on a hero's behavior, and other critics have added
the sense of propriety,[88] prudence, and excellent counsel (euboulia).[89]
Since the heroes concede the force of these considerations, it seems
fair to conclude, against Finley, that they take a place alongside honor
in the heroic code.[90] M. Schofield argues that honor may be seen as
the "goal" of the heroic life, and that success in battle and the defense
of the community, prompted by pity, justice, and so forth, may be
viewed as its "intended results"; that the two aims may obviously
come into conflict, as in the quarrel of Agamemnon and Achilles and
the disagreement of Poulydamas and Hektor; and that excellent
counsel, to which the hero is committed, has a chance of resolving
the conflict.[91] Schofield's analysis is surely persuasive, but I would
add to it my explanation of the nexus between honor as a "proxi-
mate" sanction, reinforcing the claims of the other, "ultimate" con-
siderations, and as a pressure that can have the reverse effect of
blinding the heroes to these. The heroic code has an internal ambigu-
ity when the claims of honor override those of affection, justice,
prudence, and appropriateness, which in turn minimizes the chance
for heroic generosity.

---

87. Finley 1978, 113–15.
88. Long 1970, 129–39.
89. Schofield 1986.
90. So Schofield 1986, 16–18.
91. Schofield 1986; see also Taplin 1992, 6f., 50–52.

A Text-based Reading

This book studies ethics and character in the *Iliad*, and the relationship between them, principally through the character of Achilles. As with no other field of literary criticism, the study of intentions, motives, and characterization in a work of literature needs humility and open-mindedness. I am here subscribing to a text-based reading of the *Iliad* and attempting to avoid the pitfalls of the documentary fallacy.[92] We have only the text as the source of the characters' actions and words, and from these we are invited to draw conclusions about motives; we cannot talk of characters as if they were historical persons, but as something to be constructed by means of the *Iliad*. In representing behavior, a work of art gives its readers or audience clues, whether by word, action, or gesture, encouraging us to construct things behind the words, actions, and gestures. We cannot expect that our reading will be accepted by everyone in all ages, or even by ourselves at different stages of our lives. The more powerful the poem is, the more it will encourage the audience to elicit clues about things like motives. The more mysterious the motives are, the more interesting they become, because they chime in that much more with our own experience. Furthermore, authors may choose to make a character behave in a certain way for a number of reasons. We may be prompted to opt for one particular motivation because it makes particular dramatic, psychological, or rhetorical sense, but this should not blind us to the possibility of other readings: all the clues may be equally coherent in their potential for meaning. So our real questions should be: what is the strategy of this text, and what is going on behind a character's behavior at any point, *as it is implied in the text*?

The words and actions of the Iliadic characters suggest to readers a range of emotions and motives (often conflicting) for which the readers will have different terms and analytical concepts according to their place in history.[93] The *Iliad*'s values and institutions can be

---

92. I have found particularly helpful in these matters the remarks of Edwards (1987, 231f.) and Easterling (1990).

93. A fascinating instance of this phenomenon is Simone Weil's *The Iliad; or, The Poem of Force* (1956). For "Emile Novis" immediately after the fall of France in 1940, "force" was "the true hero, the true subject, the centre of the

seen to be constructed on the basis of a range of experience that includes such emotions and motives, even if they are not explicitly acknowledged or even implicitly identified. Moreover, the relationship between emotion and motive may be extraordinarily complex, as we found with the *Iliad*'s notion of pity, which feeds into moral considerations in a way foreign to present-day thinking and sentiment. Take Achilles. People will differ over what he is doing at many junctures in the *Iliad*, but he is presented in such a way that he engages us more than enough to try to search out, empathize with, and understand what is motivating him, even when that may be unexpressed, or on an occasion when it cannot be expressed. (If, for example, I am right in suggesting that in book 24 he is generous to Priam out of magnanimity, there is no word in Homeric Greek to cover that disposition.) Here we are back with the consideration that we all draw on the experience of our times in our interpretation of the text before us, thus enlivening ourselves to the full complexity and potential for meaning of a richly suggestive work of art. My model of the values and motivations in the *Iliad* is designed to accommodate this state of affairs.

Older criticism talked of Achilles as a real person, with firmly definable motives. But such criticism was too much determined by its own engrained patterns of thought, and modern studies have shown the value of pluralistic approaches.[94] The more estimable an instrument art is, the more it creates characters who fascinate us, especially

---

Iliad," while the poem itself registers the dehumanizing process of force with a hideous bitterness, made bearable only by the gentleness of a Patroklos or the "rare" "moment of grace" in the scene between Achilles and Priam (Weil 1956, 25, 29). Weil's eye was trained by her experience of life during the occupation of France, and what it so often lit on in the text of the *Iliad* was, as Edwards (1987, 319) remarks, the speeches of the heroes in the fury of battle, without observing the softening frames of the "thumbnail obituaries" and other vehicles of "the poet's voice." But the experience of her times led Weil to a precious insight into the brutalization that, I argue, has set in by the dramatic date of the poem. How much insight will a book like the present derive from being written during the close of the cold war, the period of the civil liberties groups and the environmental lobby, with the progress they can record in establishing right, cooperative relations in society and with the planet?

94. See in particular Easterling 1990 and Gill 1990.

by the multifaceted nature of the portrayal of their motives, to the extent that we want to think about their "real" springs of action; in effect, such a work of art invites us to treat the characters as if they were "real" characters. Consider Orestes' motives for killing the usurpers in the *Choephoroi*. Orestes reports that Apollo said inaction would bring with it certain undesirable consequences; but grief for his father and himself, fear of Apollo, his hatred for his mother, a sense of aggrieved *tîmê*, and anger that his patrimony has been plundered are also at work (*Ch.* 269–305). All we have is the text, which works in such a way as to make us try to imagine what possible frame of mind he can be in when he confronts the duty to kill his mother and Aigisthos. Then we see the techniques by which Aischylos forces the audience to make up their minds. The text gives us material on the basis of which we want to postulate motives. We may choose to see Orestes' rehearsal of his motives as a means of reinforcing his resolve and, in particular, of helping him overcome the pressure of his revulsion at the thought of matricide. In a comparable way, Homer encourages us to meditate on what the inner life of his characters might be. But we are expected to do a lot of the spadework. That the figure of Achilles is particularly suggestive is shown by the way he has persistently been read and reread over the centuries. One thing this book aims to bring out is precisely this power of suggestiveness and the sense of complexity of motive in Achilles. I suggest that the complexity of Achilles draws us to an understanding of the difficulties and contradictions of the value-system that Homer invites us to construct and of the more sublime thought-world of the narrator. It also intensifies the sense of a dynamic, indeed dramatic, interplay, which is utterly precluded if we assume that life in the *Iliad* is all a matter of the mechanical operation of *tîmê*, or even a mixture of the promptings of such honor and justice.

2

Values in Tension

Indeed so intimate is the relationship of practices to institutions—and consequently of the goods external to the goods internal to the practices in question—that institutions and practices characteristically form a single causal order in which the ideals and the creativity of the practice are always vulnerable to the acquisitiveness of the institution, in which the cooperative care for common goods of the practice is always vulnerable to the competitiveness of the institution. In this context the essential function of the virtues is clear. Without them, without justice, courage and truthfulness, practices could not resist the corrupting power of institutions.

—A. MacIntyre, *After Virtue*

Cooperation Eroded

We have now, I believe, surveyed the main reasons why the Iliadic warrior should want to act loyally or kindly to his group or to outsiders like suppliants or *xeinoi*. However, they are clearly inadequate to curb the disaffection and violence that feature so prominently in the *Iliad*, let alone to ensure generosity. How can we account for the subversion of these constraints and the ensuing quarrels and acts of cruelty in the poem?

The essential factors are that the war is in its tenth year, that both sides are exhausted, and that feelings have become brutalized, a state that has ushered in the fragmentation of loyalties and moral values. The *Iliad* offers many scenes of the horrors of war, but a passage that perhaps speaks with a particular directness to readers today is the moment when the Achaians, spurred on by Diomedes, refuse Priam's offer to restore the possessions that Paris took with Helen to Troy—Paris will not part with Helen—but Agamemnon takes up Priam's request for a truce so that both armies might bury their dead. They meet soon after sunrise, coming face-to-face, but they find that it is difficult to recognize the individual corpses, and they have to wash off the gore for their identification before carting them away and burning them, which the Trojans do in silence, because Priam has forbidden lamentation out loud (7.421–32).[1] Priam has no difficulty maintaining discipline and curbing his men's non-Greek habit of crying aloud,[2] and thus he preserves his entourage's dignity before the Achaians. But it is a bitter and horrific thought that the two armies should intermingle in a brief truce, confronted by images of death, disfigurement, and namelessness, immediately after an attempt has been made to bring hostilities to an end once and for all. The passage's pathos also underlines the naked brutality of Diomedes' recommendation to the Achaians not to accept Paris' acquisitions or even Helen, the object over which the whole war has been raging (as if she were on offer), simply because Troy's doom seems imminent (400–402), an impression probably fostered by the fact that Hektor has just had a mere draw in single combat with Telamonian Aias. Although the herald, Idaios, has just reminded everybody present that Paris is the cause of the war (388), Diomedes appears to have forgotten the original reason for the Achaians' expedition, which has become submerged in his mind by a desire to press on to nothing less than the total destruction of Troy.[3]

Elsewhere, the origin of the war is remembered all too clearly, but the drive to restore Menelaos' honor results in excessively cruel reactions. A familiar example of this is the episode where Menelaos and Agamemnon dispatch the unfortunate Adrestos (6.37–65). Three as-

---

1. For discussion, see Griffin 1980, 48, 137f. Recently, critics like Marg (1973, 10), Griffin (1980, 94f., with lit.), Mueller (1984, 68–76, 77–89), Schein (1984, 67–88, with lit. at 67 n. 1), and Silk (1987, 73–78) note such gruesome moments but prefer to view the *Iliad* as a poem of death rather than war, reflecting the current opinion of the epic as a "cleaned up" version of the Trojan theme; see also now the disturbing picture sketched by Fehling (1989) of the Trojan story before the *Iliad* and the *Odyssey*. When I draw attention to the *Iliad*'s depiction of the brutalization of values, one of my aims is to demonstrate that, for all the epic's purgation of the gruesome, the grotesque, and the gratuitously cruel, it can still analyze the effects of war in their full horror, while accepting war as a datum of human life.

2. So Leaf 1886–88, ad loc.; cf. Kirk 1990, on 7.427.

3. See Mueller 1984, 67, for the view that Homer "holds that war does not come into its own until its 'original' cause is lost." On brutalization in the Trojan War, especially when the plan of Zeus has been initiated, see Redfield 1975, 167–69.

pects of the scene are of special interest here. First, there are the words of Agamemnon to his brother as Menelaos is on the point of accepting Adrestos' formal supplication, which is backed by the offer of the ransom customary in such cases. Agamemnon asks why Menelaos should have any concern for Adrestos; have the Trojans, he asks, shown the best treatment of Menelaos' household? The mention of Menelaos' household makes us think of Paris' seduction of Helen, but the reference to the Trojans tout ensemble is likely to have been prompted by Agamemnon's continuing fury over the attack on Menelaos during the truce. In any case, Agamemnon is right in implying that the Trojans have impugned the honor of Menelaos, though he has spread the responsibility noticeably wide. But does Paris' and his people's offense really justify Agamemnon's wish that no Trojan whatsoever escape the Achaians' retaliation, not even the Trojan child still carried in his mother's womb or the man who flees, but that they all die without distinction, unlamented, and leaving no trace? Second, there is the hideous moment when Menelaos breaks the physical contact between himself and Adrestos that is an obligatory and obligating step in the supplication ritual, and Agamemnon stabs him in the flank. The honor-incentive for vengeance and death has overridden the honor involved in sparing a suppliant and, in this case, acquiring the ransom-gifts. Moreover, there are instances of captured warriors being ransomed during the earlier stages of the war, though the prevailing mood is no longer one of mercy. Quite apart from Achilles' change of heart when he comes across Lykaon for the second time, Agamemnon kills Isos and Antiphos, even though he recognizes them as warriors whom Achilles once spared (11.101–12); the recognition throws Agamemnon's choice to kill into stark relief. These examples of former mercy demonstrate the hardening of feelings now. Third, immediately after the killing of Adrestos, we find Nestor shouting general advice to the Achaians not to hold themselves up by accumulating as many trophies as they can but to get on with killing, leaving the collection of spoils till afterward, when it can be done with ease (6.66–71). Nestor is saying that the pursuit of honor-trophies is actually hindering the progress of the battle: individual warriors are jeopardizing the corporate endeavor of the army by their imprudent concern with the pursuit of personal honor. Nestor recognizes that the quest for honor is becoming undisciplined and that the communal enterprise is in danger of being fragmented. Coming where it does, it seems likely that Nestor's advice is meant to include Menelaos and Agamemnon, in which case it is a further reflection on the excessiveness of their cruelty to Adrestos. The Adrestos episode as a whole signals the degree to which feelings have become brutalized by the time of the events depicted in the *Iliad*, illustrating the obsessiveness with which warriors are now prepared to assert themselves and the shattering of the norms of proper behavior toward any outsiders at their mercy and toward their own group.[4]

A further indication of the volatility of the warriors' ethical world is provided by their changing attitudes toward returning home and the thought of peace, though other quite natural impulses, such as simple homesickness and war-weariness, are at work here. When Agamemnon makes his fatal test of his force's morale, he repeatedly talks of the shame in which he will return to Argos, his purpose unaccomplished against the numerically vastly inferior Trojans, but he concludes in feigned despair that the whole force should head for home (2.140–41); and, we are told, "in their eagerness for home their shouts reached heaven" (153f.). Now that the king has effectively undermined the hope of honor and promised the reverse, the army is left with nothing more than their natural inclinations, which dictate their movements without hindrance. But once the king's authority has been reasserted and Nestor feels confident enough to state that Zeus guarantees the success of the Achaian expedition, presumably

---

4. Recently, Taplin (1992, 162f.) has explained Agamemnon's attitude toward Adrestos on the grounds that, as he sees it, in battlefield supplication scenes the captor gains ransom-gifts and "gives out some κῆδος (concern)"; because concern for a Trojan like Adrestos is "inappropriate," Agamemnon is at liberty to order Adrestos' immediate dispatch. I am unconvinced by this "anthropology" for reasons that should by now be apparent; in particular, I find the honor-component in the ransom-gifts sufficient obligation on the captor's benevolence and respect, where considerations of "concern" (which Taplin does not fully explain) are much less compelling than Taplin allows. A comparably hideous example of the contravention of normal correct behavior is Odysseus' rejection of Dolon's supplication at 10.454–64, where Odysseus actually turns around and devotes Dolon's armor and weapons to Athene. The Doloneia is, however, unlikely to be part of the monumental *Iliad*; see most recently Danek 1988; Taplin 1992, 11, 152f. See also Taplin 1992, 53f., for Agamemnon's rejection of Chryses' supplication at the very beginning of the poem, entailing a lack of *aidôs* for Chryses as a priest; but the ransom-gifts offered by Chryses command respect as well.

referring back to the portent at Aulis that confirmed that the Achaians would take Troy in the tenth year of the war (301–29), the yearning for home recedes: "at once war became sweeter to them than returning in the hollow ships to their beloved homeland" (453–54).[5] In contrast with such bellicosity is the constant longing for peace expressed by both sides. When Paris and Menelaos come forward to settle their differences in single combat in book 3, Achaians and Trojans alike have a real moment of hope that hostilities will cease once and for all (111–12), and they even pray that they will have a *philotês* ratified by trustworthy oaths (319–23). The case of Helen is interestingly different, for she is now so conscious of her responsibility for the war that when Iris tells her of the truce and the single combat between her two husbands, she is overtaken by a "sweet longing" for her former husband, her city, and her parents (130–45), and her sense of guilt over following Paris is all too clearly expressed to Priam in the Teichoskopia (172–80). The war has sensitized Helen, so that she now desires to return to her home, whereas once she had willingly and, as she now sees, culpably fled from it. This change of heart is made more poignant when she fails to see her brothers, Kastor and Polydeukes, in the Achaian force, and we are informed that they are dead and have been buried in their homeland (236–44). So complete is Helen's separation from the home that she longs for; she can only explain her brothers' absence on the grounds that they are avoiding the shame that attaches to their sister.

Apart from a figure like Helen, the people of the *Iliad* undeniably show the effects of brutalization, so neither a sense of justice, nor affective considerations like the longing for home, nor even the incentive of *tîmê* any longer provide infallible guides for behavior. In such an atmosphere, where the gentleness of the past is contrasted with the harshness of the present, it hardly comes as a surprise to find warriors on the battlefield operating often with no other motive than naked self-assertion, which may increase their personal *tîmê* but does not necessarily at all make them feel bound to "honor" either unprivileged outsiders or even the interests of their own group. Shorn of these applications, the drive for honor becomes a matter of every man for himself, more obsessive and more excessive.

This state of affairs is thrown into sharp relief by the occasional

---

5. Cf. 11.13–14, 19.339.

vignettes in the *Iliad* describing the part justice plays in times of peace and normality. The trial scene on Achilles' shield is particularly instructive. In it, a quarrel has arisen because a man's relative (no further details are given) has been murdered. There are two major rival views of what is going on. One argues that the murderer claims he has paid the blood-price in full (εὔχετο πάντ' ἀποδοῦναι, 18.499), but the kinsman denies having received anything (ἀναίνετο μηδὲν ἑλέσθαι, 500), and that they are both eager to "accept the decision at the hands of an arbitrator" (ἐπὶ ἴστορι πεῖραρ ἑλέσθαι, 501). Elders plead on either side of the case before the arbitrator, who will assign two talents of gold to the elder who "pronounces his judgment in the most straight manner" (508). The other interpretation, probably to be preferred, maintains that the quarrel is over whether the kinsman of the dead man should accept a ransom from the murderer or demand revenge (in the form of execution or exile); the murderer is claiming that he has a right to pay everything and so avoid other penalties, the kinsman is refusing to accept the option of monetary compensation, and the court is setting the "limit" (πεῖραρ) of the penalty. In either view, the sense of justice will be the decisive factor, and the litigants will be expected to abide by the arbitrator's decision.[6] Elsewhere, as we have seen, Aias argues with Achilles that he should accept Agamemnon's gifts because normally men accept blood-price for the murder of a brother or son, and the killer remains in the community (9.632–36). Here, justice, in the form of worthy compensation and involving the concept of *tîmê*, is expected to restore peaceful relations. And if men pervert the course of righteousness and justice and "pronounce crooked rulings," justice will be restored by Zeus' punishment of that community, the doctrine of the simile at *Iliad* 16.384–92.

Another prime example of the part justice can play in moments of normality is provided by the altercation between Menelaos and Antilochos after the chariot-race of the funeral games for Patroklos (23.566–611). Antilochos' claim to the prize mare is challenged by Menelaos. In a solemn procedure reminiscent of the assembly, the herald gives Menelaos the scepter and commands general silence

---

6. For discussion of the court scene see especially Edwards 1991, on 18.497–508, 498–500, with lit.; Edwards argues persuasively for the second interpretation.

(567–69). Menelaos makes his accusation that Antilochos was guilty of foul play and reckless driving in the race, thus unjustly impugning Menelaos' excellence as a charioteer. He calls on the Achaian leaders to act as an impartial, mediating jury (574) to ensure that he will not lay himself open to the charge of having pulled rank (575–78). But then he says he will adjudge the case himself, without fear of anyone taking exception, because "it will be done straightly" (580). This "straight judgment" takes the form of demanding that Antilochos swear an oath to Poseidon that he did not mean to commit a foul against Menelaos' chariot (581–85). This has the immediate effect of making Antilochos adduce his "flighty" youth as the cause of his behavior, a face-saving method of admitting to the charge; moreover, he claims that he will hand over the mare and that he is prepared to do anything rather than fall in Menelaos' esteem and be an offender against the gods (587–95). Relations are restored peacefully. Menelaos' heart is warmed, and with a warning to the young man not to try to trick his superiors again, he compliments Antilochos by saying that he has been persuaded more readily by him than he would be by any other Achaian, because Antilochos has fought hard for the Atreidai. He even gives him the mare, saying that he is responsive to his plea for it, which puts Antilochos in the position of a petitioning subordinate; and the Achaian witnesses see that the king can be generous (596–611).

These glimpses of moments of peace and normality show that justice is expected to prevail. How different the standard behavior of warriors in battle is, at least as the *Iliad* presents it. Moreover, the vignettes of peace and normality seem to suggest that when war has become as protracted and desperate as it is in the *Iliad*, how much more necessary a factor that will finally predispose people to fairness is. Such a factor will be Achilles' sympathy for and consequent generosity toward a fellow mortal in suffering.

The Case of Hektor

The fragmentation of ethical values can be seen clearly in the person of Hektor, who is presented, if anybody in the *Iliad* is, as the mainstay of his community. Perhaps the most important text in this regard is Hektor's angry rejection of Poulydamas' advice that the Trojan force should retreat into the city when Achilles returns to the Achaian cause (18.285–309). His main reason for fighting on beside the ships is that Zeus has granted that he will win *kûdos* there and will drive the Achaians into the sea (293–94), which prompts him to declare that he will face Achilles himself, in man-to-man combat (305–9). With this reasoning, he is jeopardizing his city, because he is the lesser warrior. He admits as much to Achilles (20.434), his father shares his assessment (22.40), and so does Achilles (22.333). During the pursuit around the walls, he is called "noble" while Achilles is styled "much the superior" (22.158), so his inferiority must have been tacitly accepted long before it is expressed in so many words. But the background reason for his choice is also important. We can under-stand all too well his frustration when he asks Poulydamas whether he hasn't yet had enough of being cooped up inside the city's towers and when he backs up his challenge by recalling how men formerly used to talk of Troy's wealth whereas its treasure is now exhausted, much of it having been sent as payment to allies in Phrygia and Maionia, "since great Zeus was angry" (18.287–92; cf. 17.220–26). It is legitimate to assume—reconstructing the direction of Hektor's thinking from the text—that Hektor's frustration over the thought that his city has been reduced to such dismally inglorious straits is a major factor in his desire to bring matters to a head. It is equally legitimate to conclude that he is to some extent compensating for his frustration over the faded glory of his city by pursuing individual glory and honor for himself. Now that the Zeus who has caused the Trojans to empty their coffers is offering him personal glory, should he not make the best of his opportunity? In this context, Hektor makes his decision not to retreat. The passage illustrates just how much the war has sapped the Trojans' morale. It also shows how in circumstances of such desperately low morale, the hero grows ob-sessed with his personal glory, to the detriment of his community. Later, Hektor will call this pursuit of glory "recklessness" (*atasthaliai*, 22.104), and he will see that it has led to the destruction of his com-munity, but knowledge of that fact will in no way encourage him to subordinate his need for personal glory to the common good.

In his attempt to convince Hektor to retreat, Poulydamas argues that because Achilles is at large again, he will move the battle from the plain to the city, and the Trojans will be fighting for their city and their women (18.261–65). He touches on an area of human life, the family, which might seem to exert an indefeasible claim on the warrior's loyalty, a claim based on affection, but no less compelling. In his rejection of Poulydamas' advice, Hektor nowhere explicitly addresses this argument. His family has been relegated to being associated with being "cooped up inside the towers" and has been overridden in his mind by the desire for the only *kûdos* that he seems to think he can aspire to with any confidence.[7]

This is a development of the way Hektor thinks and speaks in his farewell to Andromache and Astyanax in book 6. His famous reply to Andromache's plea to him to come inside the walls and save her from becoming a widow and their son from becoming fatherless is based on his shame in the face of the community at not living up to his reputation for winning fame for himself and Priam (441–46). When he pictures the inevitable fall of Troy, he says that he will sense no greater pain for the Trojans, his father, his mother, or his brothers and sisters than for Andromache, by which it is clear that he by no means lacks love for his family. But even so there is a strong indication that shame also permeates his thinking, because he wishes that he will be hidden beneath the earth before he hears Andromache's cries as she is dragged into slavery, and he imagines with horror how her captors will say that she was the husband of Hektor, "who was best among the Trojans at fighting" (447–65). He seizes the other end of the stick and shows his preoccupation with honor when he prays that Astyanax will grow up to be "renowned" among the Trojans and that people will say of him that he "is better by far than his father" as he brings home the armor of his enemies (476–81). Already in book 6, the constraints of shame and honor have proven stronger than that of the family; precisely shame at the thought of what will become of his family, love them as he assuredly does, forms the greater part of his decision to return to battle. By book 18, however, there is no more talk of his wife and son at all, and by book 22 Hektor is too far caught up in the web of his honor and his sense of dishonor to be persuaded by the appeals of Priam and Hekabe to fight Achilles from inside the walls, although Priam gives Hektor the explicit advice

---

7. On the analysis of Schofield (1986, 18–22), the debate between Hektor and Poulydamas demonstrates the "dynamism" inherent in the heroic code, the conflict between the "intended results" that the code sanctions—defense of one's community and so forth—and its "goal,"—glory; that may be so, but Schofield seems to me to ignore the emotional aspect of Hektor's decision.

to do so to save the whole populace of Troy (56f.); and Hekabe is even more direct in her plea than Priam is, as she holds out her breast in a mother's desperation (82–85). The potency of the image of the family as a reason for caring behavior is reserved for reassertion until book 24, when Achilles is reminded of Peleus by the sight of the grieving Priam (503–12). Until that moment, family ties provide no effective sanction for social cohesion—at one point Achilles too subordinates Peleus and his son, Neoptolemos, to Patroklos in his affections (19.321–37)—and they are restored to that role not by the side in the Trojan War naturally most often pictured in the context of their families but by a member of the Achaian force, physically separated as he is from his family, and in the end painfully aware of the rift.

The Attenuation of Sanctions

We can detect signs of fragmentation in all other areas of social contact—in relations with people outside the group, such as suppliants and strangers, and in the relations of people inside the group, with the result that the leader of the group can disaffect his fellows, who can then elect to be unresponsive to the group's needs. The sanctions, both ultimate and proximate, that govern right behavior in the case of outsiders have become attenuated. We have seen just how attenuated from Agamemnon's treatment of Adrestos and of Isos and Antiphos. In the case of Adrestos, Agamemnon's desire for *tîmê* has become excessive and is directed to individual profit. In that of Isos and Antiphos, his progress to glory makes him ignore the ties that the two Trojans have with a member of his own group. In both cases, Agamemnon's cruelty contrasts with the right behavior that Achilles once showed to suppliants like Isos and Antiphos and to Lykaon, which points up the distance between the past and the present in the warriors' ethical outlook.

To outsiders who pose some threat to his claim on an honor-gift (*geras*), Agamemnon is no respecter of rank or sanctity, as his attitude toward Chryses shows. Chryses is a suppliant and a priest of Apollo, so Agamemnon's rejection of his plea to accept his ransom and return Chryseis is especially charged. When he supplicates the Achaians, he does so with the fillets and golden staff that go with his priestly office (1.14f.), he frames his request moderately, and he states that by complying the Achaians will be respecting Apollo (20f.). The

Achaians respond by approving the idea of reverence for the god (22f.). Though Agamemnon sends him away "ignobly," he tacitly admits that the priest should be respected, when he says that if he catches him in the camp again, the god's staff and fillets will not be any protection (26–28). The king is thus said to have treated the priest dishonorably (atîmazô, 11, 94). The general reaction of the Achaians, the comment about Agamemnon's "ignoble" dismissal of Chryses, and his giveaway disclosure about the respect he feels for priestly trappings reveal that it is intrinsically good to honor a priest, so when Apollo sends the plague in punishment, it is not merely a matter of reinstating his tîmê and that of his earthly representative, though that factor persuades Agamemnon to honor the priest. Moreover, there is an element of affection between the god and his priest in return for past services: Chryses seems to use that as a bargaining point in his prayer to the god when he mentions the construction of a temple and the sacrifice of bulls and goats (39–41). None of these considerations sways the king for the moment, though the practicalities of the situation finally force his hand. At a juncture when the drive for honor has become such an excessive and individuated affair, neither respect and honor for a suppliant on their own nor even respect and honor for a suppliant with a god's special backing are capable of ensuring right relations toward an outsider.

Within Agamemnon's group is a seer who has knowledge of factors that represent a threat to the king's tîmê, to whom there is every likelihood that the king will respond with excessive self-assertion and, in a word, badly. This seer, Kalchas, feels it necessary to win Achilles' protection against Agamemnon, whom he knows he will anger (78) when he explains the causes of Apollo's displeasure. He comments that "a king is the stronger man when he is angry with an inferior" (80), and that such a king will be unable to restrain his "anger" and "wrath" for long (81–83). Agamemnon only offers verbal abuse to the seer, though he proceeds from it, after accepting the fact that Kalchas' advice is correct and should be acted on, to his more menacing demand for compensation for the loss of his geras. In this highly charged atmosphere, especially after Agamemnon's treatment of Chryses, Kalchas is wise not to put too much reliance on his status as the Achaians' soothsayer.

Through Achilles it is shown most clearly how the king's overinsistence on being paid due honor can disaffect a member of the group.

That Agamemnon's demand for Briseis is excessive and hence bad is beyond reasonable doubt. Nestor's advice that Agamemnon should give up his claim to the girl "even though he is an *agathos*, as the Achaians gave her as a prize to Achilles in the first place" can only be taken to mean that Agamemnon, as a man of high standing, might expect to have a claim on the girl, but would be a morally bad *agathos* if he acted on such a claim.[8] A few lines earlier, Agamemnon advises Achilles, "even though he is an *agathos*," not to cheat him (131f.), which obviously entails morally reprehensible behavior, and in book 24 Apollo threatens Achilles with the gods' *nemesis* "although he is an *agathos*," because he has passed the bounds of fair behavior in his treatment of Hektor's corpse (53f.). Apollo's phraseology is particularly illuminating, because it shows that among the gods some connection is perceived between the word *agathos*, with its primarily social reference, and the expectation that a man so designated will behave "in accordance with his station" or, if he does not, will earn the gods' "indignation" as a person acting beneath his position, which appears to be the mental process denoted here by *nemesis*. This is a god's view; men like Nestor and Agamemnon use *agathos* in a purely social sense and talk separately about the advisability of fairness. Apollo and, following him, Zeus seem to make the connection between social and moral nobility more directly, "sanctioning" the expectation that men in positions of significance will behave "becomingly." Poseidon puts it similarly when he comments that Zeus will move beyond the bounds of acceptable behavior for an *agathos*, if he tries to restrain him, a deity "of equal honor" (15.185f.). In any case, the conclusion is inevitable that Agamemnon's self-assertion is excessive. The ultimate moral constraints to behave fairly have broken down, and all constraints proximately based on *tîmê* are ineffec-

---

8. Against Adkins 1960b, 37f.: Dover 1983, 37f.; Rowe 1983, 264f.; Schofield 1986, 29. Cf. Long 1970, 126–28, with Rowe, loc. cit.; Gagarin 1987, 303–6; Cairns 1993, 95–103. Moreover, when Nestor points out to Achilles that Agamemnon has superior *tîmê* as a scepter-bearing king (278–79), he may be again tacitly criticizing the king, because in Homeric thinking the Zeus-given *tîmê* of the king imposes on him the obligation to wield the scepter and pronounce *themistes*; so, e.g., Odysseus at 2.197, 205–6. It is therefore "appropriate" that the man with the highest *tîmê* exercise the greatest moral and legal force and also act appropriately. In that case, Nestor could be suggesting that Agamemnon in particular should "live up to his position."

tual. Agamemnon associates the impulse to assert *tîmê* so totally with the defense of his personal worth and dignity that he nullifies all the applications of *tîmê* to relationships in society.[9]

The *Iliad* describes this disaffection in terms of *cholos*, "anger," and *eris*, "strife." These are negative drives: *eris* is commonly coupled with the adjective "soul-destroying."[10] In one remark, significant for the light it sheds on the *Iliad's* results-culture, Agamemnon describes his argument with Achilles as one of the "strifes which take away the fulfillment of one's purpose" (2.376), admitting how the strife which he started (378) has destroyed the cooperation that would have achieved more immediate results in the war.[11] In Achilles' case, anger and strife are preconditioned by Agamemnon's unacceptable assertion of his dignity. Later, he rejects and curses anger and strife, even wishing that the object over which they had arisen, Briseis, had been killed the day he took her in captivity from Lyrnessos (18.107ff., 19.56ff.), and he rejoins the group and furthers its interests, even if for reasons that the group would not have understood. Social cohesion and the prevailing reasons for commending it have thus been shattered, at least for one member of the group, but we have seen enough to convince ourselves that at the time of the *Iliad's* events, the problem is general, if less acute than in the case of Achilles, whose disaffection is what the *Iliad* is about.

A Son's Feelings of Guilt

We have now seen examples of the heroic sense of fairness that exists in the *Iliad* and even more instances of its repudiation. From the period before the main narrative we have the moment of respect, heroic propriety, and fair play when Achilles gives his enemy King Eëtion a funeral with full military honors (6.416–20). One final and fundamental question remains in our analysis: does the text of the

---

9. My analysis differs from that of Schofield (1986), who considers that "excellent counsel" is necessary to adjudicate between the claims of honor and is therefore external to it. I would accept that rationality is a heroic virtue, but I suggest that, in the settlement of conflicting claims to honor, honor gives a more direct indication of "appropriate" behavior than Schofield allows.

10. See, e.g., 19.58; cf. 16.476.

11. See further, e.g., 5.890f. (= 1.177f.).

Iliad permit us to see any other stimulus for the Iliadic warrior's sense of fairness and, beyond that, his feelings of generosity?

As with the constraints to act loyally, the psychological machinery operates on two levels, one ultimate, one proximate. It operates ultimately on the level of guilt and proximately on that of shame, not on just one or the other, though some scholars have opted for a more exclusive model.[12] D.L. Cairns' discussion of shame and guilt carefully defines the emotions. Broadly speaking, Cairns accepts the view that

> when one feels shame at one's moral conduct, one focuses on the kind of person one is, on the whole self, on one's failure to match one's self-image or to manifest a prized moral excellence; guilt, on the other hand, focuses on the specific transgression of an internalized injunction, dealing not with the whole self but with the discrepancy between one's moral self and one's (immoral) act.

Cairns is, however, at pains to point out the difficulty of distinguishing between focus on the self alone and focus on self as agent of special acts; he rightly doubts that popular usage respects the distinction, and he admits a degree of overlap.[13] His abstract models of shame and honor correspond easily with my layering of proximate and ultimate pressures.

Hektor's debate with himself whether to retreat behind the walls of Troy (22.99–130), often regarded as a key text in this connection, is couched in terms of shame. He fears the rebuke (100) of Poulydamas for not following his good tactical advice, has shame (*aideomai*, 105) in the face of the citizens of Troy and what they will

---

12. Championing shame: Dodds 1951, 17f., 28–63; Finley 1978, esp. 108–26; Adkins 1960b, 48f.; 1971, 4f. Lloyd-Jones (1983, 2, 15, 24–27; 1987a, 1–7; 1987b, 307f.) and Dickie (1978) accept the importance of shame in Homeric society, but Lloyd-Jones underemphasizes it to discover a guilt-based sense of justice in the *Iliad*, while Dickie seeks "internalized moral imperatives" alongside the shame-factor. I agree that a shame-culture could never be totally devoid of some element of guilt and some internalized sense of what is intrinsically right. See Lloyd-Jones 1983, 15, 25–27; 1987a, 1f.; Gould 1973, 87–89; Cairns 1993, 27–47 (with extensive argumentation and lit.).

13. Cairns 1993, 22, 23–25.

say about his disastrously misplaced confidence in his own might (106–7), expresses the preference to die "with fair fame" (110) before the city rather than face his shame, and finally rejects the possibility that he might offer restitution to the Achaians on the grounds that Achilles would have no reverence for him in any case and would kill him once he had taken off his armor and was naked and like a woman (124f.). As he expresses it, honor demands that he stand his ground, even if it is his last stand, and even more so now than in his speech to Andromache in book 6, where in similar phraseology he refused his wife's entreaty to fight from inside the walls, talking of his shame before the Trojans if he were to avoid combat like a coward (6.441–46). Now he has the added shame of knowing that his self-confidence has proven inadequate and that a lesser warrior is in a position to rebuke him for it.

Hektor's words and reasoning require closer inspection. He may express his reactions to his situation in terms of shame and honor, but here and in general, what function could shame and honor fulfill unless some anterior impulse were present? It is difficult to imagine a society cooperating or not cooperating on the basis of shame and honor alone, and we have already considered the likelihood that a sense of fairness lies behind such sanctions. We can in turn, I suggest, discern the workings of guilt behind the notion of justice. At the back of Hektor's honor-terminology, a core of guilt seems to exist over his having destroyed his community through his own "recklessness" (22.104). If ruining his people were purely a matter of shame and honor, we might justifiably still feel a little puzzled over what the shame and honor were about—why they were there in the first place. The sense of guilt is the ultimate driving force, though in Hektor's speech and in Iliadic society generally, its voice, like that of justice, is heard only faintly. In the case of justice, words like *just* are rare, because, as I argue, the quality is not effective by itself and needs the more tangible mechanisms of honor-based social institutions to make it so.[14] Likewise, guilt more often than not can only be expressed and actuated through the more immediate sanctions of honor and shame.

14. See Hoffmann 1914, 39ff., esp. 43, 107; Gagarin 1973, 87. On Hektor's sense of guilt, Dickie (1978, 94) argues that Hektor's speech to Andromache in *Il.* 6 provides evidence "that men have personal convictions about the right thing to do." His point is amplified by Cairns (1993, 79–83), who argues that in *Il.* 22 Hektor has an awareness of his misdeed that is likewise subjective

That guilt is a living impulse in the psyche of the Iliadic hero is demonstrated by a passage that has received surprisingly little attention from scholars interested in such things. In book 24 Achilles responds to Priam's supplication for Hektor's corpse with the image of the two jars of Zeus, a consolatory explanation of the mutability of human fortune. But from the beginning he is amazed by the "iron heart" of Priam, who has dared to enter the presence of the man who has killed so many of the king's sons (518–21). His thoughts easily turn to his own father and Peleus' mixed fortunes. Peleus, he says, was preeminent in wealth and sway, but Zeus allotted him the misfortune of having only one son, who was to be "completely untimely" (540), in terms of his early death. Achilles goes on to say, in reference both to Peleus' misfortune and to his own feelings about his father, that he is not "caring for" Peleus in his old age but is sitting idly before Troy causing "care" for Priam and his children (540–42). How are we to interpret the emotions behind these words? We may justifiably see here regret about the misery he is causing Priam and his family. Moreover, care for aged parents had a sanction in honor and shame,[15] and shame may be something else that we can legitimately impute to Achilles. But can we not plausibly identify the dominant feeling that Achilles is expressing as guilt over the fact that he is not supporting Peleus in his old age, brought on because of the deaths

---

and thus demonstrates the "germ" of an idea of retrospective conscience. Cairns' discussion of both passages seems to me, however, to underestimate the operation of *tîmê* on Hektor's mind. In both cases, the negative, inhibitory drive of *aidôs* is present, but equally powerful is the positive impulse of the "learnt" desire to be *esthlos* among the front-line fighters and to win *kleos* (6.445f.), or to face and kill Achilles or die "with fair *kleos* in front of the city" and see whom Zeus will give the triumph, ideas picked up later with the wish to die not "without *kleos*" but "having done something great for men to come to learn of" (22.110, 130, 304f.). What Hektor naturally feels, *aidôs*, and what he has "learnt" (and internalized) are not the same thing, though they are, as I have expressed it elsewhere, "opposite ends of the same stick." This is an important reservation, which I sense generally in Cairns' treatment of the pressures on Homer's warriors, however excellent its analysis of the shame-component.

15. At *Works and Days* 185–88, for example, Hesiod complains that the young in the present Age of Iron "do no honor to" their aging parents, by, among other things, not paying them back for rearing them; see also, in the *Iliad*, 4.477f., 17.301f.

he is dealing out at Troy? The passage demonstrates the need for us to be receptive to pluralistic interpretations—sorrow for an enemy, shame, guilt—rather than to be straitjacketed into reductive, minimalist approaches like Adkins'. Achilles allows guilt to speak more directly here perhaps than anywhere else in the poem.

This is even true of when Achilles recriminates himself for not being present to defend Patroklos from death. He tells Thetis that life has no pleasure for him now that his "dear" friend is dead, whom he "honored" (18.80–81), not until Hektor has "paid the penalty" for killing Patroklos (apotînô, 93), who needed Achilles' defense (98–100); so now he will rejoin the battle and win "noble glory" (121), reminding the Trojans' wives of how long he has been absent from the fray by killing many of their men (122–25). The coexistence of affection and honor in friendship in the *Iliad* is brought out very well here, but not a sense of guilt. Achilles expresses his emotions exclusively in terms of affection, shame, and honor, though now that we have reason to believe that guilt was a reality in the human world of the *Iliad* and that the heroes characteristically translate into shame what we would call guilt, we are at liberty, if we choose, to postulate the activity of guilt-feelings behind Achilles' reactions and words. In a later speech of lamentation, a direct address to the corpse of Patroklos, Achilles states that he could not suffer more, even if he were to be told of Peleus' death or that of his son, Neoptolemos (19.321ff.). It is interesting to compare his words on Peleus with those in book 24. In his speech over the dead Patroklos, he pictures his father in Phthia shedding tears of longing for his son while Achilles is abroad fighting the Trojans over Helen (19.323–25), and he surmises that Peleus is either already dead or grieving in his old age and ever expecting news of his son's death (334–37). These are undeniably words of rift and sadness, even if those feelings are subordinated to Achilles' overriding emotional concern for Patroklos, but they are not words expressly of guilt, however significant a factor that emotion may be behind the words.

The presence of such guilt is the ultimate mechanism behind the Iliadic hero's sense of justice—for example, when he is revolted by displays of excessive self-assertion. A hero's feelings of guilt may be swamped by other considerations, such as the desire for honor when the deed is hot: guilt hardly plays a role in Agamemnon's decision to insult Apollo's priest and his own prophet and to rob his loyal followers of the spoils of war that have fairly been allotted them. A mediator like Nestor, however, can, presumably by his experience of guilt at some juncture in his own life or by the transference of the feeling from the collective conscience, judge that Agamemnon should feel guilt as a consequence of his injustice. For his part, Agamemnon reacts to his internal guilt-feelings and realizes that he has acted unjustly (though he admittedly expresses his repentance without any recourse to guilt-terminology), but only when the impulses that have overridden his sense of guilt have evaporated. The expectation is, therefore, that the sense of guilt will deter men from unjust behavior. Moreover, Zeus and other gods reduplicate the motivation of guilt and therefore emphasize its importance.[16] The trouble is, as the example of Agamemnon illustrates, that the sense of guilt is all too easily ignored in the pursuit of the very values that normally substantiate its claim on the heroes to behave appropriately and worthily. The problem is especially pointed in the ethical climate of the warrior-society at the stage of the Trojan War at which the *Iliad* takes up the tale. At least in part, the crisis in values that exists in the *Iliad* is based on what have turned out to be the conflicting claims of guilt and shame or honor, though ironically shame and honor are normally expected to buttress the claims of guilt and the fairness-principle that originates in guilt. As we have seen, the balance has tipped in favor of honor and shame, though it is redressed at the end of the poem, when the voice of guilt is heard once more, and a hero responds with generosity.

A Tragedian Reflects

The tension that could arise between an essentially honor-based heroism and the claims of affection and fairness on heroic behavior apparently fascinated the Greeks into at least the fifth century. Proof of such an interest is provided by the *Aias* of Sophokles, which is in important respects a meditation on the *Iliad* and its ethical world.[17] Because Sophokles' play explores the ethical tensions within heroism and nobility in terms that are strikingly similar to those of the *Iliad*, it lends support to the model that I have proposed in this chapter and proves that the problems inherent in heroism that I have suggested

16. Lesky 1961, 27f., on "Nachdrücken."

17. Discussions of the influence of the Homeric view of heroism on the *Aias* include Knox 1961, 1–37; Winnington-Ingram 1980, 15–19; Gould 1983, 32–45, esp. 38–40; Easterling 1984; Goldhill 1986, 154–61; Easterling 1987, 52–61. What follows is a modified version of my remarks at Zanker 1992.

lie at the very heart of the *Iliad* were perceived by Greek society in Sophokles' day not as mere poetic constructs but as live issues. This increases the likelihood that at least this aspect of Homeric society was historical.

In the course of its analysis of what it means to be "noble" (*eugenês*), that is, to be nobly born and to behave appropriately, the *Aias*, I suggest, pits the claim of *tîmê* against those of affection and justice, *dîkê*. It resolves the tension by acknowledging the different sorts of nobility involved in both sets of criteria and by demonstrating the need for a combination of fairness and a generosity that is based on such human emotions as pity and on friendship.

The champion of the *tîmê*-standard is Aias. At lines 764–75 the messenger recalls the parting advice of Aias' father, Telamon, to his son as he set forth on the expedition to Troy—that Aias should desire to be victorious in battle, but to do so with the gods on his side (764–65). We saw the motif of the father encouraging his son to be preeminent and at the same time entering a caveat when we examined Peleus' words to Achilles. In the *Aias* the caveat has been turned from advice about being cooperative into a stricture about the need to maintain right relations with the gods, which is a comparatively minor element in Peleus' counsel. In both cases the advice is directed at the son's particular weakness, and in the *Aias* Telamon's suggestion is met with Aias' proud insistence that even nonentities can win might with the aid of the gods. Aias has confidence that he will win *kleos* even without their support; he later tells Athene to stand by other sections of the Achaian army on the grounds that wherever he is there to defend the line, it will never be broken (766–75). The idea that a hero might boast that he does not need divine aid is foreign to the *Iliad* and belongs more properly to fifth-century tragedy,[18] but a hero's confidence in his own prowess is quite within the realm of Iliadic concepts of heroism.

---

18. N.B. 127–33 (Athene on self-restraint). Aias' *hûbris* is absent from his words at *Il.* 17.634, but the concept is present in the *Odyssey*, when the Locrian Aias defiantly asserts that he will cross the sea in safety "without the good will of the gods" (4.504); Sophokles seems to have transferred the *hûbris* of the Locrian Aias to the Telamonian; see Kamerbeek 1953, on *Aias* 767, 768. The handling of this theme in the *Aias* has most recently been discussed by Crane (1990, 89–101, esp. 99–101); for prior studies of Sophokles' fifth-century perspective on Homeric heroism see the preceding note.

Aias is devastated by shame after his failure to be allotted the
armor of Achilles and his subsequent crazed attack on the cattle and
sheep. When Tekmessa and the Chorus first meet him after the car-
nage, which he now recognizes as such, he makes a bitterly ironic
comparison between his former martial prowess and the might with
which he has attacked mere animals, and he grieves over how he has
been reduced to a laughingstock and how he has been shamed (364–
67).[19] Later, addressing the River Skamandros, he uses a vaunting
tone typical of epic when he claims that Troy never saw his equal,
but he closes his assertion with the comment that he now lies pros-
trate, without honor (418–27); the epic tone and sentiment—we think
especially, perhaps, of Achilles' remark that he has no equal among
the Achaians (Il. 18.105), a remark made precisely when he is racked
by feelings of shame, guilt, and grief on hearing of Patroklos' death—
add significantly to the bitterness of Aias' reference to his loss of tîmê.
The thought is developed in the speech that immediately follows, in
which Aias compares his achievements with those of Telamon, who
came to the same place and through his prowess won Hesione, the
fairest prize of all the army (435), bringing home "all glory" (436),
while Aias, after no less effort, is perishing without tîmê among the
Greeks (440). Aias deplores the thought of appearing before Telamon
without gifts of honor, the source of Telamon's "great crown of
glory" (462–66).[20] He declares it ignoble that a man who has unvary-

---

19. The effect of Aias' dishonor on his followers graphically illustrates the
socially competitive aspect of shame. At 141–47, 154–61, 173f., and 187–91
the Chorus of Aias' men bewail their insignificance and their consequent
inability to defend themselves on a competitive level against the charges of
dishonor to which their master has exposed them.

20. With ironic appropriateness, therefore, it is the gift of Aias' enemy
Hektor, the sword that the Trojan gave him when they ceased hostilities at
Il. 7.303ff., with which Aias chooses to end his life (815–22); because he
obtained it from Hektor, he has received nothing "of value" from the
Achaians, which on the heroic logic of esteem must include any gift (661–65).
Moreover, Sophokles makes Hektor and Aias guest-friends as a result of the
exchange, so the sword is a gift given in guest-friendship, and the dramatist
can play on the incongruity of the inauspiciousness of the gift (665) and of
the idea of a guest-friend being "most hated" (817f.); see Herman 1987, 60
n. 56, with Easterling 1984, 6f. The case of Hektor, whom Sophokles makes
receive Aias' belt after the duel, is similarly ironic, for the belt is used to bind
Hektor's corpse to Achilles' chariot; together with the irony of Hektor's gift

ingly bad fortune should want to have a long life (473–74), and he concludes that the man who is nobly born, *eugenês*, should either live nobly or die so (479–80).

Here is heroism's competitive drive in all the shapes in which the *Iliad* presents it, apart, that is, from Aias' proud disclaimer of the need for any divine aid. Sophokles confronts it head-on, first with the claims of affection, or to use his own word, *charis*. In her answer to Aias' speech of shame, Tekmessa uses almost all the arguments with which Andromache implores Hektor to fight from within the walls of Troy,[21] but she also uses some of those with which Priam supplicates Achilles for Hektor's corpse. Significantly, she echoes the Iliadic Hektor as he pictures Andromache's captors gloating over the depths to which his wife will sink and as he hopes that he will be dead and buried before hearing her cries in captivity (*Il.* 6.459–65). She picks up the shame motif and makes a forceful point out of it: "These words will be shameful to you and your family" (505).[22] So shame does form part of her entreaty. But the burden of her plea is directed at Aias' affections. She argues that Aias should have reverence for his old father and for his mother, who longs for his homecoming (506–9), a thought that in all likelihood goes back to Priam's persuasive words to Achilles about Peleus.[23] He should pity their son, Eurysakes, whose fate she goes on to describe (510–13), just as Andromache does for Astyanax at *Iliad* 22.490–98, after she has seen that Hektor has been killed. And he should pity Tekmessa. She introduces this consideration early in her speech, when she reminds Aias that she is his allotted slave and has shared his bed, so she is concerned for his well-being and can entreat him in the name of Zeus of the Hearth not to abandon her to his enemies (487–99). Later she argues that Aias is all to her (514–19). Here she echoes Andromache's famous words to Hektor (*Il.* 6.411–30), with the difference that Achil-

---

to Aias, it makes Teukros conclude that the gods have planned the neat coincidence (1028–39).

21. See Easterling 1984, 1–5.

22. Her reminiscence of Hektor's evocation of what an anonymous man will say in time to come powerfully amplifies the shame/honor-aspect of her appeal; on such speeches, see Wilson 1979, 1–15; de Jong 1987b.

23. *Il.* 24.486–94; see esp. 487, and cf. *Aias* 506f., for the similarity of phrasing on the *gêras*, the "old age," of Peleus and Telamon.

les, the enemy, destroyed Andromache's homeland, but Aias destroyed Tekmessa's, making Tekmessa's dependence on Aias even more poignant.

All this is merely a prelude to the appeal that forms the climax of her speech. She reasons that a man should not forget "if he has anywhere enjoyed something pleasant," because kindness, *charis*, always begets kindness, *charis*, and whoever forgets being treated well is not a nobly born man or is not acting in accordance with his station (520–24). With these words she directly challenges Aias' competitive definition of the noble man as one who must either live or die nobly, and with the word *pleasant*, she is answering his question about what "pleasure" the day can bring when a man's misery is unrelieved (475–76). She is doing nothing less than defining the noble man as one who is responsive to kindness and affection. Aias' reaction is instructive. He admits that at Tekmessa's appeal, even he, who formerly was as hard as tempered steel, felt his edge grow soft, "unmanned," "made like a woman" (ἐθηλύνθην),[24] and that he feels pity for her and Eurysakes (650–53), though this is insufficient to change his resolve to die.[25] The word for "made like a woman" illustrates the honor-driven warrior's contempt for the affective appeal, but Aias is far from entirely unmoved.

This is by no means the sum total of what the play has to say about *charis*, "kindness" or "kind favor." For one thing, there is the thought that "gratitude" should be shown for past services. Aias gives indirect expression to this when he says that if his old repute has been destroyed, he will have nowhere to flee, and the Achaians will kill him (404–9). The Chorus lament the fact that the Atreidai do not appreciate Aias' former deeds of the greatest *aretê* (616–20). Teukros makes the point most clearly, perhaps, in his speech to Agamemnon, when he turns to address the dead Aias and takes the ingratitude of the Atreidai as proof of how quickly *charis* disappears (1266–71). In all this we remember Achilles' complaint to the embassy at *Iliad* 9.316f. that there has been no *charis* forthcoming in return for his

24. Cf. his low estimation of men who weep, reported by Tekmessa at 319f., and his impatience with the tearfulness of women, expressed at 525–28 and 578–82.

25. See Easterling 1984, 5f., on the limited but real softening of Aias' attitude toward people dear to him (*philoi*) that is discernible in the Deception Speech; see now also Crane 1990, 89–101, esp. 94–99, with lit.

continual fighting against the Trojans, so here too Sophokles seems to be picking up a theme cardinal to the epic.[26]

It is time to consider the thought behind the arguments of the characters in the play who are prepared to take Aias' part before Agamemnon and Menelaos. Teukros concludes his speech to Agamemnon by saying that it is more noble for him to labor on Aias' behalf than on that of the Atreidai over Helen (1310–12). He has just been defending himself against Agamemnon's taunts about his low, barbarian birth (1288–1307; cf. 1228–35, 1259–63), so context would seem to suggest that the word for "noble" here, *kalon*, involves the aristocratic *agathos*-standard of virtuous behavior, from which Teukros never really deviates. At 1125 he urges the claims of justice, and he does so in the face of Menelaos' insistence that as a mere archer he has no right to have "high thoughts" (1120–25). But he does so only after he has defended his bowmanship against the charge of being a "skill unworthy of a free-born man." At 1299–1303, he argues that his parentage was "really" noble; and at 1093–96 he expresses the traditional thought that the nobly born should set an example for the lowborn.[27] Within the competitive *tîmê*-framework, Teukros praises Odysseus as "best," *aristos*, for his justice and generosity toward Aias (1381, 1399).

The attitude of Odysseus is most important for our inquiry. Tekmessa and Teukros, as people dear to Aias (*philoi*), have reason to defend the hero, but Odysseus and Aias are rivals and enemies, and Odysseus still extends *charis* to his dead opponent. When Agamemnon expresses surprise at this, Odysseus admits that Aias was an enemy but says he was noble all the same, and he says that Aias' competitive *aretê* moves him more than their enmity (1354–57). He says he cannot approve of "a hard heart" (1361). What are Odysseus' reasons for wanting to see the body of his enemy honored with decent burial? To Agamemnon he says that he himself would not dishonor Aias, for he was "the best" among the Achaians after Achilles, and he says further that the king would be unjust (1342) to dishonor him: Agamemnon would be attacking not him but the laws

---

26. The motif is also used in connection with Tekmessa, when she is made to say that she has been cast out of "the favor [*charis*] in which ⟨she⟩ was formerly held" (807f.).

27. See Adkins 1972, 65–67.

of the gods, and it is in any case "not just to harm the morally noble man [*esthlos*] when he dies, even if you happen to hate him" (1336–45). Here a sense of justice, located in the laws of the gods, tempers the heroic *timê*-response illustrated by Agamemnon. Odysseus reveals even deeper motives much earlier in the play, when Athene has goaded Aias into attacking the cattle and sheep. The goddess has just asked Odysseus whether it is not the "sweetest mockery" to mock one's enemies, and he has replied that it would have been sufficient for him that Aias stay inside, an oblique way of saying that he did not want to look on Aias' misery (79–80). After the display of Athene's power, Odysseus can only say that he pities (121) Aias because he has been yoked to an evil doom, and he perceives that his own position is no less precarious than Aias', because all humans are mere images or insubstantial shadows (121–26). Here, as in the *Iliad*, we have the ultimate factor preconditioning the just and generous response: pity for one's fellowman, even one's enemies, motivated by the experience of the suffering that human life can entail. Near the close of the play, Odysseus even offers to join in and help with the burial and to do all that mortals should do in the case of "the best men" (1376–80), which prompts Teukros to praise him, in traditional terms maybe, for his generosity and for his sole defense of his former enemy (1381–99); "Be assured," he says, "that you are an *esthlos* as far as we are concerned" (1398f.).

Once again Sophokles is evidently thinking of the *Iliad*. The model for Odysseus is the Achilles of *Iliad* 24, who pities his enemies Priam and Hektor in part because of his experience of the meaning of mortality (*Il.* 24.503, 516, 540). Achilles is prepared to bend the rules and keep Priam's presence a secret from Agamemnon (650–55), he has Hektor's corpse washed and anointed, and lifts it onto the wagon himself (580–95), and he promises an eleven-day truce while Hektor is buried. Sophokles has shaped the model in his own way, in particular by making the theme of justice more explicit and direct, but the use of Odysseus to mediate in the denouement of the quarrel over Achilles' armor is even more powerful when we realize that his sentiments and moral outlook are based on those of the "original" Achilles. Thus Odysseus' generosity represents the crowning form of nobility of birth and the behavior expected of it in the *Aias*. However grand and awe-inspiring Aias' devotion to *timê*, however moving the appeal to affection given expression by Tekmessa, Odysseus' combination of the sense of justice and the conditioning factor of emotional responses like pity finally succeeds in resolving the quarrel over Achilles' armor in its last stages.

In Aias' unwillingness to compromise himself in his standing as a *tîmê*-warrior, in Tekmessa's appeal to him (partly) in terms of affection, in Teukros' and especially Odysseus' insistence that the Atreidai behave justly toward Aias' corpse, and in Odysseus' generosity in accepting that he has a duty to his rival and enemy that is founded on the pity he feels for a fellow mortal, we have all the ingredients of the tension in moral values that I suggest operates in the *Iliad*.[28] The remarkable overriding similarity between the two sets of heroic values helps to substantiate my reading of the *Iliad*'s values and points to the probability that the problems posed by the conflicting claims of honor and generosity were as real and engaging for the early audiences of the *Iliad* as they evidently were for those of a dramatic production like the *Aias*.[29]

---

28. Gill (1990, 19–22) argues persuasively that in the *Aias* we can see the operation of his "character"-"personality" distinction, which he bases essentially on, respectively, perspectives of character that are objective and moral, and perspectives that are subjective and empathetic; in the Deception Speech, for example, we see Aias presented from the perspectives of both "character" and "personality." Gill's distinction is by and large compatible with my ethical model, "character" comprehending the proximate drives, "personality" the ultimate.

29. In the *Philoktetes* of 409, we observe Sophokles in some ways reduplicating the scheme of values that he explores in the *Aias*. He reflects not only on his sources from epic, in particular the *Kypria*, *Little Iliad*, and *Iliou Persis*, but on the plays of the same name by Aischylos and Euripides, by introducing Neoptolemos as the agent for securing Philoktetes' bow. Neoptolemos is characterized as compassionate, generous, and thus ultimately concerned to see that Philoktetes is treated fairly (906, 965f., 1074f., 1224–34), in stark opposition to Odysseus, whose exclusive interest is to achieve his purpose (75–85, 108–34, 1049–62); see in general Jebb 1898, xixf., xxivff. Success, which Odysseus calls "victory," is an essential component of the competitive *tîmê*-mentality. This opposition of values is very different from what we can glean of the *Problematik* of Aischylos' and Euripides' plays on Philoktetes; see Jebb 1898, xiv–xxvi. It is possible that in the *Philoktetes* he uses the tension to shape his cast and their characterization. In the case of the *Elektra*, however, Sophokles' reading of Homeric epic, this time the *Odyssey* with its revenge theme, feeds into a very different set of moral concerns; see most recently Davidson 1988, 45–72. This suggests, perhaps, that Sophokles particularly regarded the tension as one inherent in the warrior-ethic of the epic tradition.

3

Achilles' Disaffection

Seit ich das Grab seh, will ich nichts als leben,
Und frage nichts mehr, ob es rühmlich sei.
—The Prince, in H.v. Kleist, *Prinz Friedrich von Homburg*

In chapter 1 I stressed how Homer's people responded to the stimulus of honor as a means of ensuring social cohesion and the success of a corporate venture like a military operation. The apparent paradox, that "competitive" drives motivate cooperation, thus turns out on closer inspection to be purely terminological. However, as I hope has become clear from the preceding chapter, the *Iliad* presents the negative aspect of honor, showing in particular how by the dramatic date of the poem it has been molded by the brutalizing effect of ten years of war into an aim in itself, severed from the promptings of affection and justice that it should normally protect, and how the rift becomes a threat to the very existence of the whole community, when Hektor chooses glory over the defense of Troy, of which he knows he is the last bastion. Now we come to Achilles, who, I argue, initially threatens his community for reasons strikingly similar to Hektor's, but who restores its fortunes—even if only as a kind of after-thought—when he is jolted back into action by intensely emotional and personal concerns. Over and above that, he finally comes to reinstate the motives of affection and fair play as the most potent reasons for acting cooperatively, doing so from a deepened sense of mortality, in his behavior toward an enemy, and with a regard for honor-gifts that plays an appropriately ancillary role in his human relations. Moreover, though the *Iliad* presents Achilles' insight as a unique, temporary thing in the long term of the Trojan War, it is, I suggest, the poem's central gift. That historical Greek society had room for such an ethical view is made clear by the reflection of the *Iliad*'s ideal in the poetry of Sophokles' *Aias*.

If we want to gauge the real nature, extent, and intensity of Achilles' reactions to the various situations that he faces in the *Iliad*, our first step, logically, is to form some picture of him as he was before the fatal assembly of book 1, especially because the poem presents an economical and judiciously pointed profile of the hero in his pre-Iliadic days. Formerly, we learn, Achilles was obedient to Peleus' command "always to be *aristos* and superior to the others" (11.784). This command was quite traditional for fathers to give their sons as they leave home for war, as we know from Glaukos' report of his father's command, to which Glaukos is proudly obedient (6.208–10). But even before the war, Achilles must have shown signs of unruliness, because Peleus on the same occasion also commanded him to "hold his mighty passion within his breast, for a cooperative attitude is better," and to leave off "evil-devising strife, so that both the young men and the old of the Argives may honor you the more" (9.255–58). Menoitios also seems to have recognized this side to Achilles' personality, because he conceived of Patroklos as an apparently necessary moderating force on Achilles, able through seniority in age to influence Achilles for the good (11.786–89). But Achilles had been a more than willing member of the Achaian army. In his great speech to the embassy in book 9, he claims that he has continuously been risking his life in battle, selflessly fighting day and night for the cause of the Atreidai, like a mother bird collecting food for her young while she goes without (9.321–27). He levels similar charges against Agamemnon in the assembly of book 1, stressing that he has no quarrel with the Trojans (1.149–71). At neither point does anyone deny the truth of his claims. Achilles was not subject to the oath of Tyndareus, so his support of the Achaians seems even more voluntary. Toward the enemy, moreover, he had shown kindness and even respect, accepting ransom from men like Isos and Antiphos (11.101–12) and Lykaon (21.34–48), with whom he shared a meal when he captured him (21.76–77), and cremating Eëtion with full military honors—without stripping his corpse of its armor—out of respect (6.414–19).[1] When Helenos compares Diomedes with Achilles, he claims that Diomedes is "excessively" battle-mad, implying that Achilles is not (6.99–101). In the course of the *Iliad*, Achilles suffers

---

1. On Eëtion as a means of measuring Achilles' "transformation after the death of Patroklos," see Mueller 1984, 38f.; Easterling, forthcoming. On the similarity of *sebas* to *aidôs*, see Cairns 1993, 137f.

a number of massive changes from his former self, and the movement
is sudden. It is only twelve days since Lykaon has been resettled in
Troy and probably less than a month since Achilles fed and released
him for ransom, and now the Trojan is slain in the ritual act of
supplication. Why and how did the changes come about? How does
the text invite us to construct Achilles' change of heart? The analysis
of the Iliadic warrior's motivation to virtuous behavior that I have
proposed will justify itself amply if it sheds any new light on this vital
question.

In book 1 Achilles still demonstrates kindness and fairness. His
patronage of Kalchas when he promises to protect the seer against
anyone who might find his advice unpalatable (1.85–91) is in glaring
contrast with Agamemnon's shameful treatment of the priest Chryses,
whom he dishonors (11) though the Achaians to a man feel that the
priest should be respected and his ransom for Chryseis accepted
(22–25), and whom Agamemnon sends away "shamefully," warning
him that his priestly status and trappings may be of no protection to
him if the king finds him by the ships again (26–32). The last affront
is an indirect recognition of the priest's rights and privileges in normal
circumstances, which can only increase Agamemnon's culpability.
Even after the king has publicly humiliated him, Achilles shows con-
sideration and even kindness to the heralds Talthybios and Eurybates,
who are sent to confiscate Briseis and whose natural fears as the
bringers of bad news Achilles is at pains to allay (330–35). Such
displays of tact and kindness underline that Achilles' grievance is
with Agamemnon alone. He reminds Agamemnon of his past record
of selfless loyalty, stressing how he had no quarrel at all with the
Trojans but supported Agamemnon solely to win him and Menelaos
tîmê, and he insists throughout on the king's break with the honor-
incentive of the heroic code as the principal reason why he now
wishes to withdraw his services from the Achaian cause (149–71).
As he puts it to Thetis a little later, Zeus should vouchsafe him honor,
though as things are, he is not doing so at all, because Agamemnon
has dishonored him by taking his *geras* (352–56).

The conflict between Achilles and Agamemnon is particularly
charged for a number of reasons. It is a conflict between near equals,
a situation heralded by the seventh line of the whole poem, when,
in an impressive deployment of traditional phraseology for an effect
of unique significance, Agamemnon is presented with his standing

epithet "king of men," which establishes his preeminence in rank, and Achilles is styled as brilliant, *dios*, which emphasizes his active *aretê* as a hero-warrior.[2] The matter of near equality becomes more acute if we follow the attractive thesis that being a "king," *basileus*, at Troy "was a matter of degree rather than rank."[3] If that is so, then Nestor at lines 277–81 advises Achilles not to rival Agamemnon qua the king to whom Zeus has given the *kûdos*, or, as he puts it, the king who is "more powerful [*pherteros*] . . . , since he rules over more men." Achilles' physical strength, conveyed in Agamemnon's adjective "mighty" (*karteros*, 178), cannot prevail over Agamemnon's collective domain. Dangerously, therefore, Agamemnon can lay claim to supreme political strength, Achilles to preeminent individual physical strength. The theme of rivalry is sustained—for example, when Achilles says to Kalchas that he need not fear anyone, even if he means Agamemnon, "who proclaims that he is by far the best of the Achaians" (91), and yet asks Thetis to beseech Zeus to cause the Achaians great losses so that "even wide-ruling Agamemnon, son of Atreus, might recognize his madness, that he did no honor to the best of the Achaians" (411–12). Again the traditional epithets significantly point out the opposition between the two men. Achilles has designed his revenge precisely to show the hazards involved in dishonoring "the best of the Achaians." Agamemnon feels in his conflict with Achilles a need to humiliate Achilles to put him in his place, or, as he puts it, "so that you may know well how much mightier I am than you, and others as well might shrink from claiming equality to me and from putting themselves on the same level as me in open opposition" (185–87). Such humiliation is only called for when a real threat is involved. Nestor describes the rivalry in a more balanced way, perhaps, but the basic picture is strikingly consistent. In his attempt at mediation, he reminds him that the *tîmê* of the king is superior to that of other mortals, because Zeus gives him the *kûdos*, and because he rules over more people. Achilles may be "mighty" and the son of a goddess, but Agamemnon is "more powerful"; so the hero should not challenge his king (277–81). Nestor recognizes Achilles' special physical might but contrasts it with the social rank and greater sway of the king.

---

2. Griffin 1980, 52f.
3. Taplin 1992, 47–49.

The passionate disagreement over the allocation of *tîmê* demon-
strates the serious shortcomings of the whole heroic value-system.
Normally, as we have seen, praise or rebuke in terms of honor se-
cures cooperation, supporting the weaker motives for such an atti-
tude, namely, the sense of reciprocity and fair play and the feelings
of affection. But given the intensity of the conflict over honor in book
1, these ultimate motives are swept aside. As we saw in chapter 2,
Nestor's speech makes it obvious enough, despite its deferential tone
to Agamemnon, that the king is wrong to take Briseis: "Do not rob
this man of the girl, though you are of high standing [*agathos*] ⟨and
might therefore be expected to act as your will leads you⟩, but leave
her be, as the sons of the Achaians allotted her to him in the first
place" (275–76). Agamemnon soon comes to accept that he is in the
wrong.[4] In Achilles' view, Agamemnon is not showing any consider-
ation for Achilles' selfless support (160), a contention with which
Agamemnon agrees when he defiantly orders Achilles to go home
with the Myrmidons (179–81). Moreover, dishonor of this kind obvi-
ously "dis-affects," so that the honor-element in the heroic code is
stripped of the other motive for cooperation that it more standardly
supports, and it becomes an aim in itself. Minus the two weaker
drives and in the face of the anger caused by conflicting claims for
tîmê, the honor-system of incentives has in the terms of our analysis
lost all the mechanisms that could mediate between the conflicting
parties and is at loggerheads with itself. The system has broken down
in every way. Moreover, as O. Taplin has recently pointed out, when
a "summoned" *basileus* claims his summoner has reneged on "grati-
tude," *charis*, the claim is politically charged, because a war-prize is
allocated by the whole army. In that case, Achilles is complaining,
partly, that Agamemnon is taking away something given him by the
whole Achaian host. Achilles is therefore far from the insubordinate
egotist he is often said to be.[5]

Also intensifying the conflict between Agamemnon and Achilles
is the latter's special view of the value of honor. His concern with

---

4. 2.375–80, 9.115–20, 19.137–39; Nestor (9.104–13), Poseidon (13.111–
14), and Odysseus (19.181–83) agree with him.

5. Taplin 1992, 60–63; Taplin (63–66) also usefully discusses the
"backlog of resentment" between Agamemnon and Achilles, expressed, for
example, in Agamemnon's words about Achilles' incessant quarreling (176–77).

honor here and in book 9 is often put down to his particularly pas-
sionate nature. There is much truth in this, but I think it pays to ask
whether there is not some impulse behind Achilles' passion. We have
seen Nestor conceding to Achilles' near equality to Agamemnon
when he says "the mother who bore you was a goddess" (1.280), and
the importance of the hero's divine birth is evident from the scene
with Thetis. Achilles' first words to her are "since you bore me, of
brief life though I be," Zeus should grant me *tîmê* (352), and Thetis'
response to his description of his quarrel with Agamemnon is "Alas
my son, why did I rear you, doomed when I gave birth to you? If
only you could sit beside the ships without tears or harm, since your
life is to be brief, of no length; as it is, you are both doomed to an
early death and are miserable beyond all of the men, so it was to an
evil destiny that I bore you in my chambers" (414–18). It is estab-
lished very soon in the *Iliad* that Achilles' mortality is a pressing
matter. His divine mother knows that he is to suffer an early death
and has communicated the fact to him. The knowledge weighs heavi-
ly on him, and the absolute certainty that he will die soon is some-
thing no other warrior in the *Iliad* possesses.[6] This certainty, together
with the fact that his mother is immortal, which can do nothing but
deepen his understanding of mortality, makes Achilles unique
among the warriors, Sarpedon, the son of Zeus, included. Sarpedon,
in his famous speech laying bare the nature of heroism, reveals the
belief that death is in fact a spur to win *tîmê:* if men were immortal,
there would be no point to entering "battle where men win glory,"
but, *since* they are ineluctably mortal, they must try to win glory
(12.318–28), which is the warrior's greatest compensation. There is,
therefore, a particular point to Achilles' cry that *since* Thetis has borne
him to a brief life, Zeus should grant him *tîmê* (1.352–56). Unlike
Sarpedon, he knows that he is to die an early death, and the need for
compensation is all the more urgent, even though Sarpedon's short
life hardly differs formally from Achilles', in the sense that the fact
of fateful war makes death immanent for all and mortality poignant.
Achilles' specially privileged knowledge that his life is to be short is

---

6. Edwards (1991, 7f.) doubts that Achilles knows in book 1 that his death
is imminent (cf. Edwards 1987, 183); this does not seem to take adequate
account of, in particular, Thetis' words to her son at line 416 that his life is
soon to run out: ἐπεί νύ τοι αἶσα μίνυνθά περ, οὔ τι μάλα δήν.

therefore a root cause of his passion for glory. The word *since* at the beginning of his appeal to Thetis makes this conclusion inevitable, in contradistinction to the *since* of Sarpedon's rallying speech, which marks as a reason for heroism only the general consideration that mortals are subject to death.

Achilles' thinking about honor at this point is entirely traditional. We have seen his passionate desire for *tîmê* and the reasons why it is so passionate. And we have the poem's picture of him once he has withdrawn: "Neither would he ever go to the assembly where men win glory nor ever into battle, but as he stayed there his heart pined and he longed for shouting and battle" (490–92). But book 1 closes with Achilles in a unique position to see the flaws in the *tîmê*-system of incentives. His anger prevents him from cooperating with Agamemnon, so he has firsthand experience of the need for positive emotions in the community, which will culminate in his later curse of strife and wrath, *eris* and *cholos* (18.107–10). At the same time, he has experience of the way injustice too can disaffect.[7]

The tensions that Achilles' experience reveals in book 1 are developed to a point of crisis in book 9. The hero can articulate his attitude to them clearly enough, as I hope to show, though I am aware that previous scholars have held very different views. We fortunately seem to have left behind us A. Parry's contention that the formulaic structure of Homeric verse precluded Achilles from expressing his reservations to the traditional concept of heroism except by "misusing" traditional language.[8] Less fortunately, in some ways, critics

---

7. Mueller (1984, 34f.) argues that Achilles' request to Thetis at 407–12 is an Aristotelian *hamartia*, because it goes beyond Athene's prophecy at 212–14, and "in acting to ensure its success [Achilles] fatally taints the manner of its fulfillment." Though I cannot agree with Mueller's contention that therefore "the causal chain leads back to an action by Achilles rather than, as Redfield ⟨1975⟩ (pp. 102, 122), has argued, to his reaction to the arrogance of Agamemnon," his more general observation further elucidates the tensions inherent in the *tîmê*-sanction.

8. Parry 1956, 6f., refuted by Reeve 1973; Kirk 1976, 51, 74f. (but cf. 205); Griffin 1980, 100; Lynn-George 1988, 93–101, 123–28, 133f. Schein (1984, 106, 108f., 115) still finds Parry's thesis "fundamentally correct" (106 n. 25). On 9.378–405, 387, Hainsworth (1993) finds Achilles' "'pay me back my shame' i.e. 'undo what he has done . . . ,'" "impossible" as a demand; Hainsworth takes account of Parry's thesis but concludes that "It is likely therefore that the obscurity is intentional: if Akhilleus were to state his terms in clear language we should want a reason why the Achaeans did not meet them."

have tended to discount the more interesting part of his thesis and
to deny that Achilles in book 9 is in any way unheroic, pacifist, or
disillusioned, ascribing his rejection of the Achaian embassy to his
"unquenchable thirst for glory" and the like.[9] S.L. Schein argues that
"Achilles comes to question and contradict the validity of the norma-
tive social value system."[10] M. Lynn-George's deconstructionist read-
ing suggestively presents an Achilles contemplating the hero's death,
which for him has been "deprived of any heroic possibility of distinc-
tion"[11]—though Lynn-George does not draw any direct conclusion
from this picture about Achilles' heroism. C. Gill, illustrating his
distinction between "character" (an "objective" view of a person or
literary figure, to do especially with his or her alignment with the
dominant morality of his or her world) and "personality" (a "subjec-
tive" view, "empathetic rather than moral"), sees in Achilles' attitude
an actual "ambivalence" that arises out of a shifting of our viewpoint
of him from one of "character" to one of "personality," whereby "an
interrogative mode of writing" tends to result, as in tragedy.[12] For
O. Taplin, Achilles is "coming off the gold standard" in his "rejection
of any simple or direct equation between *tîmê* and material goods."[13]
Here again it seems to me that the ethical reference points I have
located in the text of the *Iliad* will help us arrive at a useful reorienta-
tion.

---

9. In the phrase of Mueller 1984, 45f.; see also Redfield 1975, 105f.
("Achilles' refusal of the warrior's role is an affirmation of the warrior
ethic . . . "); Kirk 1976, 51f. ("It is because Achilles has been robbed of his
geras, and for this reason alone, that he questions the war"); Griffin 1980,
74–76 (at p. 76 n. 48 we read that while Achilles questions the nature of
heroism he does not reject it, but by p. 100 Griffin rather shifts his ground
and says that Achilles does not "really regain his belief in heroism"); Silk
1987, 71 ("Achilles withdraws from the fighting because of an affront to his
tîmê; he returns to win *kléos*"; see further 89–93); Reeve 1973, 195 (at 9.378–97
Achilles experiences no "disillusionment" and sets "an absurdly high value
on his honour"; but "The disillusionment is introduced in 398–416"); Hains-
worth 1993, on 9.307–429 ("Akhilleus is disillusioned, but he is disillusioned
primarily with his place in the heroic scheme of things . . . ").
   10. Schein 1984, 71, 104–10.
   11. Lynn-George 1988, 120.
   12. Gill 1990, 6f., 13–16.
   13. Taplin 1992, 66–71, rightly stressing Achilles' sense of deception, ex-
pressed at 312–13, 344–45.

In his interview with Thetis in book 1, Achilles regarded the brevity of life foretold him by his mother as a particular reason for his desire that Zeus grant him *tîmê*. By book 9, however, his attitude toward death has undergone a remarkable about-face. This dramatic change is encapsulated in his words to Odysseus at lines 318–20. At line 318 he says that men have "an equal portion," *îsê moira*, whether they "hang back" or fight hard. That the malingerer whom he has particularly in mind is Agamemnon is made likely from his statement a few lines later that the king habitually "hung back" by the ships, divided up a small portion of the booty among his men, and kept the greater part for himself (332f.); and Achilles regards himself as a prime example of the energetic warrior (321–32). The incommensurability of effort and reward is dispiriting enough, but in his choice of the word *moira*, "portion," Achilles is thinking beyond rewards to death. When we first encounter the word, we have no reason to give it any other meaning than "portion," especially after Achilles' complaint that he never won any *charis* from Agamemnon and the other Achaians for his continuous fighting (315–17). But the context, defined at line 320 in our text, demands that we reappraise our first reading and give *moira* its more specialized sense of "doom" or "death." Achilles follows up line 318 with his famous statement that the ignoble (*kakos*) and the noble (*esthlos*) are held "in a single honor," *en . . . iêi tîmêi* (319). But here again we are forced to reinterpret and to conclude that by "honor" he means nothing less than death. We must redefine *moira* and *tîmê* because the text has Achilles immediately glossing his assertion of the valueless equality of effort in war by saying that both the nonachiever and the achiever alike *die* (κάτθαν', 320), and he continues by complaining that ceaselessly risking his life in battle has won him nothing (321–22).[14] This might be

---

14. The "standard" heroic application of the phrase "in a single honor," *en iêi tîmêi*, is illustrated when Diomedes tells Agamemnon not to hold his and Sthenelos' father "in a single honor" with them, because they are "superior" in their performance of heroic feats (4.404–10). At 6.488f., moreover, Hektor tells Andromache that neither an ignoble man (*kakos*) nor a noble man (*esthlos*) escapes death (*moira*), but committed to honor as he is, he does not make the logical jump that Achilles does. It has been thought that line 320 is an interpretation, on the grounds, e.g., that the notion of death as a leveler is not elaborated until lines 401–9; see Hainsworth 1993, on 318–20. But the theme of putting one's life on the line is something with which Achilles makes explicit play at 322.

thought of as one of those moments when Achilles "misuses" a tradi-
tional term, but if he does, the solecism is surely intended; Achilles
sarcastically equates honor with death, and for sarcasm to be effec-
tive, you need to know very precisely what the standard term means
and how you wish to subvert it. The acts of redefinition that we are
invited to undertake are, rather than being the result of any "misuse"
of language, put to striking rhetorical effect, as we are arrested by the
paradoxical nature of Achilles' phrasing and thinking. Death is for
Achilles no longer a reason for heroic striving for *tîmê* and the *kleos*
traditionally supposed to follow it; death is a leveler. The simile of
the mother bird selflessly feeding her unfledged young (323f.) em-
phasizes that Achilles has lost all interest in fighting the battles of the
Atreidai, though he has continually fought on their behalf until now
(325–27), and that he has lost all "affection," especially now that
Agamemnon is allocating rewards so arbitrarily and is not taking part
in the fight (332f.).[15]

As we have seen, Achilles is "privileged" as no other warrior is in
the *Iliad* because he knows for an absolute fact that his life is to be
short. But to this knowledge, as Achilles reveals to the ambassadors,
there is a cruel refinement: Thetis' supplementary information about
his "double destiny," *dichthadiai kêres*, according to which he will win
"unperishing glory" if he stays to take Troy, or a long life, albeit
forfeiting his "noble glory," if he returns home to Phthia (410–16).
The apparent contradiction between Achilles' certain knowledge of
his early death and his belief in the prophecy giving him a choice can
perhaps be resolved if we accept that Achilles' destiny is that he will
not choose the alternative *kêr*, however real it may be as an alterna-
tive, and Achilles knows these things. The explanation may lie in the
two different kinds of fate denoted by Achilles' choice of words.
"Fate," *moira*, found in the adjective describing Achilles' short life,
ôkumoros (1.417, 505, 18.95, 458) and "doom," *aisa* (1.418), are un-
avoidable; Hektor says at one point that no one has ever avoided his

---

15. It is going beyond the text to argue with Gagarin (1987, 302) that "what
Achilles is here rejecting is a moral sense of disinterested concern for others,
as he dismisses even the most minimal, instinctive concern of a mother for
her children as unprofitable," and to conclude that here we have "Achilles'
error in moral terms." Cf. Adkins 1987, 320.

fate. But "avoiding *kêr*" is a common formula.[16] It thus appears that one's *kêr* involves a degree of flexibility, but that one's *moira* and *aisa* do not at all, and that this "theology" shapes Achilles' thinking. Most modern critics assume, perfectly reasonably, that the choice of Achilles was invented at this point, whether by Achilles or the narrator, to make Achilles' argument more impressive.[17] But however we account for the double destiny, Achilles concludes that *because of it* (so the "for" of line 410), not even Agamemnon's gifts of restitution, the wealth of Troy before the Achaians came, or even the wealth of Delphi are equal in value to life for him (οὐ γὰρ ἐμοὶ ψυχῆς ἀντάξιον); though herds and precious objects can be taken as spoils (*leïstos*), life cannot be taken as booty (*leïstos*), nor can it be captured once it has passed from the body (401–9). The idea that a man's life can be taken back in a kind of act of plunder, as a trophy that will bring honor, involves a sarcasm akin to his equation of honor and death, and the whole of this passage can be taken as an elaboration on the earlier lines, with Achilles there responding in particular to his treatment at the hands of Agamemnon and the Achaians, while here he has generalized his thinking about honor.

The text, therefore, reveals an even deeper layer to Achilles' thinking about his death than merely knowing that it is imminent. It signals his uniqueness in this regard in an interesting way. When Achilles tells Odysseus at the beginning of his great speech that he hates dissemblers as much as the gates of Hades (312f.), which among other things indicates the depth of the defiance with which he will reject Agamemnon,[18] he unconsciously echoes Agamemnon's statement (unreported by Odysseus) about the implacability and

---

16. Hainsworth 1993, on 9.411. Edwards (1987, 224) compares the legendary choice of Herakles (Xen. *Mem.* 2.1.21–34) to remind us that the idea of a choice "is not unparalleled."

17. E.g., Willcock 1976, ad loc.; Edwards 1987, 224; Hainsworth 1993, on 9.410–16: "The usual point made is that Akhilleus *is* short-lived, therefore he has a claim to fame. But it is easy for him (or the poet) to reverse this argument and imply that renouncing fame even at this late date would entail long life."

18. Parry (1956, 5) suggests rightly, I think, that Achilles' words reflect on the optimistic rhetoric of Odysseus' preceding speech and on his general assumption (but see the next paragraph) that Achilles will accept Agamemnon's gifts "as adequate symbols of honor."

hatefulness of death (158f.), which is part of his appeal to Achilles to relent. Achilles thereby draws attention to the difference between his understanding of death, as he will reveal it later in his speech, and that of the other warriors: neither Agamemnon nor anyone else can have anything like Achilles' apprehension of death's hatefulness and implacability. As I argue he reasons, precisely his unique exposure to death's hatefulness causes his own "implacability."[19] Achilles, therefore, has come to regard *tîmê* as the literal equivalent of death, and no amount of gifts can compensate for the loss of life. It follows from this premise that Achilles will not respond positively to any plea based on the honor-incentive for virtuous behavior.

The first appeal is Odysseus' speech, with its catalog of the gifts that Agamemnon will offer. As critics have noticed, although Odysseus suppresses Agamemnon's argument that Achilles should relent because the king is "more kingly," *basileuteros* (160), and older (161), he also omits to report Agamemnon's admission of having wronged Achilles—"I was deluded (*aasamên*), nor will I deny it" (116). He insists on the condition that goes with the gifts, that Achilles should cease from his anger (299; cf. 157), and the cumulative effect of the gift-catalog makes it seem like a statement of regal superiority.[20] It would be quite wrong, however, to underestimate totally Odysseus' insight into Achilles' frame of mind. He appeals first and best to friendship, vividly picturing the plight of the Achaians and calling on Achilles to save them in their exhaustion (225–61). He even shows that he expects Achilles to hate Agamemnon's gifts, when he says that even if Achilles hates Agamemnon and his gifts, he should pity the rest of the Achaians (300–302), thereby reverting to his first affective appeal. Nonetheless, Odysseus interlards his speech at crucial moments with what he takes to be the irresistible incentive of *tîmê*, even, for example, in the passage on the advisability of "a friendly attitude toward others" (*philophrosûnê*, 249–61). First is the suggestion, couched in terms chosen for the power of alliteration and word-play, that it will be a matter of remorse, *achos*, for Achilles, because

---

19. Taplin (1992, 196f.) comes tantalizingly close to this analysis, stopping short at the idea that Achilles might have deprived himself of any moral coordinates.

20. Redfield 1975, 15f.; Mueller 1984, 44f.; Thornton 1984, 123, 126f., 132–34; Lynn-George 1988, 86–92, 106–21, 141–44, 165f.; Taplin 1992, 72–73.

there will be no device, *mêchos*, for discovering a remedy, *akos*, once the harm is done, *rechthentos*. This is an emotional appeal to Achilles' sense of fairness. Next follows the report of Peleus' commendation of *philophrosûnê*, with all the paternal authority that Odysseus reasonably assumes it will command. Yet the purpose of yielding to such emotional impulses is, as Odysseus construes it, so the Achaians might honor Achilles more, and so Agamemnon will give him "worthy gifts." The argument from *tîmê* is put more insistently at the close of Odysseus' speech: the inhabitants of the seven cities that the king will give him will honor Achilles with gifts, like a god (297), and if he persists in his hatred of Agamemnon but pities the other Achaians, they will honor him as a god, because he will win great *kûdos* when he slays Hektor. The continual association of pity and a kindly disposition with the *tîmê*-incentive can at this juncture only meet with Achilles' angry rejection: Odysseus has unconsciously undermined what he thinks is his most compelling argument, however subtly he has otherwise seen into Achilles' mind, which Achilles has not yet spoken.

Phoinix' appeal is based even more than Odysseus' on affective and fair-play considerations; yet it ultimately comes to grief for the same reasons as Odysseus'. Phoinix owes his position in the embassy to his close emotional ties with Achilles. He is almost a surrogate son to Peleus and an exclusively dear friend and tutor to Achilles (478–95).[21] The picture of the Prayers, slow, wrinkled, and looking sideways, graphically underlines the need for pity toward the suppliant, whose mental attitude the image mirrors, and Phoinix makes it clear that Zeus' will is that the petitioner should meet with *aidôs* (508–12); there is a sense in which it is a moral obligation to yield. Yet Phoinix addresses the old underpinning arguments: that Achilles should accord *tîmê* to the daughters of Zeus, the honor that bends the mind even of "men of superior standing" (*esthloi*, 513–14); and that he would not be advising Achilles to yield if Agamemnon were not offering many gifts (515–19). The last thought is expanded in the tale of Meleagros. The Aitolian elders had supplicated the hero, promis-

---

21. See Preisshofen 1977, 32; Tsagarakis 1979, 237–42; Lynn-George 1988, 131–40. Cf. Köhnken 1975, 1978. For general discussions of the "superimposition" of Phoinix on book 9, see Kirk 1962, 217f.; Rosner 1976; Willcock 1976, on 9.182; Mueller 1984, 174.

ing a great gift (534–36), but his late deliverance of the Aitolians brought him no gifts, and he saved his community "in vain" (599). For that reason, Phoinix concludes, Achilles should not wait until the Achaian ships are burning, but, in view of the gifts, he should come, and the Achaians will honor him like a god (602–3). The last two lines of Phoinix' whole address contain the advice, offered as if a trump card, that if Achilles enters the battle without gifts he will no longer be held in the same honor, even though he repulses the Trojan onslaught (604–5). Achilles' first words in reply confirm the inefficacy of the *tîmê*-appeal with a resounding finality: "I have no need of this honor at all" (οὔ τί με ταύτης / χρεὼ τιμῆς, 607f.).

Achilles goes on in a significant way to explain his reaction to the honor offered by Agamemnon. He says that he thinks he is honored already by the will of Zeus, which will continue to accompany him by the ships as long as he has breath and movement in his body (608–10). Such is his desire for forceful expression that he illogically contradicts his threat to leave for Phthia on the following day, but in other respects he is telling the simple truth. What being honored by the will or dispensation of Zeus involves is explained for us earlier in book 9, in the conversation between Nestor and Agamemnon (109–18). It involves Achilles' superior physical strength, as Nestor recognizes (110), and Zeus' destruction of the Achaians, as Agamemnon, agreeing with Nestor, makes clear when he says, "Worth many warriors is the man whom Zeus loves in his heart, as now he has honored this man, by conquering the army of the Achaians" (116–18). Achilles seems to be saying that he has no need for the gift-centered *tîmê* of Agamemnon, because if it comes to honor, he has it from the highest level: Agamemnon's gifts are thus relativized into meaninglessness. He does not repudiate Zeus' honor; his reference to it may suggest that Achilles is sardonically asserting that in terms of realpolitik he has the upper hand. But he makes no further point of it, by which we are to infer that he is really beyond such considerations at the moment.[22] What does the text lead us to suppose is on his mind? First, he has made it abundantly clear that life outweighs all the value of *tîmê*, and that he is concerned with the thought of his early death.

---

22. Pace Macleod 1982, 23f., therefore, it need not at all necessarily follow from Achilles' words about Zeus' honoring him that at 319–20 Achilles is "protesting too much."

But a second layer to his thinking is revealed in the words immediately following his comment on Zeus' honoring him (611–19). He advises Phoinix not to disturb him by grieving for the Achaians, thus doing a favor, *charis*, to Agamemnon, when he should not be a friend to the king lest he be hated by Achilles, who loves him; he further advises Phoinix to join him in harming his enemies, and with a hyperbole charged by the emotion of the moment, he asks Phoinix to be a king on equal terms with him and sharing half his honor, and to stay in his hut for the night. Central to these words to Phoinix is a feeling of deep emotional attachment and a sense of hurt and betrayal that Phoinix is pleading Agamemnon's cause; his statement that Phoinix is gratifying Agamemnon is particularly pointed after Achilles' claim that Agamemnon gave no gratification to *him*. Phoinix was on the right track when he based his appeal on affection: Achilles is here demonstrating how much more important personal relations are to him than heroic *tîmê*. This sets in motion a strand of the plot that stretches from the present moment to Achilles' behavior over Patroklos and ultimately over Priam, when, in the face of death, which comes prematurely to both Priam and Achilles, Achilles chooses to respond to affection and act magnanimously toward his unexpected friend.

Is Achilles disillusioned with the honor-code in book 9? All the responses expressed by Achilles indicate that he most assuredly is. Yet it has been argued, for example, that when Achilles demands that Agamemnon should "pay back all his grievous injury" (387), "Far from renouncing heroic ideals, he is setting an absurdly high value on his honor."[23] The text suggests that the point lies elsewhere. Achilles has claimed that all human endeavor is leveled by death and that death is the sole *tîmê* (318–20), and he later explains this thought by saying that literally nothing material is of value equal to his life (401ff.). This is quite sufficient cause for him to find Agamemnon's gifts hateful and refuse to honor the king at all (378). By asking him

---

23. Reeve 1973, 195. On 387, πρίν γ' ἀπὸ πᾶσαν ἐμοὶ δόμεναι θυμαλγέα λώβην, cf. Hainsworth 1993, ad loc., who writes "Literally the meaning is 'pays me back all the heart-grieving outrage' (not, or not literally, 'pays me back *for* all the outrage,' which is expressed by τίνειν λώβην, 11.142). Akhilleus appears to mean that he has 'paid' as it were a measure of humiliation to Agamemnon, who must now 'pay' back an equivalent measure."

effectively to undo what has been done, Achilles shows that, within the framework of the honor-incentive in the heroic code, absolutely nothing will compensate him.[24] Moreover, it seems perverse to argue that "Achilles's refusal of the warrior's role is an affirmation of the warrior ethic," in the absence of absolute honor, and given Achilles' own alleged moral absolutism. Once Achilles asserts that life is irreplaceable and too valuable for any adequate compensation, he is breathing a different air from Sarpedon, for whom honor actively softens the finality of death.[25]

Achilles is by no means impervious to every appeal, and it is useful to locate the moments at which he yields and the reasons why he does so. Phoinix says to Achilles that Agamemnon has selected those "best men" among the Achaians who are "most dear," *philtatoi*, to Achilles (520–22; Phoinix is distorting the truth in Agamemnon's favor, because Nestor chose the embassy, 165–70), and book 9 makes much of the emotional closeness of the embassy, from Achilles' greeting at lines 197–98 and 204 onward, quite apart from Odysseus' misdirected association of *philotês* and *tîmê* and Phoinix' reminder of his special relationship to Achilles from his childhood. But Phoinix adds an important thought to his words about Agamemnon's selection of the "most dear" Achaians to supplicate Achilles: he urges Achilles not to bring shame on the journey and overtures of such *philtatoi*, though there has been no cause for indignation (*nemessêton*) at his wrath up until now (522–23). In line with his thinking in the parable of the Prayers, he uses traditional shame/honor-phraseology to support the "weaker" impulse in emotional affection alone, but in the story of Meleagros, he tells how the hero relented, not as a result of the elders' supplication and promises of gifts, or even from the formal

---

24. "Setting an absurdly high value on his honour" appears, therefore, to be in fact an ironical means of debunking it, a common enough linguistic ploy. See further Griffin 1980, 99f.

25. Redfield 1975, 105f.; cf. Griffin 1980, 74 n. 46. According to Schofield (1986, 21f.), Redfield's and Griffin's alternative explanations of Achilles' supposedly exclusive concern with honor are not genuine alternatives: the high ranking of *euboulia* in the *Iliad* gives "ample scope for criticism of Achilles . . . ," and Achilles need not have been trapped by the logic of his heroism if he had listened to *euboulia*. From what I have said, I hope it is clear that Achilles is far indeed from exclusively concerned with honor, and that not even *euboulia* has a chance of bringing Achilles back to the "code" at present.

supplication-ritual of Oineus (531, 583) or the entreaties of his mother, sisters, and "dearest comrades," but from the tears and supplication (591) of his wife, Kleopatra, and her picture of what happens when a city is sacked (574–96). Once again, the more purely affective plea proves successful. Affection seems to emerge from the Meleagros story as a surprisingly potent means of securing moral behavior, especially in view of the lack of any *tîmê*-support that a Kleopatra might be expected to bring to bear. There are signs in book 9 that Achilles is sensitive to the pull of affection between a man and his woman. One of his grievances with Agamemnon is that the king has robbed him of a woman "whom he loved from the bottom of his heart" (342f.), as any man does who is *agathos* and "sensible" (341).[26] His feeling for Briseis is, however, one of the reasons for refusing to fight on behalf of the Achaians, but Kleopatra, through her appeal to Meleagros' emotions, can succeed in inducing the hero to defend his community. Different again is Achilles' argument from the case of the Atreidai and Helen: Menelaos' love for Helen prompted the whole expedition to Troy (337–41). This is no real attack on the expedition,[27] but Achilles once more stresses emotional ties over and above the necessity of winning back the *tîmê* lost when a man has been robbed of his wife or concubine. This point has rarely received the emphasis it deserves.

In the face of persuasion based on affection, Achilles, like Meleagros, relents. Despite the honor-argument adduced by Phoinix at the end of his speech, his person and the authority that it lends his plea (together with the image of Kleopatra, possibly) are the principal reasons Achilles repeats an earlier request that Phoinix stay the night. But they are also the reason why he postpones until the following dawn his decision whether to leave for Phthia or stay (617–19). Odysseus' more exclusively honor-based speech had, by contrast, been met finally with the firm statement that Achilles would leave "tomorrow," together with Phoinix, without the offer to deliberate whether

---

26. On the "special 'romantic' relationship between Achilles and Briseis," see Taplin 1992, 214–16.

27. Reeve (1973, 194, n. 3) is convincing in his refutation of Parry's view (1956, 6 n. 12) that Achilles' question at 337–38, "Why should the Argives fight the Trojans?" makes us "feel that the justification of war itself is being called into question."

he and his troops should leave or not (427–29). Aias' speech is also significant here (624–42). Throughout the *Iliad*, Aias shows an agreeable, if rugged, sincerity,[28] and in his speech in book 9, he demonstrates that he can combine his sincerity with impressive skill as an orator. Addressing Odysseus as if Achilles were not present, he begins by proposing that they leave immediately because Achilles is unresponsive to the friendship with which the Achaians honored him and is without pity (630–32). We have seen that Aias' words illustrate how Iliadic friendship and pity are reinforced by the sanction of *tîmê*, and that Aias is faithfully reflecting standard heroic thought on the connection. We also have cause to suspect that the honor-component mentioned by Aias is unlikely to impress Achilles at this point. But at the close of his plea, Aias talks passionately and more and more in terms of "pure" friendship. He appeals to Achilles to be amenable (639) and to respect that the embassy is in his dwelling and is thus entitled to his compliance. He points out that the embassy comes from the Achaians as a whole, not just from Agamemnon, and consists of his "dearest" friends (642). This affective aspect of Aias' speech prompts the final "concession" that he will rejoin the war, even if only when Hektor reaches and sets fire to the ships of the Myrmidons, and that he will hold off Hektor beside his hut (650–55). His other arguments are based on a soldier's no-nonsense inability to understand what Achilles' problem really is.

The complex conclusion from all this seems inevitable. Achilles' special awareness of the significance of death has almost totally undermined his drive for *tîmê* and for the resultant *kleos* traditionally thought to offer some compensation for the hero's death. Achilles' experience at the hands of Agamemnon has shown that of itself, *tîmê* is a labile commodity. The two discoveries effectively deprive Achilles of any strong reason within the system's honor-based incentives for heroic action. In the absence of the traditional reasons for heroic action, he loses moral orientation and is thrown back on his affective impulses, visible in book 9 in the warmth of his greeting to his "most dear friends" and in his partial concessions to their requests where *tîmê* plays a lesser part than emotional ties. Still, the desire for *tîmê* and *kleos* acts at least as a vestigial force. The ambassadors come across him singing of the "glorious deeds of the heroes," on the lyre

---

28. Edwards 1987, 229f.; Edwards 1991, on 17.626–55, 645–47.

he took as booty from his heroic exploit against the city of Eëtion, Andromache's father (186–89);[29] he can level the old charge that Agamemnon showed him no gratitude (315–17, 328–33) and has treated him like a dishonored vagabond (646–48); and he has still not made up his mind on a long life without *kleos*. This state of indecision, whose roots are in Achilles' horror at the implacability of death, puts the hero in the wrong in practical terms, as we can sense in Phoinix' comment "Up till now your wrath has not been a matter of *nemesis*" (523);[30] and a Diomedes can dismiss Achilles as an obdurately proud man whose pride Agamemnon has merely consolidated by supplicating him (697–700). Aias' reaction is also instructive. Aias assumes that the Achaians' friendship and honor should be enough to stir some pity in Achilles, and he argues that most men are willing to accept compensation even from the killer of a brother or son, but Achilles is unwilling to accept a most handsome compensation for just one woman (632–39). For Aias, nobody could reasonably refuse the transaction, and it has been fairly remarked that his response "must be considered the opinion of the ordinary, down-to-earth Greek captain."[31] Such a soldier's soldier would find it impossible to understand Achilles' questioning of the value of *tîmê* and his apprehension of the value of life. Objectively, at least, Achilles is not acting as a hero is expected to.

The narrator has let us see that for Achilles the traditional reasons for heroic virtue have lost their cogency and relevance, a situation that neither Diomedes nor Aias can understand and that they hopelessly misconstrue. He is not acting in accord with the internal premises of good and noble behavior, because he contravenes the morality present in the image of the Prayers, that one should yield to suppliants as a matter of honor, an incentive Achilles is hardly disposed to respect at this point, even though Phoinix' description of the Prayers as allegorical presentations of the suppliant in his disadvantaged situation implies that pity is a factor. This stimulus to pity, just like the strong emotional tie between Achilles and Phoinix (not to mention

---

29. Cf. Griffin 1980, 93; Mueller 1984, 45; Schein 1984, 26; Lynn-George 1988, 150f., 154.

30. To say nothing of the Achaians' general agreement that the guilty party is Agamemnon: see n. 4 above.

31. Edwards 1987, 230.

his other friends), is inevitably washed aside by Achilles' other preoccupations. On both counts, Achilles' refusal of the Achaians' supplication is an offense against the one effective means in the heroic code of restoring broken relations.

I have drawn a picture of an Achilles fearful of death, responding only to affective impulses and yet not totally impervious to the claims of the *tîmê*-component in the heroic code. The structure of his response to his situation is therefore multilayered and even self-contradictory, though one consideration seems to be dominant. This complexity of response is familiar in both life and literature, and we have gained an insight, if we are persuaded by it, that is possible only from the pluralistic approach I introduced in chapter 1. I hope that I have demonstrated conclusively the usefulness of this approach, with its capacity to admit both disjunction and conjunction, over and against the more reductive analyses of the Adkins model or that of Adam Parry. I hope that I have set up referends in which I may offer a more persuasive reconstruction of the thought-world of Achilles in book 9.

Deprived of a clear ethical standard, Achilles is exposed to motives for action other than the most compelling standard heroic ones, especially the impulses of emotion, which can issue forth in behavior that is confusedly well-disposed, unacceptably cruel, or uniquely generous. Book 9 leaves Achilles adrift from traditional honor, a state that permits his excessive self-assertion and cruelty toward Tros, Lykaon, and Hektor, but that also leaves the way open to an Achilles responding purely to the sense of fairness and compassion that the incentive of *tîmê* more normally supports. He will still be swayed by considerations of *tîmê* and *kleos* (in books 16 and 18 in particular), but after Patroklos' death, they lose their driving force. With the embassy (and later with Hektor), his nature has become emotion-driven, "passionate," but with Priam his sense of fairness is recalled largely through emotional responses, and acting in tandem, the two form a heroic generosity of an unprecedented kind, which accords *tîmê* only a secondary status as a sanction. The roots of heroism are reinstated, with its traditional support-system restored to its proper ancillary social function. Achilles finally, if briefly, attains to a refined heroism that I argue we may call magnanimity. But his rejection of the code is a necessary precondition for that magnanimity.

The ethical vacuum in which we leave Achilles in book 9 is maintained through books 10 to 17. Analysis of these books in terms of the tension we have been seeing at work will, I hope, shed light on Achilles' state of mind in them and on certain textual problems that critics have suggested they contain. Achilles is notable for his absence from the battle. At one point Poseidon rallies the Achaians by admitting that Hektor's present show of confidence is based on the knowledge that Achilles has withdrawn but urging that they will not miss him too much provided that they defend one another (14.364–69).[32] The Trojans are aware that Achilles' return will put an end to their current run of success. Poulydamas, for example, has a presentiment that Achilles' return is not far away and that it will restore the Achaians' fortunes, an argument by which he succeeds in persuading Hektor to call a council (13.740–48).

Though Achilles is generally perceived to be vital to the outcome of the battle, it is equally felt that he is behaving wrongly. Poseidon suggests to Agamemnon that Achilles' "murderous heart" must be rejoicing at the Achaians' discomfiture, because he has no "feelings," not even to any small extent (14.139–42). The Achaians see his culpability very much in terms of his "excellence," *aretê*. In his long speech to Patroklos in book 11, Nestor comments that though Achilles is of noble degree, he does not live up to the expectations held of a person of such a rank, because he does not show the appropriate concern or pity for his fellows (11.664f.).[33] Later, Nestor claims that Achilles will "have the profit of his excellence all to himself," even though he will have reason to regret the deaths of his comrades (762–64). The thought that Achilles is not fulfilling his *aretê* is also present when Nestor recalls Peleus' parting words—very much to suit his purposes, just like Odysseus when he quotes Peleus' advice about *philophrosûnê* in book 9—that Achilles should always strive to be "best"

---

32. Poseidon's words "there will be no excessive longing [*pothê*] for him" pick up Achilles' words of defiance at 1.240 that the time will come when a longing (*pothê*) for him will come over the Achaians.

33. The "of noble degree though he be" formula here may remind us of its usage by Nestor to convince Agamemnon to give back Briseis, but there is a significant difference in its application: here an ethically sound response like pity is assumed to be something that the superior man, the *esthlos*, should feel, but in book 1 the assumption is that the *esthlos* can be expected to do as he pleases, as an irresponsible autocrat, even against the dictates of morality, though in this case Agamemnon should nevertheless yield to them. The excellence-criterion operates on a sliding scale.

and to surpass all others in his excellence (11.784). Nestor clearly regards Achilles' *aretê* as a positive thing, something to be exercised to the full. Patroklos sees it quite differently. In his appeal to Achilles to let him go into battle in Achilles' armor, he addresses his friend as *ainaretê*, "you of dreaded *aretê*," because later generations will not derive any benefit from him if he fails to defend the Achaians (16.30–32). It is clear from the context that Patroklos thinks Achilles has insisted on the potency of his *aretê* to the point at which it has become a negative thing, driven by "anger" (30), so that he has become inhumanly pitiless (33–35). This is really only an extreme development of words that he has spoken to Nestor in book 11 in apology for Achilles' behavior. His defense there is that Achilles is essentially a man who is both to be respected (*aidoios*) and is "capable of indignation" or "easy to anger" (*nemesêtos*),[34] and Nestor knows what a "terrible" man he is, quick to find fault even in a guiltless man (11.649–54).[35] The general profile of Achilles at this point is one of a man destructively insisting on recognition of his traditional excellence and could not be more misleading.

Though the common opinion is that Achilles is behaving wrongly, it is also still felt that Agamemnon is the original guilty party, apparently in spite of his attempt to make amends. Poseidon, in the guise of Kalchas, urges the Achaians to keep on fighting, even if Agamemnon is "truly guilty in every way" because he dishonored Achilles (13.111–14). And we are told explicitly that Zeus was still honoring Achilles and his mother, even though he did not want to see the Achaian army destroyed (13.347–50). Agamemnon indirectly admits his responsibility for Achilles' anger when he gloomily predicts to Nestor that all the Achaians, not merely Achilles, will now nurse "anger" in their hearts (presumably because he has been an unsuccessful general, 14.49–51). Achilles continues to refer to his dishonor,

---

34. So Leaf 1886–88, vol. 1, on 11.649. Leaf is followed by most translators and critics in taking the adjective *nemesêtos* here actively, hence "easy to anger"; however, as an anonymous reader suggests, if it were taken in its more normal passive usage, Patroklos would be calling Achilles respected and "blamed," which would yield an attractive ambivalence and oxymoron.

35. The phrase is traditional and standardly involves finding fault with people over the matter of their excellence, as when the chastened Alexandros says to Hektor at 13.775, "You are moved to find fault in a guiltless man."

at least in public. Thus, as our text stands, Achilles, on the very day after the embassy, makes his infamous cry of jubilation, that "now" the Achaians will supplicate him, because their need is no longer tolerable (11.608–10). In book 16, too, we are faced with an Achilles who chides Patroklos for showing pity for the Achaians who are dying beside their ships because of their own transgressions—that is, because they have failed to stand up against Agamemnon (17–18)—and who claims to Patroklos that the real reason for his abstention from the war is the grief that Agamemnon caused him when he took back his hard-won "war-prize," merely on the basis of superior sway, dishonoring him like an honorless vagabond (52–59). Perfectly in line with this are his instructions to Patroklos to win him great *tîmê* and *kûdos* in the eyes of the Achaians and to make them give back Briseis and give other gifts in addition (83–86); Patroklos should proceed no further after driving the Trojans from the ships and should not go on to fight the Trojans by leading on his troops to Troy, because he would merely make Achilles "less honored," by which Achilles seems to imply that the Achaians will no longer see such a pressing need to honor him if Patroklos can save the day alone (87–96). Patroklos seems to consent wholeheartedly to this program, at least up to lines 269–74, where he spurs on the Myrmidons, so that together they might bring honor to Achilles, "by far the best" Achaian, and make Agamemnon realize his deludedness in not honoring "the best of the Achaians."[36] Achilles gives every appearance, then, of talking the traditional language of *tîmê*. Hence, in part, the old tug-of-war continues between those who wish to delete the whole of the Embassy as a later interpolation and those who would purify the text of the passages where Achilles slips back into the traditional *tîmê*-terminology and harps on the old grievance, as if nothing had happened to Achilles since book 1.[37]

---

36. Cf. Long 1970, 138: "In the case of Patroclus, whose ranking is considerably lower than that of Achilles, the latter can simply say, without argument, that Patroclus is not to storm Troy without him because this would bring dishonour." Taplin (1992, 177f.) also accepts the full operationality of *tîmê* here.

37. See, e.g., Leaf 1886–88, vol. 2, on 85. See further Lynn-George 1988, 170–72, against Page 1959, 304–10; see further below, p. 97, on the decisive connection between 16.61–63 and 9.650–55. On the alleged incompatibility of ll. 609f. with the Embassy, see Schadewaldt 1966, 81; Thornton 1984, 133:

Yet something has happened to Achilles, and we are justified in postulating what it is precisely because the text presents him as trying to hide it. In book 11 Nestor suggests to Patroklos that Achilles may be holding back because of some prophecy, θεοπροπίη, that his mother has passed on to him from Zeus, in which case perhaps he will send Patroklos in his armor to make the Trojans think Achilles has returned to the colors (11.794–804). Nestor's suggestion about the prophecy is relayed to Achilles in book 16, lines 36f., only to meet with Achilles' flat denial that he has any concern for any prophecy that he knows of from Zeus through the mediation of Thetis: οὔτε θεοπροπίης ἐμπάζομαι, ἥν τινα οἶδα, / οὔτε τί μοι πὰρ Ζηνὸς ἐπέφραδε πότνια μήτηρ (16.50f.). What are we to make of this disinformation? Other scholars have not made very much of it,[38] but it offers a vital clue to the reconstruction of Achilles' thinking and to the problem of the text. It is truly disinformation, first because Achilles has known, at least since book 1—and Thetis has told him—that his life is to be short (1.414–18), and second because Achilles has told the ambassadors, in a speech prefaced by the declaration that he hates dissemblers like the doors of Hades, that he recognizes the finality of death (9.404–9) and that his mother has given him precise knowledge of his twofold destinies (9.410–16). To expunge book 9, then, you must do more than that: you must expel the whole network of references to the prophecy announced in book 9. To athetize the

---

the Achaians did not supplicate Achilles "kniefällig" (cf. "around my knees," 11.609).

38. E.g., Willcock 1976, on 9.410–16: "Achilles's fateful choice is never referred to again, and in 16.50–51 he explicitly denies that he has had any warning from his mother." According to Lloyd-Jones (1983, 19), Achilles replies to Patroklos "that he is in no way moved by the prophecy." De Jong's (1987a, 280 n. 59) example of apparent contradiction, 9.410–16 and 21.274f., is much less serious than the passage under review, which one cannot explain away as an "Augenblickserfindung," or on any other ground mentioned by de Jong. The formula "neither do I care about any prophecy that I know of etc." (οὔτε θεοπροπίης ἐμπάζομαι, ἥν τινα οἶδα / . . . μήτηρ) has a curious but evident association with dissimulation. At *Od.* 1.413–20 Telemachos, in the course of hiding from Eurymachos his knowledge that Mentes is really Athene, fudges the issue by saying that he no longer believes reports that his father is still alive, "Nor do I care about any prophecy . . . " (οὔτε θεοπροπίης ἐμπάζομαι κτλ). The Odyssean use of the formula perhaps supports the suspicion that Achilles is dissembling in *Iliad* 16.

"traditional" sounding passages of book 16 entails the same mea-
sures, because Achilles' denial that he knows of a prophecy is made
only to restate the old grudge. Moreover, when Achilles claims he
said that he will cease from his wrath only when the fighting reaches
"my" ships (16.61–63), he is clearly echoing the concession he made
to Aias in book 9, lines 650–55, that he will not involve himself in the
battle until Hektor reaches the tents and ships of the Myrmidons and
"my" own tent and ship; he is not echoing his much less specific
original oath that all the Achaians will feel his absence as Hektor slays
them in great numbers (1.239–44). This simple fact alone should have
made it clear that the narrator of 16.61–63 knows of book 9. Argu-
ments about the presence of Phoinix in the embassy may make it
certain that he has been grafted on to an earlier version of book 9,
but Achilles' apparent ignorance of the compensation offered there
is no argument for deleting the whole book. It seems far better to
conclude, with Mueller, that the superimposition of Phoinix is the
work of the monumental composer of the *Iliad*.[39]

Achilles in books 11 and 16 slips back into the turn of mind and
phrase associated with the traditional *tîmê*-incentive. He does so in
public, after he has eroded the authority of that incentive at its very
roots, expressing his deepened awareness of the nature of death.
He denies the knowledge of the prophecy, or rather prophecies, that
have led him to this private awareness, and he talks in *tîmê*-concepts
and phraseology. Why this persistence with honor-talk? Here is one
of the most notorious places where Homer "leaves a gap."[40] The text,
together with my reading of the overall situation, opens up the possi-
bility that Achilles wants to conceal an unexpressed motive for refus-
ing to rejoin the Achaians, namely, his personal realization of the
reality of death, which he may, for instance, also think others may
take as a fear of death. His recourse to the traditional *tîmê*-thinking
would in that case be a means of reassuring Patroklos, and anyone
else who wants to hear, that he is still recognizably worth the title of
"the best of the Achaians," but it remains a camouflage. If we accept
this as a reading of the denial of the prophecy, it only demonstrates
how hollow his honor-talk has become. Accordingly, when Achilles

---

39. See n. 21 above.

40. See Janko 1992, on 16.49–50, for a summary of the problems seen in
the passage.

reverts to the traditional phraseology about honor, we should see behind his words much more than a feeling that the embassy was in some way or another inadequate: given his deeper concerns, it never could have been adequate.[41] Again the Achaians fail to understand what they are dealing with, though Nestor and, through him, Patroklos come close to the truth. It is significant that Achilles is so sarcastic about Patroklos' show of emotion and pity for the Achaians, comparing him with a little girl holding on to her mother's skirts (16.7–10), because Achilles is speciously discounting affective impulses as against the "hard facts" of the Achaians' "transgression" and their dishonoring of him. Yet the affective supplication (16.46) cuts at least some ice, and Achilles yields to Patroklos' plea, thus unconsciously confirming the truth of Nestor's words, that Patroklos, as the older of the pair, will have particular persuasiveness for Achilles, and that a friend's persuasion is a good thing (11.785–91). As Achilles says in his concluding prayer to Zeus, Athene, and Apollo, if only it could be granted that the two friends could together alone sack Troy (16.97–100). The underlying assumption is that both friends will remain alive to share the glory, their friendship intact. The prayer is hopeless.

We are dealing here with a lie, which the narrator has depicted "objectively," without telling us explicitly, "Here is a lie." Yet there is every reason for us to accept it as a lie, and none against our accepting it as such. If a lie can be thus "objectively" represented, what prevents us from trying to recover multilayering of thought and motivation on other levels? It is surely more reasonable to accept a pluralistic reading of the lie rather than a surface one (at worst falling back on the desperate expedient of expunging it from our texts). I suggest that the lie of Achilles is further vindication of my mode for reading character and ethics. And critics cannot talk of any circularity of argument, because in chapter 1 I was at pains to avoid consideration of texts precisely like the ones before us. A more reductive analysis could never do justice to the lie of Achilles, and the same will hold true a fortiori of all other moments in which we experience difficulties in assessing motivation.

---

41. Cf. Lynn-George (1988, 167f.), who (rather intentionalistically for a deconstructionist) construes Achilles as attempting "to create time for the renewal of the offer of recompense by sending Patroklos into battle."

What does the text present as the thoughts and impulses that operate on Achilles when he decides to rejoin the battle after Patroklos' death? Certain things suggest, in ways that I do not think have always been adequately appreciated, that Achilles' personal sense of grief is above all else, and that his sense of loss informs all his thinking. The essential component of Achilles' reaction to Patroklos' death is perhaps most clearly expressed in the simile that compares Achilles in his grief with a lioness who angrily stalks a hunter who has taken her cubs from their lair (18.318–22). Such similes demonstrate the existence of affection in the animal world and in the human world that they reflect, and in this instance the poet emphasizes Achilles' personal affection and grief for his friend. The emotion of grief is further explored in the speech that follows, in which Achilles laments that he cannot now fulfill his promise to Menoitios that he would bring Patroklos home with him, though Thetis and Peleus will have enough to mourn (324–32). The emotion of wrath is developed as Achilles determines not to bury Patroklos until he has killed and despoiled Hektor, with the additional promise to cut the throats of the twelve Trojan youths before Patroklos' pyre, "angered at your death" (333–37).

The warrior, who mutilates his face and hair and is so distraught that Antilochos fears that he might commit suicide (22–35), can claim to his mother that he has no pleasure (80) any longer in the fact that Zeus has fulfilled his promise that the Achaians would be driven back among the ships for lack of Achilles (73–77) and that the warrior would be honored in the process. He now sees that such honor is a joyless thing when weighed against the death of his friend. It is significant in this connection that Achilles says of Patroklos that he "honored" (81) his *philos* above all his companions, as much as his own life (80–82), because we remember his difficulty with accepting as indefeasible Aias' claim that the Achaians "honored" (9.631) him with a *philotês* beyond anyone else. Though Aias' emphasis on the honor-component in friendship was so eroded in Achilles' mind that it partially weakened the emotional appeal of the relationship, the death of a friend has reactivated the affective component to make Achilles seek emotional compensation in exacting vengeance from Hektor, or, as Homeric Greek puts it, taking *tîmê* from him (*apotînô*, 18.93). As nothing else could have done, Patroklos' death has made Achilles alive to the power of affective appeals, and the parallelism

of his and Aias' phraseology brings this out with striking forceful-
ness. This sharpened awareness drives him to rejoin the battle in the
full knowledge that reentering it will mean his death[42] and with the
explicit wish that he might die immediately (98) because he was not
present to defend his friend when he was killed far from his home-
land (98–100). When Achilles remembers that even Herakles had to
die (117–21), we may certainly talk of a bitter resignation, which adds
to our impression that death goes very deep with the hero. It is a
thing from which, against all his hopes, he now realizes he cannot
escape, jolted into an acceptance of it by his loss of Patroklos; so in a
very real sense he is mourning his own death as much as his friend's.
In book 9 death had cast doubt on the value of action and inhibited
it, but we find Achilles now pushed beyond any such considerations,
to the point where, paradoxically, death has totally lost relevance to
his decision-making processes.

Beside Achilles' extreme, affective response is an admixture of the
emotions of shame and guilt. Shame is evident in his statement about
his failure to defend Patroklos, particularly in his realization that he
is "sitting beside the ships, a useless weight on the ground" (104),
unfulfilled in his function as an unequaled warrior, though, as he can
now see, others may be better than he is in the assembly (104–6). His
emotional trauma has made him realize all this. At the other end of
the scale of shame and honor, Achilles can now wish that he might
win "noble glory," showing the wives of the Trojans how long he has
been absent from the battle by giving them cause to rend their cheeks
and groan with sorrow (120–26), a cruel compensation for his own
loss, which demonstrates that the desire for "imperishable glory" is,
like his sense of shame, motivated by predominantly affective drives.
His vengeance on Hektor is one on a "destroyer of a dear life" (114).
All this leads us to detect an element of redefinition in *kleos* here.
Achilles' whole decision to face death at this juncture should be seen
against the background of the double destiny of book 9.[43] Gone now
are all thoughts of his return home (90, 101) and of a homecoming to
an inglorious old age. What has driven him to wish for "noble glory"

---

42. 18.95f., 117–21, 330–32; 19.408–23; 21.110–12, 277f.; 22.359f. For Achil-
les' "death while still living" see Mueller 1984, 58; Schein 1984, 25–27, 131f.,
155f.; Lynn-George 1988, 212–14.

43. Taplin 1992, 196f.

can reasonably be read as an overwhelming sense of personal loss, so *kleos* is a much more internally and affectively motivated thing here than in the rest of the poem, something to be contrasted with the external type of *kleos* that Hektor desires while quelling all affective ties to his family and community.[44] Guilt is also present. In book 19, Achilles says that he could suffer no more dreadful loss, not even if he heard of the death of Peleus, whom he pictures back at Phthia in old age close to death, constantly waiting for news of his son's death, while he himself is fighting at Troy (19.321–37). Intense sadness is evident in these words and in what he says about his son Neoptolemos, away in Skyros, whom Patroklos will now not be able to show over Achilles' estate. There is also a sense of guilt that he is not looking after Peleus in his old age, a thought that Achilles develops when he meets Priam.[45]

The "competitive" considerations are present to some degree at least. So, in two further examples, Achilles responds positively to Thetis' opinion that it is "truly no ignoble thing" to defend one's comrades when they are hard-pressed (18.128–29), and Iris at least thinks she is on firm ground with him when she says he should have a sense of awe and revulsion, *sebas*, against the Trojans' mutilation of Patroklos' corpse, and when she claims that it would be a disgrace if Patroklos' corpse were to be brought back "degradingly mutilated" (18.178–80).[46] But again the competitive drive is subordinated to the affective impulses, as is made clear by Achilles' striking insouciance over Agamemnon's gifts of compensation, which Achilles says the king is free to give as is "seemly" or to withhold, given Achilles' desire to start the fray (19.147–49). This last is consistent with Achilles' lack of pleasure over Zeus' fulfillment of his promise.

Hence the claims of *philotês* that bound Achilles and the ambassadors in book 9 have been raised above those of honor, and even above those of life, the contemplation of which in the earlier book had stifled all action. Hence, in turn, he makes the impassioned curse of wrath and anger (18.107–11), and he wishes that Briseis, whom he tells the ambassadors he loved "from his heart," had died when

---

44. Cf. Silk 1987, 71, cited in n. 9 above.
45. See above, pp. 62–64, below, p. 121f.
46. Later, when Achilles fears that the flies will "disfigure" Patroklos' corpse (19.23–27), the concern is purely affective.

Achilles had taken Lyrnessos (19.56–62). Hence, also, he renounces his wrath, which comes, however, almost as an incidental to his impetuous desire to start the battle again—"Now, I swear, I cease my anger, nor should I be angry for ever; but come now, send the Achaians to battle . . ."[47] Hence, finally, he vows not to eat or drink now that his comrade is dead, until, that is, he has avenged the disgrace (199–214).[48] Just how this predominantly emotion-driven vengeance will manifest itself, divested as it is of the *tîmê*-sanction and of justice, and how acceptable it is, is made grimly apparent in books 20 through 22.

The most important index of Achilles' emotional state and of the opinion we are meant to form of the morality of his actions is provided by his rejections of his suppliants Tros, Lykaon, and Hektor. The rejection of Tros' supplication, briefly narrated (20.463–72), contains a surprising amount of judgment by the narrator. Tros is said to have tried to supplicate Achilles in the hope that Achilles might pity him on the grounds of his coevality with Achilles, but he only earns the narrator's epithet "fool" (*nêpios*), because, the narrator continues, Achilles was not in any way "sweet-minded" nor "gently disposed," but rather "impassioned." Leaf felt the description "wholly alien to the Epic style," but it is not really much more so than the phrase "swaying him with fateful words" (αἴσιμα παρειπών), which is used of Agamemnon when he persuades Menelaos to dispatch that other exemplary failure of a suppliant, Adrestos; and it seems an appropriate way, given the brevity of the narrative, to mark the enormity of flouting an institution as vital as supplication.[49]

---

47. 19.67–75; cf. 19.147–49, the dismissive remark about Agamemnon's gifts, and the wish to start the fighting immediately. There is a flash of bitter self-assertiveness at 63f., when Achilles surmises that the Achaians will remember his and Agamemnon's conflict for a long time—though now such things should be forgotten, and their anger should be tamed out of necessity (65f.).

48. Griffin (1980, 15f., with lit.) holds that Achilles refuses to eat because he is still unreconciled with Agamemnon; so also Taplin (1992, 211f.). But the quarrel and the gifts with which Agamemnon hopes to soothe it seem rather to have become *parerga*.

49. De Jong (1987a, 87, 261 n. 55, 268 n. 32) accepts 20.466 as illustrating the "omniscience" of the "primary narrator focalizer" and 464 as depicting the character's point of view, but she curiously neglects the evaluative adjectives of 467f.; on her scheme of things, they would probably belong to the

The rejection of Lykaon's plea (21.34–135) is obviously a more developed affair. Despite the evident pathos of Lykaon's fate on an individual basis,[50] it should be seen against Achilles' overall attitude toward all the Trojans. As he says to Lykaon, the death of Patroklos is the reason it is no longer "more dear" to him to spare the Trojans or take them alive, as he used to do (100–102). Moreover, evidently referring to Thetis' prophecy that he will die as a consequence of reentering the battle and killing Hektor, he announces to Lykaon that even he, Achilles, despite his beauty, might, and illustrious parentage, will die (108–13). By the bitterly sardonic consolation that he offers in these words, Achilles demonstrates that he also has his own death on his mind, which feeds into his impassioned sense of loss, guilt, and dishonor over Patroklos' death. This emotional state has become an absolute matter, and will not be assuaged by anything less than the destruction of *all* Trojans, in an act of veritable genocide. Achilles tells Lykaon that now, after Patroklos' death, not one of the Trojans will escape death; this becomes true of all the Trojans, but particularly of the sons of Priam (103–5). There is no room here for mercy or privileged treatment, only special harshness toward a par-

---

NF_1, but could they not also be the "characters'"? On 6.62 in the Adrestos incident, Goldhill (1990) suggests the meaning "swaying him with fateful words" for αἴσιμα παρειπών; cf., e.g., Mueller 1984, 70; de Jong 1987a, 204f. ("proper things," NF_1's evaluation of Agamemnon's speech); Taplin 1992, 51f. At 21.99 Achilles addresses Lykaon as "fool," but that is in a speech, for which there is no room in the Tros episode, so the adjective, typical in scenes of rejected supplication, has to be put in the narrator's mouth. When the poet says that Lykaon heard an "inflexible voice" (21.98), that is as much a judgment by the narrator as "not in any way sweet-minded" and so forth. De Jong (1987a, 200) regards "inflexible" here and at 11.137 as "focalized" by the suppliants. Again, I find it hard to assign these perspectives with such precision. How can we be sure that both the "narrator focalizer" and the suppliant focalizers are not involved? De Jong is followed, with reservations, by Taplin (1992, 6, 51f.), who emphasizes that the absence of "moral judgement by the primary narrator-focalizer" by no means precludes the extrapolation of moral values or the audience's assessment of moral questions.

50. Lykaon is mentioned in 3.332f., where Paris has to borrow his breastplate, because, as an archer, he usually wears lighter armor, at this point the leopard-skin of 3.17. Lykaon, therefore, as a man who toils for a "lightweight" like Paris, is doubly tragic when he is mown down in the service of Paris.

ticular group, of which Lykaon happens to be a member, despite his
desperate claim that he is only Hektor's half-brother (95–96). Again,
when he first sees Lykaon, Achilles conjectures that, if Lykaon could
escape death, the Trojans whom he has actually killed will next be
rising from the dead, and he wonders whether the earth will succeed
in checking Lykaon where the sea failed, because he has returned
from Lemnos where Achilles had shipped him (54–63). Achilles evi-
dently now regrets his former mercy, though he must remember the
bread that he had broken with Lykaon, to which Lykaon does not
omit to refer in his plea (75–76); now he wants an absolute finality to
the lives of Lykaon and the Trojans. Finally, after his grim epitaph
over the corpse of Lykaon, he turns to the Trojans in general and
literally commands them to die until the Achaians have taken Troy,
and he predicts death for them until they have all paid in full for the
killing of Patroklos and the other Achaians who died without Achilles
to protect them (128–35).

The absoluteness of Achilles' passion means that individual vic-
tims like Lykaon are treated with a strange and horrifying impartial-
ity.[51] This is true in the case of Lykaon even though he has been
ransomed mercifully by Achilles in the recent past; now offers "three
times" the value of the cup worth one hundred oxen with which he
was ransomed before (89f.); has entered a formal and at least partially
affective relationship with Achilles by virtue of the shared first meal,
so that Achilles can even now address him as *philos*;[52] and comes

---

51. Taplin's (1992, 220–24) "terrifying scream," "merciless logic," though
I doubt his interpretation of Lykaon's gesture of dropping his sword and
spreading his arms as a "gesture of acceptance" whereby Lykaon establishes
complicity with Achilles' "logic"; it is rather a gesture betokening utter vul-
nerability with which to implore Achilles' mercy, as Gould (1973, 80f.) ar-
gues. Like Taplin, Cairns (1993, 113–19) thinks that Lykaon is abandoning
his supplication of Achilles, which Cairns takes as evidence that "the desire
for vengeance, when such vengeance is justified against an enemy or one
who has affronted one's honour, may legitimately override both the sense
of *aidos* and consideration for the rules of supplication." In precisely what
way is Achilles' rejection of Lykaon "justified"? Why does any enemy, qua
enemy, bother to supplicate his vanquisher? Where does the "tone" of the
Adrestos episode support this?

52. Leaf (1886–88, vol. 2, on 21.106) argues against the scholia in seeing
"a mocking allusion to the claim of hospitality. It rather indicates a real touch
of pity." This does not square with 98, "he heard an inflexible voice." See

before Achilles "as good as a suppliant, who should be revered" (75), especially because Achilles was the first person to break bread with him on his capture. Even in this instance, Achilles' resolute passion ignores the claims of the honor that might otherwise accrue from the ransom (99), the affective claims that have come into being, and the claims of the institution of supplication. Achilles' response is implacable: his voice is "inflexible" (98), and he addresses Lykaon as "fool" (99). His absoluteness admits a degree of a sort, however, as he reveals when he reminds Lykaon that even Patroklos died, who was "by far the better man than you," and that he himself, Achilles, will die, in spite of all his magnificence, for which reason Lykaon should not grieve over his death so much (106–13). The "degree" in Achilles' absoluteness is that alongside the deaths of Patroklos and Achilles, the death of Lykaon is "relatively" trivial, the only real point of comparison being located in Lykaon's description of himself as "short-lived," *minunthadios* (84), the word used by Achilles of himself in his conversation with his mother in book 1.[53] The relativity is grim.

Achilles' absoluteness informs his terrifying command to Lykaon, "Friend, you die too" (106). By using the word *friend*, he is admitting the affective and ritual claims that Lykaon has on him, doing so in the very moment of announcing his death. Hence, too, is the particular cruelty of the epitaph in which Achilles pictures the fish as cleaning Lykaon's wounds, "uncaring" (*akêdees*), which is surely a play on that word's connotations of a lack of burial;[54] and hence is the savagery of his statement that instead of a mother to lament over him on a bier, the River Skamandros will hold him in his "bed," *kolpos*—again a terrifying wordplay, because *kolpos* means not only riverbed but a woman's bosom, on which she holds the head of her dead son as she laments him.[55] Hence in part, too, is Skamandros' anger and

further Gould 1973, 79 n. 36; Griffin 1980, 55; Mueller 1984, 71; Schein 1984, 98f., 148; Thornton 1984, 139; Lynn-George 1988, 205; Taplin 1992, 223; Richardson 1993, on 21.99–113.

53. 1.352; cf. Thetis' "of swift doom," *ôkumoros*, at 18.95; Lynn-George 1988, 204.

54. Cf. 24.554, *Od.* 24.187f. In its passive sense, *akêdês* means "unburied," in its active use standardly "uncaring"; but here the context suggests "not giving due burial"; so also Richardson 1993, on 21.122–23.

55. See 24.710–12, 723–24; cf. Achilles at 23.136 and Thetis at 18.71 with the remarks of Mueller (1984, 58); Schein (1984, 131f.); Edwards (1991, 8, and on 18.22–31); and Richardson (1993, on 21.123–25).

revulsion, though Achilles has also insulted him directly by saying
that the river, to which the Trojans had shown special veneration,
will be unable to contain the corpses of the Trojans, and the river
naturally wants to protect Troy (130–32, 138). The Lykaon incident
thus gains at least part of its particular, horrible significance from the
fact that Lykaon, who stands as one victim of Achilles' absolute pas-
sion and hatred of the Trojans in their entirety, is presented as having
the strongest claims on Achilles' mercy. Lykaon is, apart from Hek-
tor, the most individually characterized of the Trojan warriors whom
Achilles comes across, and he is on the most personal terms with
Achilles, but Achilles' only response is most chillingly impassioned
impartiality. The affective drive that must normally precede mercy
has paradoxically become so overwhelming that it absolutely rules
mercy out of court. How is Hektor to survive where Lykaon failed?

Achilles' response to Hektor's pleas for the honorable treatment
of his corpse is the culminating moment in the development of the
motif of rejected supplications. Achilles reaches the zenith of his
fury—or rather the nadir, because his behavior is presented as that
of an animal. He rejects Hektor's suggestion of a compact not to
mutilate one another's corpses (22.250–59) by saying that it is no
more possible for them to be on terms of agreement and friendship
(265) than it is for pledges and promises to exist between lions and
men or among other animals who are naturally hostile and continu-
ously bent on one another's destruction: there can be no question of
exchanging oaths until one or the other of them is dead, which is
nothing other than a paradoxical way of absolutely denying the possi-
bility (261–67). This brutal state of mind will not countenance the
sort of human reciprocity that Hektor seems to think is reasonably
likely to meet with assent. In the ensuing fight, Achilles' fury is called
"wild" (312f.), and later, when Hektor is down and begging for de-
cent burial in his home, Achilles expresses his wish that he could eat
Hektor's flesh (346–47). The logic of the wish probably demands that
Achilles thinks its fulfillment inconceivable,[56] but that does not alter
the fact that he wishes he could bring himself to cross the barrier
between human and animal behavior, which is the most extreme

---

56. So Leaf 1886–88, vol. 2, on 346 and 24.213. See further Griffin 1980,
19–21; Mueller 1984, 69; Taplin 1992, 244 ("That is unthinkable—yet even to
wish for the unthinkable is bad enough").

statement of the savagery of his hatred that can be expected. Given the animal state of mind to which his emotions have driven him, it is no surprise that he rejects Hektor's final offer of ransom-gifts for his body, *apoina* (349), even if ten times as much were brought to him and promises were made for more over and above that (349–50); the only possibility is exposure to the dogs and birds.

This absolute denial of the incentive of honor comes pari passu with the rejection of Hektor's supplication in terms of the full ritual and even of its appeal to Achilles' parents: "Dog, do not entreat me by my knees or by my parents" is his explicit response (345). Any honor-terms used by Achilles at this juncture should be seen in this light. For instance, when he is chasing Hektor and forbids his men from intervening, the only *kûdos* that he wants is to be the sole executor of the coup de grace, in exclusive and absolute fulfillment of his passion (205–7), though he tells the Achaians, "We have won great glory: we have killed Hektor, whom the Trojans prayed to as a god" (393–94), a "public" statement in language that the Achaians will understand. The only significant way by which the honor-machinery still operates is negatively—for example, when Achilles says the dogs and birds will drag Hektor's corpse "shamefully," while Patroklos is accorded full burial (335–36); when he strips Hektor's corpse of its armor (368, 376); when he contrives the shaming treatment of Hektor (395); or when Zeus grants that Hektor's enemies treat him shamefully in his homeland (403–4). And as before with Lykaon, Achilles shows a sullen resignation over the fact that he is to die soon, a moment that Hektor describes with a specificity unprecedented in the poem so far, mentioning his death at the hands of Paris and Apollo at the Skaian gates (358–66): "Die," Achilles says. "I shall accept my doom when Zeus and the other gods want to bring it about." All this is because, as Achilles puts it, he will remember his dear comrade Patroklos while he himself is alive and even when he is dead, even if the dead in Hades normally forget their dead (389–90). It is significant that after this statement, Achilles immediately turns to the mutilation of Hektor's corpse.

But a resolution to the absolute impasse is already being prepared, as the theme of "pity," *eleos*, and "respect," *aidôs*, is set in motion. Its first statement is when Hekabe implores Hektor from the walls to have respect for her breasts, which suckled him, and pity for her herself (82–83). Its second statement is when Hektor rejects his idea of offering Achilles restitution, because Achilles will not pity or respect him (123f.). Its third statement is in book 22, when Priam determines to supplicate Achilles in the hope that he might pity and respect his advanced years (418–20). Most importantly, Priam conceives Achilles' father, Peleus, as a lever for effecting the change, and he continues by saying that "Achilles also" has a father like Priam (420–22). Moreover, Hektor begs Achilles for burial among his people by supplicating him in the name of his parents. Evidently, Achilles is as yet unreceptive to such an appeal. Nonetheless, the book opens the possibility that affective ties might be activated and might condition Achilles to respond to the human appeals to pity and respect. Even now Achilles shows some sign of relenting. In book 19 we saw him so eager to fight the Trojans that he wanted his troops to begin the offensive without eating (19.199–214), but in book 22 he cuts short his desire to press home the Achaians' advantage and test the Trojans' will to fight now that their champion is dead, because Patroklos lies a corpse, unlamented and unburied (22.378–90). He immediately turns to exact his "shaming" vengeance on Patroklos' killer, but his vendetta against the Trojans in general has abated, and he is addressing the loss of Patroklos more directly again. The absoluteness of his passion has been relativized.

For the moment, however, as the supplication motif shows, now that the honor traditionally associated with sanctions like supplication has been removed, Achilles is left only with his passion to guide him.[57] It has become an all-consuming passion, and it overrides the affective drives of pity and respect to which the honor-sanction is standardly meant to lend conclusive support, as it did with his treatment of Eëtion.

With the obsequies for Patroklos, Achilles' passion reaches its turning point. As he begins to face his comrade's death squarely,

---

57. He does not lose his sense of his own, personal *tîmê*; he disparages Asteropaios' lineage as the grandson of the river, Axios, claiming that not even Okeanos could vie with Zeus, Achilles' progenitor through Aiakos (21.157–59, 184–99). Later, when threatened by the River Skamandros (whom he must have needled with his words to Asteropaios), he laments the impending loss of his destiny to kill Hektor, when, while he would have preferred death as an *aristos* from Hektor, himself an *aristos,* he will now die like a mere swineherd lad (21.275–83).

Achilles is enabled to give the fullest and most direct expression to his affection and grief, and in the process, he attains a state of resignation and acceptance over his own death and reestablishes harmonious relations at least with his community, if not yet with his enemy, though there is a hint of change even there. When Patroklos' ghost appears to him, he expresses his hopeless wish that he and his friend might have one last embrace in mourning (23.97–98). Patroklos schools Achilles in the finality of death when he tells Achilles that they will never again take counsel apart from their friends, and he reminds him of his own destiny to meet his death beneath Troy's walls (77–81). Prompted by the apparition, Achilles draws his famous conclusion that a soul does live on in Hades, although without any corporeal life (103–4). Of similar importance is Achilles' gift to Patroklos of the lock of hair that Peleus had promised the River Spercheios upon Achilles' safe return to Phthia (141–51). The gesture betokens Achilles' grief for his friend and his acceptance of the fact that he will not return home, and it is obviously a preenactment of his own death, because the hair will be burned with Patroklos. The motif of the common grave, which Patroklos desires as a memorial to their shared childhood in Achilles' house (82–92) and which Achilles gives orders for (125–26, 236–48), highlights much the same thinking, and the simile comparing Achilles with a father lamenting as he cremates his son, who is married but has not yet had any children (222–23), draws attention to the common humanity of Achilles' feelings of grief[58] and prepares for the moment when Achilles will show compassion toward Priam as he grieves over Hektor in book 24. Significantly, the last mention of Patroklos before the games begin is of him as Achilles' "gentle" (*enêês*) companion (23.252),[59] whose bones are collected from the ash of the pyre.

Achilles begins to show the quality of gentleness to the Achaians.[60]

---

58. The image of an animal parent grieving (18.318–22) thus gives way to one of a grieving human parent; see above, p. 15f.

59. At the start of the chariot-race, however, Achilles excuses himself from competing, first because of the excellence of his immortal horses, but also because they are grieving for Patroklos, whom he describes as having "noble glory" and the quality of being "gentle," *êpios* (274–86). He thus talks of Patroklos in terms of honor and affection.

60. A sense of resignation is indicated by Achilles' sleeping, which is said to "dissolve the cares of his heart" (62f.).

His willingness in book 19 to make the Achaians enter the fray without taking food is now counterbalanced by his considerate order that they have a meal once the horses have been unyoked from their chariots (10–11), even though food is hateful to him (48). He consents to the Achaians leading him to Agamemnon's hut, even though they "had difficulty in persuading their companion's angry heart," thus introducing him back to his community proper (35–37). In the course of the games, he finally makes his peace with the Achaians, and he fully reenters his community after the cremation of Patroklos, which at Achilles' request had involved only Patroklos' most intimate associates (160, 163). When he offers the two-handled bowl to Nestor, for example, the old man accepts the gift, delighted, he says, that Achilles constantly remembers him as "gentle" and well-disposed, and that he remembers too the *tîmê* with which he should be treated (616–50), showing that the balance between honor and consideration has been restored. When the Achaians urge that Diomedes and Telamonian Aias break off their fighting-match and receive equal prizes though Aias is clearly inferior, Achilles offers Diomedes the main prize, Asteropaios' sword, and also its scabbard and belt (798–825), thus doing justice to the terms of the contest and tactfully recognizing Diomedes' superiority. Crowning all is his gift of the cauldron to Agamemnon in the javelin-throw, in which he publicly asserts that "we know" how much Agamemnon excels all and is *aristos* in strength and seniority and so needs no test to prove his worth (890–94), at last finally and diplomatically demonstrating his acceptance of the king's superiority.[61]

We see Achilles even taking a role in his community as a conciliator.[62] When the dispute arises between Idomeneus and Oilean Aias over who is winning the chariot-race, Achilles checks the "conflict" that would have arisen, by labeling their behavior as unseemly and as conduct they themselves would consider unbecoming in others (490–98). Here Achilles is using the community's appropriateness-standard to maintain social cohesion. He also soothes Antilochos' frayed temper when Antilochos refuses to part with his prize, a mare,

---

61. Thornton 1984, 137. Taplin (1992, 258f.) is rightly of the opinion that this is "a rather late and lowly 'curtain call' for Agamemnon."
62. See further Macleod 1982, 28–32; Taplin 1992, 253–60.

which Achilles wants to be passed on to the favorite in the chariot-race, Eumelos, who was "the best" (536), though his chariot had come to grief. Achilles smiles at Antilochos' defiance "because he was a dear companion," and he offers Eumelos another prize, the cuirass that he had stripped from Asteropaios (555–61). Of all the contests of the games, the chariot-race and the haggling over the prizes in it illustrate the honor-centeredness of the heroic code in its most exemplary form, with justice allowed its full play,[63] and in that event, Achilles makes full avail of the language of his peers, which is an index of his reintegration with them.[64]

Though at one with his community again, he is far from being restored to acceptable relations with his enemies. The chief areas for dissatisfaction with his attitude toward his enemies are his cruel treatment of Hektor's corpse and the sacrifice of the twelve Trojan youths that he has promised Patroklos (18.336–37, 21.26–27, 23.19–23). Hektor is stretched facedown in the dust beside Patroklos' bier, treatment designed to shame Hektor's corpse (23.24), which will not be burned but will be exposed to the birds and dogs to be eaten raw (21.182–83). It is more likely that the comment "he planned dishonoring deeds" reflects the perspectives of Achilles and the Trojans rather than conveying the narrator's evaluation, as narratological criticism has demonstrated.[65] For the narrator's view of the moral status of the "dishonoring deeds," we need other clues in the text. We may discern these in the responses of the gods. That Aphrodite and Apollo see to the corpse's preservation indicates some divine displeasure, and not even Hera will deny that Apollo is right to say that Achilles has destroyed pity and has no respect (24.44f.). Zeus says that the gods are angry, himself in particular (24.112–16). Similarly, there can be no real doubt about the moral status of Achilles' treatment of the twelve prisoners, though here the situation is more complex, because we lack the textual clues that inform our judgment of Achilles' treatment of Hektor. When we read that Achilles was

---

63. Above, p. 52f. See in general Finley 1978, 108–11. Cf. Taplin 1992, 255 n. 9; Taplin also usefully discusses Achilles' magnanimity in his dealings with the competitors.

64. Cf. 276, 280, 492–94, 536–38, 890–91.

65. See de Jong 1987a, 138; Edwards 1991, 6. The words also describe Achilles' dragging of Hektor at 22.395.

"devising evil things" (23.176), a phrase used also in book 21 when Achilles slaughters indiscriminately on the banks of the Skamandros and then takes the Trojans alive (21.19), we should again take the "evil things" as referring to both Achilles' and the Trojans' perspectives.[66] Because this allows us to reconstruct the minds of the characters, we are better equipped to form a response of our own, so the narrator is still directing our responses, even if, in the case of the twelve Trojans, we are given less to test our reactions against. Because the "evil things" are part of his punishment of the Trojans and of Hektor in particular for killing Patroklos—Achilles takes them as vengeance for Patroklos' death (21.28)—they fall into the same moral category as his dishonoring of Hektor's corpse.[67] The cruel treatment of Hektor and the twelve Trojans stands in obvious and hideous contrast to his tenderness to Patroklos. The contrast is encapsulated at the beginning of the book, when Achilles is said to have tenderly put his "man-slaughtering hands" on his dead comrade's breast.[68]

But there are signs that appeasement may be brought about even toward Achilles' enemies. Often in the games, reference is made to key prior events, as when, for example, Diomedes uses the horses he took from Aineias (23.290–92), or when Achilles awards Asteropaios' breastplate as a prize to Antilochos, and his sword, scabbard, and belt to Diomedes.[69] Of particular importance in the present context are two objects Achilles had received when he had shown mercy or respect to his victims. As the first prize in the footrace, Achilles puts down the mixing bowl that had been given as ransom for Lykaon—we are told at this significant juncture that Patroklos acted

---

66. Ibid.

67. It is true, though, that the actual slaughter of the youths on the pyre "verges on the perfunctory," as Taplin (1992, 252f.) says.

68. When the gesture occurs at 18.317, "man-slaughtering" is reflected in the anger of the lion against the man who has stolen his cubs (18.318–22) and also in Achilles' promise to Patroklos to kill Hektor and sacrifice the twelve Trojans (18.336–37). The nexus is maintained when Priam kisses the "man-slaughtering hands," for they are said to have killed many of his sons (24.478f.), but the element of affection will be radically redirected. On the way the poet uses the adjective *androphonos* to reflect not only the implied narrator's and our responses but Priam's thoughts about kissing the hands "which had killed many of his sons," see de Jong 1987a, 119f.; Edwards 1991, 4.

69. Note also the armor of Sarpedon, won by Patroklos, at 798–800.

as the intermediary (740–49). This object had been given when Achilles had shown mercy to Lykaon on the first occasion on which Lykaon supplicated him. The other prize, and the last named one of the games, is the lump of iron that Eëtion, whose body Achilles had burned with full honors out of respect, used to throw. Taken together, the two prizes remind us of the two most important moments when Achilles had shown respect and mercy to his enemies, and given in peaceful sport, they alert us to the possibility of a return to such behavior.[70]

---

70. Cf. Taplin 1992, 259.

4

A Brief Resolution: Achilles and Priam

Das Kriegsgesetz, das weiß ich wohl, soll herrschen,
Jedoch die lieblichen Gefühle auch.
—Natalie, in H.v. Kleist, *Prinz Friedrich von Homburg*

The scene is thus set for the general resolution reached in book 24. The cardinal factors that condition Achilles' ransoming of Hektor and his kindness toward Priam are his reassessment of the role of *tîmê* and of the gifts that embody it; his acceptance of the gods as arbiters of what is right behavior, especially in the matter of supplication; his rediscovery of the need for pity and respect for the disadvantaged; and the modified influence on him of his own deep passions. If this assessment is correct, my attempt at a more flexible approach to motivation incorporates factors stressed by other scholars (like *tîmê*) and also includes factors that are often ignored.

To a certain extent, *tîmê* is rehabilitated, if in a refined form. On the divine level, Hera urges, in defense of Achilles against Apollo's attack on the hero, that consideration must be given to Achilles' superiority to Hektor in point of his *tîmê*, as the son of a goddess and of a mortal who was particularly dear to all the gods, even to Apollo, who played his lyre at the marriage-feast of Peleus and Thetis (56–63). In his conciliatory speech, Zeus asserts that Achilles and Hektor shall be treated as different with regard to their *tîmê*, though Hektor was also most dear to the gods, especially to Zeus, because of his sacrifices (66–70). Even Apollo has agreed that Achilles is *agathos*, that is, a man of excellent standing in his community, though Achilles should take care that the gods do not become indignant at him (53). All the gods, therefore, take human *tîmê* as a principle to consider in their dealings with mortals. And the mortals, for their part, including Achilles, accept that *tîmê* has a role to play in their dealings with one another.

Of particular significance here is Achilles' attitude toward the ransom-gifts, *apoina*, that Priam brings, because in Homeric thinking they involve *tîmê* just as much as a *geras*. Zeus considers Achilles' acceptance of the ransom-gifts an intrinsically appropriate step and a necessary part of the ransoming of Hektor (75f.), but also a means of softening Achilles' heart (119), a perspective faithfully relayed to Achilles by Thetis (137). Achilles' reply to Thetis is immediate: if Zeus commands it, then let someone bring the gifts and take away the corpse (139–40). Both the gods and the humans involved consider that the ransom-gifts are essential to the transaction. Iris imparts Zeus' order that Priam give gifts (147); Priam tells Hekabe about them (196); they are detailed at length (228–37); they are lifted on to the wagon (275–78); Hermes, disguised as a Myrmidon, plainly thinks that he is inventing a convincing fiction when he refuses to accept a gift from the pile, designed as it is for Achilles (434f.);[1] the gifts are driven to Achilles' hut (447, 458); and Priam begs Achilles to accept them (502, 555f.), though, as if intuiting Achilles' current assessment of gifts, he does not emphasize or elaborate the gifts, in stark contrast with Odysseus' approach in book 9. Accordingly, Achilles, Automedon, and Alkimos take the "countless gifts" from Priam's wagon (578f.). That the acceptance of the gifts is more than just a formality is shown in Achilles' prayer to Patroklos not to be angry that Hektor has been ransomed, because Priam "has given honorable ransom-gifts," and Patroklos will receive his fair share of them (592–94).

Achilles evidently shares Zeus' view of the social importance of the ransom-gifts, but he also sees them in their proper perspective. The giver means more than his gifts; a token from a true suppliant counts for more than mere wealth from an Agamemnon, who will not even face Achilles in book 9 (9.372f., 11.609). Again, he permits the shrouds and a tunic to be taken from the gifts to wrap Hektor's corpse (24.580–81), no small concession in view of his still barely suppressed rage (582–86).[2] But even more important is his request to Priam that he sleep outside in the portico so that no bringer of counsel might notice him and tell Agamemnon, which would cause a delay in the ransom (650–55). His rather oblique thinking here is

---

1. On 430, Macleod (1982) points out that Hermes cannot accept it as a god either, for the gods are repaying Priam for his favors to them.

2. Taplin (1992, 274) points out that Andromache's lament at 22.508ff. "is delicately contradicted, and by Achilleus of all people."

explained by Hermes when the god commands Priam to leave imme-
diately on the grounds that, if Agamemnon and the rest of the
Achaians were to recognize Priam, his remaining sons would have
to give three times the great number of ransom-gifts that Priam had
already given, to ransom the king back alive (685–88). Achilles can
therefore see that the mere acquisition of wealth through ransom-
gifts is something at which his peers would not scruple;[3] he can also
see that such a use of gifts is inappropriate. Ironically, moreover, the
Achaians would have understood his noninsistence on gifts here,
when he is resigned to the inevitability of his death, as little as they
understood his rejection of Agamemnon's in book 9, when he was
in a state of agonized irresolution over Thetis' prophecy. Achilles
accepts *apoina* even though he had savagely refused them from
Lykaon (21.99) and Hektor (22.349–52), he preserves a moderation
concerning such matters that his peers do not share, and he achieves
a balanced attitude toward the importance and limitations of honor
in right relations.[4]

This attitude is made all the more strikingly generous because,
though the guest-friendship relationship on which Achilles and
Priam have now embarked is a ritual built on reciprocity,[5] Achilles
can have no expectation that he will receive any future hospitality
from Priam. At one juncture he recalls Priam's former territories and
wealth in general (24.543–48), but these have now been exhausted
by payments to the allies, as Hektor complains to Poulydamas in
book 18 (288–92). And with Hektor now dead, Troy's last defenses
have effectively been broken down, and the city must fall, as Priam

---

3. Hence ἐπικερτομέων (649) means "taunting," as Leaf (1886–88, vol. 2,
on 649) argues; cf. Macleod 1982, ad loc. Richardson (1993) on 649 sees the
participle as denoting "a gently provocative or mocking tone" toward Priam;
but the fact that Agamemnon poses a serious threat is something with which
the god Hermes at least, in his advice to Priam to leave (683–88), is in entire
agreement, and Achilles is therefore making a serious point, sneering at
Agamemnon rather than having a rather pointless joke with Priam. On
Achilles' "superiority to the idea of possessions" here, see Griffin 1986, 7.

4. The balance is struck by Zeus not only in the importance he attaches
to the ransom-gifts but when he says he will grant *kûdos* to Achilles by not
letting the gods steal Hektor's corpse, to maintain Thetis' *aidôs* and *philotês*
(110f.).

5. See especially Herman 1987, 60–61, 80, 92, 124.

presages in book 22. Also, Achilles will die soon, a fact of which he is all too conscious. On all counts, any reciprocation in the relationship is ruled out. The purity of the transaction in this respect is unparalleled in the *Iliad*, and it is only made the more remarkable by comparison with the encounter of Glaukos and Diomedes in book 6.[6] This is a cardinal consideration in our evaluation of Achilles' attitude, which I argue in chapter 5 can best be described as magnanimous.

The acceptance of the gods, in particular Zeus, as upholders of correct moral behavior and the recognition that mortals should maintain right relations with them are also important themes in book 24. Apollo regards Hektor's past record of sacrificing to the gods as a cogent reason for restoring his corpse for proper mourning by his family (33–38), and we have seen that Zeus considers Hektor to be "most dear" to the gods, in particular to himself, for the same reason (66–70). And when Hermes tells Priam that the gods have been looking after Hektor's corpse and preserving it from mutilation, Priam concludes that it is a good thing to sacrifice to the gods after all (425–28). As for Achilles, respect for Zeus is something he shows in full measure. When Zeus instructs Thetis to tell Achilles that the gods are angry, he softens the stern message by adding the words "if in any way Achilles might fear me and ransom Hektor" (116). That Achilles fears and respects Zeus' authority and command is made clear from his retort to Priam, the sharpness of which is construable as a symptom of an intense internal struggle,[7] that he himself intends to release Hektor to Priam, because his mother has come to him with Zeus' message (560–62).[8] He closes his warning to Priam with the

---

6. Here at least is a vital exception to the view of *philia/philos* offered by Adkins (e.g., Adkins 1963, 33f., 36f.) as based on the "need and desire for self-preservation" on the part of the *agathos*, as "not, of course, . . . altruistic," and thus as "unappetizing" to modern sentiment. Just how is Priam supposed to "reciprocate"? How will Achilles' "friendship" with Priam profit Achilles in terms of tangible "results"?

7. See Leaf 1886–88, vol. 2; Macleod 1982, ad loc.

8. Such doubled motivation does not preclude Achilles' full human responsibility for his decision; see Lesky 1961, 32–44, esp. 44f., where Lesky quotes Nestle (1942, 61), who describes Achilles' change of heart in book 24 as a "Bestandteil der Gesamtwirklichkeit, der göttlichen und der menschlichen." The same process can be seen at work at 24.503, when Priam begs Achilles to "have reverence before the gods, and pity me, remembering your father"; see Lesky 1961, 25. I would only add to Lesky's model that the gods

advice not to provoke him any further by insisting on the gifts, lest he violate Priam as a suppliant in his own home and transgress the ordinances of Zeus as Zeus Hikesios.[9] He is ready to suppress his continuing feelings of anger out of obedience to Zeus. The god, therefore, is not disappointed in his hope. Nor can he be disappointed with Achilles' response to Priam as a suppliant, a vital index of Achilles' state of mind. When he gets Iris to relay his message to Priam that he should ransom Hektor's corpse, he concludes by saying that Achilles "is neither insensitive, nor thoughtlessly impulsive, nor a transgressor, but will be careful to spare a suppliant" (157–58), which Iris duly repeats to Priam (186–87). The prediction is answered when Achilles carries the corpse out of Priam's sight, to stop Priam from displaying emotion in a way that would anger Achilles and cause him to kill Priam and, again, "transgress the ordinances of Zeus" (586).

Achilles recognizes that his rage is still powerful, but he takes active steps to control it in an attempt to respect Zeus' wishes, especially in his role as Zeus Hikesios.[10] He respects the supplication in practical terms as well. When he has the corpse washed and anointed (582f.) and lifts it onto its bier himself (589), tasks more normally undertaken by the mother,[11] he is effectively starting the funeral rites of Hektor. He offers the meal often shared with a suppliant (601–20), thus establishing greater communality with Priam than he had done with his own peers in book 19, redressing the balance disturbed by his encounter with Lykaon, and fulfilling Thetis' behest that he eat, given his short life (128–32).[12] In response to Priam's request to be

provide the stronger sanction on Achilles' compliance, his pity not being something that can yet be bargained on.

9. The identification is secured by Zeus' statement that Achilles will not be "a transgressor," ἀλιτήμων, over Priam's supplication (157f.), and by Achilles' desire not to "transgress," ἀλίτωμαι, the commands of Zeus (570).

10. On the role of *aidôs* in the scene, see in general Cairns 1993, 113–19. Achilles' initial response is postponement (508), then acceptance (515), as he masters the emotions that Priam has provoked; see Macleod 1982, on 508; Lynn-George 1988, 243; Taplin 1992, 270. Lynn-George (248) observes that Achilles' address to Priam, "Do not irritate me any more, old man" (560), "suddenly echoes the first rejection of a father suppliant in the epic," Agamemnon's of Chryses at 1.32. Taplin (loc. cit.) points out that Achilles shows pity for aspects of Priam that Hektor hardens his heart to in book 22.

11. So Macleod 1982, on 587–89, citing 720, 21.123–24, 22.352–53, and Richardson 1993, on 582–90, 587–90.

12. See further Taplin 1992, 276.

allowed to sleep—surely a sign of the trust in Achilles that Priam has built up—Achilles offers him a bed (635–48), which honors him as a guest, even more than the meal does. He obviates the possible difficulties with the ransom (649–55), and he gives his assurance of the eleven-day truce while Hektor is buried (656–70). There is a magisterial concinnity to all this. Hera insists on Achilles' superior *tîmê*, Apollo on the ethics of the situation; and Zeus' insistence on Achilles' *tîmê* and appropriate response to the ransom-gifts, on the one hand, and his emphasis on morality, on the other, constitute a neat reconciliation of Hera and Apollo's claims.

In this way, moreover, Achilles shows his reverence and pity for Priam. He belies Apollo's statement that he has lost pity and has no respect (44f.) and Hekabe's evaluation of him as an eater of raw flesh and a faithless man, together with her prediction that he will not pity or have respect for Priam (207f.).[13] Achilles was wrong to have lost pity and respect in his mutilation of Hektor's corpse, as is made clear by Apollo's words and by Zeus' statement of the gods' anger, but we can say that he is now acting morally, if only because he is doing the reverse of what Apollo and Zeus agreed was wrong. His present behavior is therefore a pole apart from his cruel rejection of the supplications of men like Tros, Lykaon, and Hektor. Homeric theology allows Achilles' present generosity, or rather magnanimity, to be based on his own volition. The habit of positing "double determination" admits without any sense of strain the possibility that the gods can command an action at the same time as men desire it independently.[14] This parallelism of agency is illustrated most graphically when Achilles tells Priam, "I am myself also minded to ransom Hektor for you, for [explanatory "and," δέ] my mother has come as a messenger to me from Zeus" (560f.). That it is open to Achilles to disobey the gods, whom he knows to be backing Priam, makes his

13. The parallelism of Hekabe's and Apollo's phraseology—and Priam's at 22.419—militates against the contention of Hooker (1987b, 123) that Apollo means by *aidôs* "(religious) awe" not "shame," in part because Apollo's remarks are made from a divine perspective to a divine audience. The word here will have the proximate force of shame, with the usual background of morality and guilt, just as when Hektor says *aideomai* at 22.105: see above, p. 61.

14. See Dodds 1951, 14; Burkert 1955, 108–25; Lesky 1961; Taplin 1992, 99f.; cf. Schmitt 1990, esp. 36–52; see also n. 8 above.

obedience all the more striking, especially when he is said to lift Hektor's corpse onto the bier "himself" (589). Moreover, it accords well with the thrust of my approach to construe Zeus' words to Thetis that he is stopping the gods from stealing Hektor's corpse to save this *kûdos* for Achilles (110) as the god's way of granting Achilles the chance to act of his own will and hence win a *kûdos* that has undergone "a kind of redefinition."[15]

We are clearly witnessing a radical change in Achilles. A sense of resignation has entered his thinking. With the funeral games for Patroklos, we saw him to some degree coming to terms with his friend's death, with his own death, and with the claims his community has on him. The scene with Priam shows that he still bitterly mourns Patroklos (511f.), but also that the gifts, of which Achilles says Patroklos will have a fair share, resolve any sense of injustice to Patroklos that might have been felt over the ransoming of Hektor (591–95). Thus Achilles can honor both his grief for Patroklos and his kindness to Priam. As for his own death, Thetis reminds him of it, recommending that he take thought for sleep and food, and even for making love with a woman (128–32; cf. 83–86). But Achilles' concern with his death is no longer directed toward himself. It is directed toward Peleus and the suffering it will cause him. After Priam has claimed that Peleus can joyfully look forward to Achilles' return (490–92), Achilles deftly and diplomatically corrects the misapprehension by saying that as a son of Peleus he is "in every way untimely," *panaôrios*, because he is not looking after his father in his old age (538–42), and that therefore Peleus is just as "in every way unfortunate," *panapotmos*, as Priam considers himself to be (493).[16] This leads

---

15. Taplin 1992, 263, 274; see further Macleod 1982, 27. Richardson (1993, on 560–70) represents Achilles as unwilling to defy the orders of Zeus only because of Thetis' mediation and his own realization that Priam must have been helped into the Achaean camp by a deity. This underestimates καὶ αὐτός, "myself also." Cf. also Richardson's statement on 101 that "κῦδος must refer at least primarily to the honour which Akhilleus will receive from Priam's ransom (cf. 119)."

16. Cf. 19.334–37, discussed above, p. 100f. Moreover, as Silk (1987, 43) observes, there is, ironically, a similarity between the positions of Priam and Peleus: "By killing Priam's son, Achilles has in effect killed himself, so that Priam's analogy between himself and Achilles' father is more exact than he knows." There are also parallels between Priam and Achilles: Achilles' wish

us to what I suggest we are invited to construe as the fundamental basis of Achilles' kindness to Priam. Priam conceived the idea of supplicating Achilles in the hope that he would have reverence and pity for his old age, in which he resembles Peleus (22.416–22). Hermes revives this idea, in a scene with Priam that is a preparation for the theme of the father and son relationship that is to play so important a part in the meeting in Achilles' tent.[17] So Priam's first words of supplication stress how similar he is to Peleus in age (as we have just seen, Achilles shows that the two fathers are comparable in more than just that respect) and how Achilles should remember his father and thus have respect before the gods and show pity toward Priam (24.486–506, especially 503f.).[18] The result is that Achilles is filled with longing for Peleus but also weeps for Patroklos (507, 511f.), which suggests that Achilles regards his relationship with Peleus in a sense as dead as that with his friend. Achilles also "pities" the old man and compares him with Peleus in point of the unhappiness that Zeus has allotted them despite their huge wealth (534–48).

The image of the two jars of Zeus that Achilles offers as the "theological" explanation of Peleus and Priam's suffering is vitally important for the perspective it gives on the view of life that Achilles has now reached. It tells that the gods allot man either a mixture of good and evil fortune or bad fortune alone.[19] Although Achilles has come to recognize the value of "honoring" in social institutions, his image is strikingly negative on the matter of social standing. Peleus and Priam, men of substance to whom material wealth has been allotted (534–37, 543–46), are suffering from the disruption in their relationships with beloved sons, so wealth and standing cannot ensure happiness on a personal level. And the man to whom Zeus grants only evil fortune will lose his material wealth so that he will suffer degra-

---

to die immediately if that is what is entailed by reentering battle is remarkably similar to Priam's desire to go to the Achaian encampment even if it is his lot to die there: "I prefer it; for Achilles may slay me immediately . . . "(24.223–27). Their willingness to face death because of the death of their dear ones gives them a moving kindred-spiritedness.

17. See especially 24.362, 371, 377, 387, 398, 425, 461. On the father theme, see, e.g., Lynn-George 1988, 230–50.

18. Lynn-George (1988, 238f.) reminds us that the only other kiss in the *Iliad* is that given by Hektor to Astyanax at 6.474.

19. So Macleod 1982, on 527–33; Richardson 1993, on 527–33.

dation—honored neither by gods nor men—and the lot of a vagrant (531–33). The image of the jars thus develops the theme of the fragility of *timê* enunciated in Achilles' great speech in the Embassy and entertains no idea of compensation for heroic or more generally human action. It emphasizes what Achilles, overwhelmed as he was by the hateful inevitability of death, had not yet contemplated in the Embassy: the centrality of human relations to human life and happiness.[20] Now, therefore, the functionality of honor-gifts is of significantly circumscribed value in Achilles' thinking. In the terms of my analysis, the ultimate promptings seem to have been foregrounded vis-à-vis their proximate sanctions. Moreover, Priam at no point bases his appeal on the ransom-gifts but concentrates on the claims of common humanity. He has judged Achilles' mood precisely in this matter, and we are left marveling at the contrast with Agamemnon's failed supplication, as shot through with the honor-criterion as it was.[21]

The theme of human relationships is developed when, during their meal, Priam and Achilles reach a moment of "admiration" for one another (629, 631) and "take pleasure in" (633) looking at one another. Achilles addresses Priam as "old man, my friend" (*geron phile*, 650), a sign that he has accepted him among his *philoi* as a guest-friend.[22] The negative emotional drives unleashed by the death of Patroklos have become positive ones, pity and respect, but also, as we can see from the vocative "my friend," affection, as Achilles gains a clearer perspective on death and its effects on human relations. Achilles' generosity toward Priam is thrown into sharp relief by a comparison with his treatment of Hektor's father-in-law, Eëtion. Achilles ultimately showed reverence, *sebas*, toward Eëtion (6.417)

---

20. Cf. Silk 1987, 97, 103.

21. Taplin 1992, 269. See Burkert 1955, 104–7 for "das rein Menschliche" in Priam's appeal in the name of Peleus, for the relegation of the importance of the ransom-gifts, for the applicability of Achilles' consolation of Priam to Achilles, and for Achilles' return to human solidarity; whereas with Lykaon a solidarity was established that was beyond the grave, with Priam it is forged between living fellow human beings.

22. See further Schein 1984, 162, on the contrast with the use of the address to Lykaon at 21.106. The construction put on the vocative by Richardson (1993, on 650–52) as fitting Achilles' "semi-serious tone here" is based on nothing more than the thinking challenged at n. 3 above.

and *aidôs* toward Hektor and Priam, in the one case by undertaking complete burial honors—because there was no one left in his family to do so—and foregoing the ritual degradation of stripping the corpse of its armor, and in the other by starting the burial rites but leaving their completion to the people by whom they should properly be carried out. Both are unquestionably generous acts: in particular, Achilles' reverence for Eëtion could never have been motivated by a hope of compensation or reciprocity. But Achilles' treatment of Priam and Hektor is based on an incomparably broader experience of suffering: Achilles has lost so much more here than with Eëtion, including his own life. So much more is at stake, so much more emotion must be overcome and controlled, and so much more companionship in suffering directs Achilles' generosity. So much greater is the victory.[23] In the Eëtion story, it is a matter of generous respect, as

23. Cf. Segal 1971, 65, who believes that Achilles only "reaffirms the gentler side of himself" shown in his treatment of Eëtion's body. It is understandable that the change goes unnoticed by Hekabe (751–56), but it is a poignant misapprehension. As a consequence, moreover, I would argue that Lynn-George (1988), whose thrust is that the *Iliad* balances "mortal loss" against "epic recompense" and doubts even its own capability to keep *kleos* alive, is prevented by the terms of his inquiry from adequately recognizing a moment of generosity that stands outside the ambit of *kleos* and that the poem on my interpretation presents as an alternative to *kleos*-driven behavior, worthwhile and commendable in and of itself. On Lynn-George's logic, could not Achilles' striking generosity, presented at the culminating point of the whole *Iliad*, constitute precisely the *kleos* that will bring some "compensation"? If an action—or anything—has not won *kleos*, it is not recorded in the poem. Cf., too, the view of Mueller (1984, 75) that "The final wisdom of the *Iliad* is not the attainment of a new and more human order born out of the destruction of the warrior code, but the temporary and ordered vision of the suffering and contradictions of human life." The "resolution" that I think is reached in book 24 has no effect on the course of the Trojan War, but it was evidently meant to have a permanent effect on the audience. I find myself in greater sympathy with the conclusion of Schein (1984, 160) that "the unique solidarity and humanity shared with Priam surpass even the earlier *philotês* characteristic of Achilles before his *mênis*," though Schein reaches his conclusion on different grounds from mine; in particular, he does not bring out the importance of Achilles' attitude toward the *tîmê* involved in his transaction with Priam. See further Silk's judicious remarks (1987, 95–97, 102–5) on Achilles as a "heightened form of humanity" and on the "subversiveness" of the *Iliad* ("Heroic endeavour *and* Achilles' eccentric version of it are both offered as realities"). Burkert (1955, 107) provides a most

opposed to the dearly won magnanimity of the scene with Priam and Achilles.

Book 24 restores harmony, which is the narrator's answer to the moral standards displayed by the characters of the poem, for whom the honor-incentive has overridden other aspects of the heroic life. The place of honor in human relations is reinstated in a refined form. Social institutions are once again accepted. Due respect is shown for their sanctions, not only shame and honor, but the gods and the fair play that they and especially Zeus seek to preserve, despite internal friction.[24] The affective drives are foregrounded, especially pity, respect, and affection, the significance of which is fully appreciated only in the experience of death.[25] Achilles' unique experience and knowledge of death enable him, alone among the warriors before Troy, to attain to the companionship in suffering that he shares with Priam and the sublime generosity that he shows toward him, a generosity that, as we saw in chapter 1, outstrips even that of the gods themselves, whose immortality debars them from the totality of Achilles' vision.

---

fitting assessment of the meeting: "Freilich ist das Beisammensein der Feinde nur Episode, noch in der Nacht ruft Hermes Priamos zur Rückfahrt; und doch bleibt etwas Weiterführendes, Wesentliches und Gültiges in dem rein menschlichen Zusammenfinden, das durch ἐλεεῖν gewirkt wurde."

24. See Macleod 1982, on 25–30, with lit., for Hera, Poseidon, and Athene's continuing hostility to Troy: "This reminds us that even if for the moment 'the gods' are to unite in allowing the ransom of Hektor's body, the gods hostile to Troy still have reason to be as angry as ever; and the city they hate must fall." From Troy's point of view, however, the "dangerous lust" (μαχλοσύνη) of Paris may be "the sweet infection that the Trojans cannot bring themselves to purge," and it "sets a dark background" to the destruction of the city through guilt by association; Taplin 1992, 261f. See further Davies 1981.

25. See Taplin 1992, 74–82, 278f., for the view that by sleeping with Briseis at 24.676 (and thereby falling in with Thetis' recommendation at 24.130f.) Achilles "assert[s] life in the teeth of imminent death."

5

The Magnanimity of Achilles

Whatever shares
The eternal reciprocity of tears.

—W. Owen, "Insensibility"

A Definition

In my attempt in chapter 1 to elicit a general picture of Iliadic coopera-
tion and its incentives, I deliberately tried to leave Achilles out of the
discussion. My strategy was to provide a model of Iliadic cooperation
that might be valid in itself, and that could also be used as a yardstick
with which to measure the attitudes Achilles shows toward coopera-
tion. His responses to the more materialistic, honor-centered incen-
tives in the heroic code vary throughout the *Iliad:* infuriation at the
theft of Briseis in book 1; an overriding doubt over the value of such
incentives in book 9; an almost total neglect of them as a reason for
reentering the battle in books 18 and 19, in favor of the personal and
emotional pull felt when he reacts to the death of Patroklos; a cruel
flouting of the rules of appropriate behavior toward suppliants like
Tros, Lykaon, and Hektor; and an acceptance of personal and emo-
tional ties as the compelling reasons for showing compassion in book
24.

   In plotting Achilles' course, my chief concern has been to question
the precise ways in which Achilles' behavior with Priam goes beyond
the demands of conventional social institutions and the respect and
pity that he showed with Eëtion but that characters like Hekabe and
Apollo doubt he is capable of any more. The salient factors are identi-
fied and discussed more fully in the preceding chapter. First, though
he accepts the ritual importance of *tîmê* and gifts to both his duty to
Patroklos and to his transaction with Priam, he shows a remarkable
insouciance over acquiring honor and ransom-gifts, as is shown by
his use of the gifts of cloth in which to wrap Hektor's corpse, and by

his sneering sideswipe at Agamemnon, who will demand ransom for Priam if he learns of Priam's presence in Achilles' hut. Second, Achilles acts generously toward Priam without any hope of the future reciprocity that guest-friendship normally entails; both men know that Troy's wealth is spent and that the city is to fall soon, and Achilles knows anyway that he is soon to be killed. Third, he respects the behest of Zeus Hikesios in accepting Priam's supplication, offering him a meal, kind words, and a bed, but he seems to go beyond Zeus' requirements by having the corpse washed and anointed, by his gesture of lifting it onto its bier—thereby starting the funeral rites of Hektor—and by his offer of the eleven-day truce. Fourth, he proves significantly responsive to the personal aspect of Priam's appeal, especially to the invocation of his relationship to Peleus, and he shows that he has recognized the value of human relations, which he is prepared to foster precisely at the moment when he knows for certain of his imminent death, and which he is ready to express through his admiration for Priam, by calling him "old man, my friend," and by clasping Priam's right wrist to reassure him that he has nothing to fear (671–72). Fifth, he is accorded Zeus' novel *kûdos* by his own moral choice to give back Hektor's corpse. Sixth, his generosity to Priam outstrips his respect for Eëtion, noble though that is within its more standard framework.

How shall we characterize Achilles' behavior toward Priam as he reverts to and surpasses the generosity he used to show before his conflict with Agamemnon, pinpointing the compelling existence of nonselfish drives? The word that I wish to propose is *magnanimity*, which has already, quite naturally crept into the discussion. I must therefore define what I mean by magnanimity and show how Achilles displays the quality, even though there is no word in Homeric Greek to describe it. I shall then examine whether Greek philosophical discussions of magnanimity and related responses, especially those of Plato and Aristotle, offer any retrospective insight into the gratuitous benevolence of Achilles, and where it stands in relation to Greek society and thought. Finally, I shall try to examine the uniqueness of Achilles' moment of magnanimity in early Greek epic. I suggest that in this respect also Homer earns the title of "the first teacher and way-finder of the tragedians" given him by Sokrates in the *Republic* (595c1f.).

I hope to have demonstrated in this book that in the meeting between Priam and Achilles, a moment exists in the *Iliad* in which we can discern a character acting in a kind way toward another, who is moreover an enemy, without any dominating sense of self-interest, motivated instead principally by a feeling of common humanity in the face of common mortality. Parallels can be drawn from modern times—for example, from the trench warfare of World War I. S. Weintraub describes the spontaneous truces on the Western Front, which "were most likely to occur in bad weather, and men emerging from flooded trenches often were not shot at by the other side even when orders to fire were in effect."[1] Otherwise, we have the incident on the first day of the Battle of the Somme, when "German stretcher-bearers came out at certain points, under white flags, and picked up British wounded near their own wire," and the occasions on which soldiers strayed near enemy lines, in foggy conditions, for example, and were merely told to go back by the sentries, who could not bring themselves to shoot an exposed enemy.[2] *Magnanimity* seems the most natural word to describe such behavior. The dictionary defines the quality as "Nobility of feeling; superiority to petty resentment or jealousy; generous disregard of injuries,"[3] but such a description does not seem to do justice to the extent of the generosity involved in the ancient and modern examples we have before us, where the rifts between the two sets of parties are anything other than "petty," and where the motivation to disregard the rifts is, each in its own way, of a highly complex kind. Nor will we find appropriate to our inquiry the sense of the haughty superiority suggested by the diction-ary's definition, whereby, for example, a general might spare the lives of a few defeated troops on the grounds that he was far too grand to bother to attend to the execution of a few more paltry, insignificant souls. Such "magnanimity" is closer to disdain. More-over, we tend nowadays to consider magnanimity to be the greater where the element of self-interest in the motivation is small. We are accustomed to assigning different degrees of moral status to different

---

1. Weintraub 1985, 4f.

2. See Ellis 1976, 170–73; there is also, from Gallipoli, the incident mov-ingly described by Facey (1981, 265).

3. *Oxford English Dictionary*, 2d ed., s.v. "Magnanimity" 4.

acts of magnanimity, and few of us would seriously demand an abso-
lute, Kantian purity of motive from altruism, of which magnanimity
is an aspect.[4] Most of us, though we might distantly admire it, would
more likely be repelled by the severity of Kant's example of the man
whose natural sensitivity for others' suffering has been displaced by
some personal grief of his own, but who nonetheless, despite the
cessation of his naturally kind inclinations, does a beneficent act,
purely out of a sense of duty that a beneficent act must be done, at
which point alone, according to Kant, his action has genuine moral
worth. We would react even more strongly in the case of the man
whose natural endurance and fortitude make him expect the same
qualities in other people, so that he is cold and indifferent to others'
suffering, and who, though he acts benevolently not from inclination
but from pure duty, wins a higher moral worth than a man of a
good-natured temperament.[5]

What, then, motivates altruistic magnanimity? The *Frontkamerad-
schaft* between the opposing sides of World War I was presumably
based on the perhaps unconsciously shared feeling that they were
both "in the same shit"—on a sense of common suffering that has
somehow been preordained by superior forces in their lives. Achil-
les shows a significantly comparable awareness of this feeling, in his
description to Priam of the two jars of Zeus from which the god
dispenses either a mixture of good and bad, or of pure and simple
bad. Priam and Peleus as fathers and Achilles as a combatant away
from his homeland are enmeshed in a greater mechanism. From
such a view of one's lot, "fellow feeling" arises, whose centrality to
magnanimity—and importance to this book—should by now be very
clear.[6]

---

4. Kant 1785, 398f., in the *Grundlegung zur Metaphysik der Sitten.* Cf.
Gagarin 1987, 287–90; Lloyd-Jones 1987b, 308; and Adkins 1987, 313, on
Adkins' use of the word *Kantian* at Adkins 1960b, 7.

5. Kant, loc. cit.

6. Largely for this reason—but also because of their failure to discuss *Il.*
24 at all—I think that the analysis by Claus (1975) of "gratuitous" heroic
behavior and even the "generalized reciprocity" of Donlan (1981–82) are in-
adequate as coverages of altruistic behavior in the *Iliad.*

Achilles' Magnanimity and Greek and
Modern Society and Thought

Some would object that the search for such magnanimous impulses (or for anything akin to altruism) in Greek morality before Stoicism was a total wild goose chase, so a brief discussion of certain texts outside Homer seems needed, in particular from Plato and Aristotle. However, the legends of self-sacrifice, like those of Alkestis, Menoikeus, and Iphigeneia, at least as Euripides formulates them in the *Alkestis*, the *Phoinissai* (834ff.), and the *Iphigeneia at Aulis*—in the latter two cases, admittedly, Euripides seems to have introduced the motif of self-sacrifice into the standard versions of the myths—and the historical example of those who risked their lives to tend the stricken during the plague at Athens, detailed by Thoukydides (2.51), should warn us against assuming a total absence of magnanimity in Greek popular morality before the fourth-century philosophers. Moreover, Phaidros in the *Symposion* of Plato mentions the stories of Alkestis and Achilles together as proof of the esteem in which the gods hold self-sacrifice out of *philia*, in Achilles' case his willingness to avenge Patroklos' death despite his knowledge from Thetis that he will die directly after killing Hektor (179b–d, 179e–180b).

Phaidros' speech shows that Plato must have known of the concept of altruism as a characteristic of Greek popular thought, and that he must have realized that people associated the quality with legendary figures like Alkestis and Achilles. In his own thinking, however, it is hard to make a convincing case for believing that altruism had any part to play. Two key passages illustrate this. In the first book of the *Republic*, Thrasymachos is made to adopt two positions. He is made to subscribe to a kind of opportunism, whereby the strong act neither rightly nor wrongly but out of mere self-interest (338c). At the same time, he accepts the view that justice is "in reality the good of someone else" (343c), whereby the weak do what is in the interest of the ruler, qua the stronger. Sokrates does not either directly attack or refute the position.[7] But this "good of someone else" can hardly entail altruism. It is not a motive for conduct but something pursued out of fear, as is made clear from Thrasymachos' ex-

---

7. Mackenzie (1981, 127f.) would have it that he merely shows that opportunism and altruism cannot be consistent with one another.

ample of the shepherd who day and night watches over his master's sheep to secure his master's profit. It has been argued that altruism is discernible in my second passage, again from the *Republic*. After the parable of the cave, in which Sokrates considers whether it would be fair to demand that the philosopher-kings return to the state after their exposure to the vision of goodness to give the state the benefit of their knowledge (520a–21b), Glaukon concludes that they would return: the command to return is "just," and the philosopher-kings are "just" (520e). The philosopher-kings' counterpart in the fable of the cave, however, merely congratulates himself on the acquisition of his grasp of reality beyond the cave, pities those who still inhabit it, and loathes the thought of his return, as Achilles in the *Odyssey* loathed his existence in Elysium (516c–e, quoting *Od.* 11.489f.). All this shows that the philosopher-kings would not want to return but would accept that they should. And the passage reveals a countervailing pressure against the philosopher-kings' natural inclination, which has been identified as altruism.[8] This is, however, unlikely. The passage parallels exactly *Laws* 731d–32a, where self-love is opposed not to a love of others but to a love of justice. Thus the love of justice of the philosopher-kings, who are themselves "just," would induce them to return to the state. As a professional philosopher, Plato discards what he evidently thinks is the common view.[9]

Something similar can be said of Aristotle. In the *Rhetoric*, for example, Aristotle says that one thing that creates friendship is doing a favor, *charis*, without being asked, and without advertising the fact, "for in this way the favor seems to have been rendered for the sake of the friend, not for some other reason" (*Rhet.* 1381b35–37). A little later *charis* is defined as the emotion of benevolence or kindliness displayed when one renders a favor to fulfill a real need, without the expectation of a return favor, and without any self-interest on the part of the donor (1385a17–19). Aristotle points out that claims in court that a favor has been rendered can be refuted by asserting,

---

8. Kraut 1973; cf., e.g., Annas 1981, 266f.—Annas regards the philosopher-kings' motivation as "very abstract" ("They are simply doing what is impersonally best")—and in general Annas 1977.

9. Bostock (1986, 16–20) argues for altruism, or at least for something other than self-interest, in relation to Plato's ban on suicide at *Phaidon* 61b–63e; he is challenged by Tredennick and Tarrant (1993, 98f.).

among other things, that the donors acted in their own interests or were paying back a favor (1385b1–5). Here we have an unequivocal case of disinterested magnanimity, especially important because Aristotle must be following a line of thought likely to be considered as orthodox by the audience of his orator. From the ethical treatises, we have the remarkable reference to women who give their children away for adoption and, though they love them, keep their identity a secret from them, to save them any discomfiture; they do this in the full knowledge that their children will not be able to reward them in the proper way; they do not insist on being loved in return but are sufficiently gratified to see their offspring faring well (*Nichomachean Ethics* [hereafter, *E.N.*] 1159a28–33). Care should be exercised with this last example, because one's well-being is conventionally assessed in relation to the well-being of one's children and parents.[10] We cannot talk of strict, Kantian altruism here, but we can talk of the mother's self-sacrifice and the magnanimous renunciation of duties owed her.

Though Aristotle admits that popular thought has room for notions of altruism, his template for the truly virtuous life, the so-called magnanimous man (*megalopsûchos*) of the *Nichomachean Ethics* is motivated principally by the greatest good—honor. The magnanimous man possesses worth and knows his worth (*E.N.* 1123b1f.). Thus he deserves the greatest external good, honor (*tîmê, E.N.* 1123b17–22), though he will be indifferent even to that (*E.N.* 1123b16–20) or to risking his life in significant circumstances, because he does not consider life worth hanging on to at any price (*E.N.* 1124b6–9). He will benefit others rather than accept benefits, because the former is the mark of a superior man and the latter that of an inferior (*E.N.* 1124b9–10), and he returns favors with interest to be the truly benefited party (*E.N.* 1124b11f.). Similarly, in Aristotle's discussion of proper self-love, the virtuous man (the *agathos* or *spoudaios*) may be motivated by the interests of friends and country, sacrificing wealth, power, and even his life if he can win for himself nobility, which Aristotle considers to be the proper expression of self-love (*E.N.* 1169a18–1169b2). And the generous man (*eleutherios*) has a propensity to excessive giving, "for not considering his own interests is the hallmark of the generous man" (*E.N.* 1120b4–6). At one point in the *Nichomachean*

---

10. See, e.g., Plato *Hippias Major* 291e–d.

Ethics, however, we find Aristotle considering why, as an observable fact of human life, benefactors love their beneficiaries more than vice versa "even if they are in no way useful nor likely to be so in the future." The philosopher offers a multiple-choice answer: the benefactor feels affection for his beneficiary; he enjoys "creating" just like an artist, because our love of existence can only be realized by activity; he enjoys the element of nobility involved in giving; as the "lover" of the beneficiary, he enjoys the more active role; and the more we put into a thing, the more we value it (*E.N.* 1167b17–1168a27).[11] This is perhaps the closest that Aristotle comes in the ethical treatises to a recognition of genuinely disinterested behavior, and it sits a little uneasily with the motivations that Aristotle proposes for generosity in the case of the magnanimous or virtuous man, although the nobility-incentive is a common factor. It is interesting to find Aristotle describing Achilles as an example of "magnanimity," *megalopsûchia.* At *Posterior Analytics* 97b7–25, Aristotle asks what is the shared feature between Alkibiades, Achilles, and Aias, and he concludes that it is "intolerance of insult." In Achilles' case, this is related directly to the quarrel with Agamemnon by the statement that Achilles "was raised to wrath" by this disposition. Though Aristotle nowhere says as much, it is tempting to think that he would have considered the Achilles of the Priam scene as an example of his ideal benefactor.

In view of the evidence that we have surveyed, ranging from popular thought to Plato and Aristotle, there seems to be no difficulty in discerning a recognition of an at least relatively disinterested magnanimity in Greek thought and society. If this book has shown that such a concept is at work in the *Iliad,* we may more justifiably suspect that it was also part of the ethical equipment of the society to whom Homer was singing. It has been forcefully argued that to deny that Homer's epics had any contact with the "conventions or values" of his age demands that we assume what is implausible, that the poet invents not only a story but a set of ethical referends unfamiliar to his audience.[12] If there is common ground between historical, documented Greek society and the ethical assumptions that Homer's epics

---

11. I am indebted to J.E.J. Altham for drawing my attention to these passages.

12. Mackenzie 1981, 68f.

make, we may have greater confidence in attributing at least certain values to the society in which Homer and his audience lived than we have been encouraged to have.[13] In that case, the *Iliad*'s original audiences will have viewed Achilles in much the same way that I have tried to do, granting Achilles in book 24 a magnanimity that, though not *Kantian* altruism, is altruistic to a high degree and morally noble.[14]

Here we inevitably face the problem of dating the society that Homer's *Iliad* reflects. I find myself persuaded by the arguments of I. Morris that "The assumptions Homer made about the workings of society will have been based on those of the Greek world in which he lived," a society that Morris locates in the latter half of the eighth century, after the introduction of writing in around 750.[15] My reconstruction of Homer's altruism would fit in easily with Morris' conclusion that the *aristoi* of the eighth century laid claim to the Homeric poems—in the form of texts committed to writing—as sanctions for their own supremacy in a time of social turmoil, even though the poems contained an evaluation of their status that was on occasion clearly critical. The assertion of a morality beyond reciprocity could have been precisely one of those "critical" elements. My argument also concurs with the analysis of J. Whitley,[16] which in some important ways represents a refinement of Morris' position, helping us to form an even more precise background. Whitley envisages a Dark

---

13. By, e.g., Snodgrass 1974. But see now Donlan 1981–82, 146, n. 18; Qviller 1981; and for Hesiod, Zanker 1986, 26f.

14. Admittedly, it was not always so in early Greek society. As H.A. Shapiro reminds me, by the fifth century, and even in the sixth, the vase-painters go out of their way to emphasize Achilles' savagery—for example, by placing Hektor's corpse on the floor nearby, under Achilles' dining couch, or beneath the dining table, while Priam entreats him; see, e.g., the cup tondo by Makron in the Louvre (Louvre G153; Beazley 1954, 15, fig. 4; 1963, 460, 14). Achilles' magnanimity is reinstated in the vases when narrative is introduced into representations of the Priam-Achilles episode, notably on the cup by the Painter of the Fourteenth Brygos in New York, Collection of Shelby White and Leon Levy (Beazley 1963, 399, 1650; von Bothmer 1990, no. 118), in the decoration of the tondo, where the corpse has been removed, and Priam and Achilles, in Shapiro's opinion, are approaching their Homeric rapprochement. The scene is discussed by Shapiro (forthcoming).

15. Morris 1986, 89.

16. Whitley 1991.

Age Greece as one of a hitherto unimagined social diversity, in which the very unity of the institutional and ethical world of the Homeric poems, especially in gift-giving, *xeniê*, and marriage, is evidence of the need for a unified code binding the distinct communities of *aristoi* in crossing "tribal" boundaries. In such social conditions the notion of altruism could easily have had an important part to play. I thus conclude that Homer constructs the heroic world from his own times, with recourse to the "distancing devices" that Morris identifies so clearly,[17] and that the ethical values of the *Iliad*—specifically the element of altruism—can with confidence be postulated as living forces in the historical Greek society, or societies, of the eighth century.

I see more of a continuity between the society depicted in the *Iliad*, Greek society of the classical age, and our own sociomoral values than Finley or Adkins did. Their point of view was much more colored by Kantian, Christian, and humanist ethics in the fifties and sixties of this century than is the case today, when thinkers like Bernard Williams and Alasdair MacIntyre have argued forcibly that Kant in particular has impoverished our moral vocabulary; they have in effect disputed the view that the Greek understanding of virtue is fundamentally different from ours, or from what ours should be.[18] Perhaps the Kantian "purity" of motive led Finley and Adkins to the reductivity of their model of the *Iliad*'s ethical world (which this book has tried to combat) and, in particular, to turn a blind eye to Achilles' behavior in *Iliad* 24: the critical moment simply did not fit their view of Iliadic society as fundamentally alien to our own. Now that Kant and Christianity can no longer claim general arbitration over what constitutes virtues like kindly, other-regarding altruism, we perhaps find ourselves back with a reading of Achilles in book 24 as a hero with a magnanimity that we can once again admire at close quarters.

---

17. Morris 1986, 85, 89f.

18. Williams' critique of Kantian moral thinking (and thus, by inference, of the underpinnings of much thinking about "guilt-ethics") is apparent in Williams 1985, chap. 10, esp. 184, 189, and 1993, 75–77, 100, 158–67; see also the (partial) linking of Aristotelian and modern approaches to ethics in Williams' chap. 3, esp. 34, 52; see now Williams 1993, chaps. 4 and 6. For MacIntyre's views, see MacIntyre 1981, chap. 14; cf. chaps. 10 and 12. Further literature can be found in Lloyd-Jones 1983, 230 n. 7.

The Achievement of *Iliad* 24

How unique is Achilles' magnanimity in the *Iliad* and in the rest of early Greek epic? My contribution to the question of social cooperation has been to offer a new model of the *Iliad*'s value-system and to use it to explore the important part that affective and moral impulses have to play, demonstrating that there is a sense in which the Iliadic warrior feels, however dimly, that he is disposed to help people because he likes them and/or because he thinks it fair play to do so. I have presented the case for believing that such promptings, though associated with the emotion of guilt, are weak stimuli for cooperation and are therefore easily neglected by the forces of a society that is intensely results-oriented and competitive. Cooperation is ensured by a system of incentives, so in general the degree of self-interest is high, if not total. My conclusion is that the guilt-based motives for cooperative behavior, which may be the "ultimate" ones, nonetheless require the underpinning of the honor and shame system, which may be called the "proximate" motives for loyalty to the group. Once this two-tiered system has been accepted, it is possible to accept the coexistence of guilt and shame and the coexistence of "inner" motives, such as affection and fair play, and "external" motives, such as honor. Therefore it is possible that disinterested magnanimity in the sense that I have allocated to it is likely to be excluded in the general run of human life (and also that of the gods), but in exceptional circumstances, affection and fair play may be foregrounded, so that other-regarding kindness might become a reality, however briefly such a moment is likely to last in a society like that of the *Iliad*.

In discussing magnanimity in the *Iliad*, we must distinguish between the motives for the magnanimous behavior and the behavior itself. Sympathy, affection—which in Homeric society, and in our own, can easily rise out of what the *Iliad* calls pity (*eleos*)—and the sense of fair play form the main motives for Iliadic magnanimous behavior; and the degree of disinterestedness in motivation determines our view of the magnanimity of any particular act. Normally these motives of "fellow feeling" are a weak constraint on cooperative behavior in general and need to be substantiated by the element of self-interest at the basis of the honor-sanction. It is an exceptional circumstance, then, if the more powerful, self-interested honor-incentive is transcended and if agents go beyond the behavior required

by that incentive. Then the "ultimate" motives, like "fellow feeling,"
come into play, and the resultant behavior is based on more disinter-
ested motives. The narrator of the *Iliad* puts the moment when this
happens, the meeting of Priam and Achilles, in a sublimely positive
light, as a thing won only after a massive struggle in Achilles' heart
that has, what is more, involved the most hideous cruelty to his
enemy.

Here again we find resonances in historical Greek society. I have
tried to demonstrate this by reference to Sophokles' *Aias* and ex-
amples from myth, history, and popular and philosophical thought,
but it is now generally accepted that the predominant results-orienta-
tion and honor-centeredness were facts of Greek life in general,
Sparta and Macedonia being only extreme examples.[19] In this respect,
too, the *Iliad* is likely to be speaking an ethical language with which
its original audiences were quite familiar.

We may now address the task of examining the behavior of the
main characters in the *Iliad* who appear to approximate to magnanim-
ity. More broadly, it will be helpful to cast an eye over the rest of early
Greek epic for any traces of the quality. We will then have performed
all that is necessary to set up the emotional and moral reference-
points for evaluating Achilles' behavior in book 24.

The most important instance of a warrior showing pity for his
comrades is Patroklos. His pity is initially the by-product of Achilles'
command to him to find out from Nestor the identity of a wounded
warrior whom he (rightly) conjectures to be Machaon; the command
is part of Achilles' excited apprehension that the Achaians will now
at last beg him, gathered at his knees, to rejoin the battle (11.596–
615). Famously, the narrator calls Patroklos' appearance at this point
"the beginning of evil for him" (604). His behavior to Nestor is concil-
iatory, for he calls Achilles *aidoios nemesêtos*, "worthy of respect but
easy to anger," thus from the outset acknowledging his companion's
positive and negative aspects;[20] similarly, when he excuses his desire
to hurry back to Achilles to fulfill his errand, he says that Nestor
knows what a terrifying man Achilles is, "quick to find fault with the
innocent" (649–54). Patroklos is therefore ripe for Nestor's appeal to

---

19. See, e.g., Mueller 1984, 6; Lloyd-Jones 1987a.
20. See above, p. 94.

him to put on Achilles' armor and join the battle in his guise, espe-
cially after Nestor has reminded Patroklos that Menoitios sent his son
to Troy with Achilles in response to supplication and as an act of
guest-friendship, and after he has reminded Patroklos of his father's
parting words to act as a moderating influence on Achilles (785–803).
When Patroklos comes across the wounded Eurypylos, his pity is at
last explicitly awakened (814f.), and he interrupts his mission to care
for his friend in distress (839–41). His pity is jolted into urgency
when he sees the Trojans streaming over the Achaian wall (15.397f.),
and he cuts short his conversation with Eurypylos to rouse Achilles,
"for the advice of a comrade is a good thing" (404). In book 16 his
tears, his pity, and his accusation of Achilles for his obduracy (chid-
ing Achilles as "dreaded in his excellence") are well known (1–45).
In his big speech, Patroklos details the wounded *aristoi* (23–29); ac-
cuses Achilles of being difficult to deal with (*amêchanos*, 29); prays
that he will never succumb to the "anger," *cholos*, that Achilles is
nurturing (30); points out that later generations will have nothing to
thank him for if he does not ward off a "shameful" destruction from
the Achaians (again the "two tiers"—Achilles should feel pity, a duty
underlined by considerations of the shame and dishonor in the de-
struction of the Achaians); emphatically denounces Achilles' inhu-
man pitilessness (33–35); and asks to be sent in Achilles' guise, "in
the hope that I may bring salvation to the Achaians" (39), who are
exhausted and in need of respite (42f.). His fatally emotional plea
("Thus he spoke in supplication, very foolishly," 46) has its effect.

Patroklos is therefore given no motive other than pity for his com-
rades, and the absence of the honor-incentive makes his response
truly disinterested.[21] With him we appear to have a clear case of
magnanimity: his pity of the Achaians is entirely other-regarding and
seeks no obvious reward in honor. All this exists in a hero whose
gentleness is constantly recalled: by Achilles' horses (17.426ff.); by
Zeus, who foretells that Hektor's death is nigh, because he has killed
Achilles' mighty and gentle (*enêês*) friend and stripped him of his
divine armor (17.205);[22] by Menelaos, who pronounces the epitaph

---

21. Though, when he is down, he is careful to assert his honor and im-
pugn Hektor's by pointing out that Hektor's coup de grace came only after
Apollo and Euphorbos had done the real work (844–50).

22. Zeus considers Hektor's stripping of the divine armor to be presump-
tuous, which seals his doom; Edwards 1991, on 17.194–209, 205–6.

that Patroklos "knew how to be gentle to all while he was alive" (17.671); by Briseis, who calls him "constantly gentle" (19.300); by Lykaon (21.96); and by Achilles, who talks of Patroklos' gentleness at his pyre (23.252, 281).[23] Sarpedon's famous dictum to Glaukos on the heroic life, that the hero should strive in battle to win glory because death is so near (12.310–28), is simply inapplicable to Patroklos' behavior, which is a yardstick by which to measure Achilles' magnanimity to Priam in book 24. Patroklos' magnanimity is a constant characteristic and comes comparatively easily to him. But Achilles' magnanimity toward Priam, however a momentary a thing it might be, is so supremely significant because it has been won after an almost superhuman struggle against the potent contrary pressures that have built up, especially through the doubts that Achilles himself has come to entertain over the value of honor and fame.

The doctrine of Sarpedon is perfectly applicable to a figure who is fleshed out much more than Patroklos, who is moreover explicitly and repeatedly said to be fighting in defense of his community, and whose imminent death is announced in the same unique, striking phrase as Patroklos': "the gods have now called you/me deathward," *dê se/me theoi thanatonde kalessan* (16.693 = 22.297).[24] Hektor's motivation for defending his fatherland is perhaps made clearest in the Andromache scene. There his love for his immediate family is elaborated more explicitly than anywhere else in the whole poem. Thus, when he voices his presentiment that Troy will be defeated, he tells Andromache that the day of his captivity will make him grieve more for her than for the people of Troy, Hekabe, Priam, or his brothers (6.447–55). When he notices her "tearful laughter" over Astyanax, he "pities" her and caresses her (483–85). But not even this devotion to his family will allow him to heed Andromache's plea for him to show pity for her and their child by staying on the tower, "from which, presumably, he is to direct his troops."[25] The overlay to this

23. Weil (1956, 25) argues that Patroklos is generous also in the sense that he "commits no brutal or cruel act," respecting life in his enemies when he is jeopardizing his own; but note his sardonic vaunt over Kebriones at 16.744–50. For further analysis of Patroklos' gentleness, see Taplin 1992, 174–78.

24. On the correspondences between the deaths of Patroklos and Hektor, see most recently Taplin 1992, 234–37; Janko 1992, 312, and on 16.751–53, 794–800, 830–63.

25. Kirk 1990, on 6.431–32.

affection is honor. Hektor cannot stay clear of the man-to-man fighting "like a man of no account, a coward," because he has "learnt" to be preeminent in the front line, winning great glory for Priam and himself (441–46). Shame and honor, those two ends of the same stick, override the ultimate emotional drives that we see him here regarding as most effectively fulfilled if he responds to the proximate drives: "I feel *aidôs*, . . . I have learnt to be preeminent . . . , for this I know well, that there will come a day when holy Troy . . . will fall." And honor has permeated every relationship with his family. He has learned to win glory for himself and Priam; he is horrified at the shameful notion of what Andromache's captors will say of her and her husband, "who among the horse-taming Trojans excelled at fighting" (460–61). His prayer for his son, after he has taken off the offending helmet and kissed and dandled the baby, is that Astyanax will be conspicuous among the Trojans and goodly in strength, that people will say that he is better by far than his father, and that his mother's heart will be delighted when he brings home the bloody spoils, stripped from an enemy's body (476–81). We might be tempted to see magnanimity in Hektor's prayer that Astyanax will live to be the greater warrior, but its disinterestedness is circumscribed by Hektor's concern with his family's reputation—a piquant mixture of emotions, nonetheless. Love, as we would know it, is present, but there is also a less familiar mechanism for "proving" that love. Already in the Andromache scene, there are signs that honor has for Hektor begun to be an aim in itself.[26]

In battle, however, the reward of honor is unalloyed. Honor impels Hektor to announce to Aias in their duel his predilection for open, honest "man-to-man" combat (7.237–43)[27] and to express the wish that he were immortal and honored like Athene and Apollo as surely as the Great Day of battle will bring suffering to the Achaians (8.537–41). During the Great Day the prospect of glory proves fatally irresistible. Crucial is the moment when Hektor angrily rejects

---

26. On Hektor's attitude here, see further Taplin 1992, 121–24; among other things, Taplin follows the logic of the "Homeric paradox"—"that victory is matched by the necessary corollary of defeat"—to the conclusion that Hektor is, ironically, praying for his son's death.

27. Cf. his criticism of Paris that he is all appearances and that he has no strength and provides no defense (3.45).

Poulydamas' advice to retreat because Achilles has now rejoined the fray and the battle will now be over the city and the Trojan warriors' wives (18.265). Hektor reveals two important reasons for refusing to retreat. First, he has had enough of being cooped up in Troy; though it was once famous for its wealth, its treasures are now exhausted, much of it on payment for the allies (287–92). Understandably, the warrior is impatient, and the sense of his city's exhaustion can only make him yearn for splendor on an individual basis. Second, Hektor believes that Zeus is granting him *kûdos* (293–94).[28] Therefore, Hektor wants to confront Achilles. There are several consequences to all this. It is generally accepted that Hektor is Troy's sole bastion. The thought is first expressed in the explanation of the nickname Astyanax, by which Hektor's son is known rather than by his real name, Skamandrios: "Hektor alone saved Ilion" (6.402–3).[29] The fact is also believed on the Achaian side; for example, once Achilles has killed Hektor, his immediate thought is to find out whether the Trojans will now desert their city or remain, "since Hektor is no longer alive" (22.381–84). At the same time, even Hektor accepts that he is the weaker warrior, as he admits to Achilles (20.434–37), as the narrator puts it (22.158), and as Achilles reminds Hektor (22.333).[30] Priam warns Hektor of this fact as he implores him from the walls of Troy (22.40). His decision in book 18 to face Achilles has therefore gone

---

28. A similar combination of frustration at having to hold back and exultation over Zeus' apparent support can be seen in his command to bring fire onto the Achaian ships (15.718–25). For Hektor's progress and Zeus' favor on the Great Day, see most recently Taplin 1992, 155–60.

29. The motif recurs significantly at 22.506f., when Andromache laments what Astyanax will have to undergo now that his father is dead.

30. See further 6.106–9 (the effect on the Achaians of Hektor's appearance in battle), 16.834–36 (Hektor announces that he is warding off from Troy "the day of compulsion"), 22.56f. (Priam entreats Hektor to come inside Troy's walls so that he may "save" his community), 24.243f. (Priam rounds on his remaining sons, saying that they will be easy meat now that Hektor is dead), 24.380–85 (Hermes asks Priam whether the Trojans are deserting Troy because Hektor is dead), 24.499 (Priam tells Achilles that Hektor defended Troy by himself), 24.729f. (Andromache pronounces Troy's doom now that its protector has fallen). See Taplin 1992, 116, for the connections made between Hektor's name and the verb "to hold," *echein*, as at 5.472–75, 24.729–30; see Taplin 1992, 248, with lit., for the identification between the fates of Troy and Hektor at 22.408–11.

past strategic sense and has become focused on much more individual concerns. The proximate sanctions for right relations with his community have overridden the ultimate sanctions. These are now so far out of kilter with one another that Hektor is actually led to jeopardize his community, as Priam observes when he tells Hektor to come inside the walls so that he might save Troy, in another affective appeal (21.56–57).[31] The rewards involved in the pursuit of honor have made this warrior, who embodies the ideal of defending his homeland,[32] the reverse of magnanimous.[33]

This does not deny Hektor a full tragic status.[34] It is striking that his final decision to face Achilles in book 22 is motivated by his sense of shame before his community at having lost so many of his men through his own recklessness and at the thought that men will say of him that he lost his men by trusting in his own strength. His decision either to face Achilles and win or to die "in great glory" in front of his city is a last-ditch attempt to reinstate his honor, literally before the eyes of his community (104–10). But at the same time, it exposes his people to what is already fairly clear destruction, and the pity-element in the heroic code has been obliterated by the code's orientation in results. There can be no doubt that on Homeric thinking Hektor's decision is a wrong decision made from traditionally noble motives, which have blinded him to other motives, in particular pity, that are also recognized by the traditional code. Driven by shame—and also guilt—at having lost what he thinks to be a major part of his community, he is prepared to endanger his whole community. There are indeed limits to heroic self-assertion.[35] Accordingly and appropriately, the only thing he is left to desire is the honorable treatment of his corpse (22.256–59, 338–43).[36]

---

31. Hekabe's appeal illustrates the same point in a different way: it is supremely affective, but this quality cannot convince Hektor to have *aidôs* even before his mother's breasts (22.79–89).

32. See, e.g., 12.243, 15.496–99, 24.383–85, 500.

33. On the tensions in heroic life, see especially Redfield 1975, 99–127; Mueller, 1984, 60–64; Schein 1984, 82; Taplin 1992, 121–24, 166, 200, with useful comment on Hektor in book 22 at pp. 234–38.

34. See Redfield 1975, 109–27, 128–59.

35. Rowe 1983.

36. This concern for the honorable treatment of his corpse is adumbrated at 7.77–91, the conditions of the single combat that Hektor offers out of a delicately expressed sense of shame (7.69f.) at the broken truce of book 3.

A section of Iliadic society that we must examine for traces of the other-regarding virtues is the women of the poem. Almost by definition, the women are excluded from a role as combatants, being obliged to tend to the household and to rear the heroes' children. Hektor does not expect Andromache to concern herself with warfare, let alone to discuss battle strategy (6.433–41, 492f.).[37] She is to go inside the house and tend to her own tasks, the loom and the distaff—though we are surprised to learn that this includes feeding Hektor's war-horses, Xanthos, Podargos, Aithon, and Lampos, for which they should repay Andromache, by their efforts in pulling Hektor's chariot (8.185–90)—and to direct the maidservants in their work (6.490f.). Following the advice of Helenos, Hektor commands Hekabe and the elderly women to pray for Athene's assistance (6.86ff., 269f.). Despite such nurturative functions, the women's position of utter dependence on their men for protection from the horrors of defeat in war inevitably imposes on their love and kindness an element of self-interest. And the horrors of war are great indeed: the embodiment of moderation and good sense, Nestor, urges the Achaians to forget about returning to their homes before sleeping with a Trojan's wife in revenge for the grief that Helen has caused (2.354–56); more predictably, Agamemnon, discouraging Menelaos from sparing Adrestos, expresses the desirability of killing all the Trojans, including the male babe that his mother still carries in her womb, again all to wreak revenge on the Trojans for their treatment of Menelaos' household (6.55–60); and Achilles expresses his vengeance on the Trojans for killing Patroklos by describing how he will make their womenfolk wipe tears from their cheeks with both hands and groan with anguish (18.122–25).[38] The women know all too clearly what the scenario will be once their city is sacked: Andromache describes her two terrifying visions of her fate (22.482–507, 24.725–45), having already experi-

---

37. See also 5.428–30, 7.236.
38. See also 6.94f. = 275f.; 11.393–95; 14.501–5; 17.26–28, 34–37, 223f.; 21.123–25. For the idea that, because the word for a woman's veil, *krêdemnon*, is the same as that for a city's walls (as at 16.100), the sack of a city is a kind of sexual assault, so that when Andromache throws down her veil at 22.470–72, she is foreshadowing her future captivity and the sack of her city, see Monsacré 1984, 68f.; Schein 1984, 9, following Nagler 1974, 44–63 (see also Nagler 1967, esp. 300f.). Cf. Griffin 1980, 2 n. 5.

enced the annihilation of her parents and brothers when Achilles sacked Thebe (6.414–28), which is the reason why she can call Hektor her father, mother, brother, and husband, thus signaling her absolute reliance on him alone for protection (429–30); and Kleopatra's picture of what happens when a city is taken convinces Meleagros to defend Kalydon (9.591–94).[39]

From the warrior's point of view, it is, as Hektor says, no shameful thing—that is, it is a matter of glory—if a warrior dies successfully defending Troy, because his wife and children will remain safe for the future (15.496–99)—hence the stress that women lay on the gentleness and protectiveness of their menfolk to them. This happens most poignantly when the women lament their dead warriors. Over the dead Patroklos, Briseis recalls how he urged her not to cry when Achilles had killed her family, and how he had promised to make her Achilles' wife, "forever gentle" as he was (19.291–300). In the obsequies to Hektor, Andromache reflects how he is now dead and gone, the hero who used to save her and all the other Trojan women and children (24.729–30), and Helen shows her particular gratitude for his gentleness to her and his kindly protection of her from the cutting remarks of her brothers- or sisters-in-law (762–75). The women can show love and solicitude for the well-being of their menfolk in ways that go well beyond mere rewards for their protectors. This in itself can paradoxically pose a threat to the heroic life: when Hekabe offers wine to Hektor to keep up his strength, Hektor refuses, saying that he will forget his fighting prowess (6.258–65), and Helen's invitation to him to sit meets with his refusal, on the grounds that he wants to defend Troy (6.360–62).[40]

One area in the relations between men and women where we can see less self-interest is the relationship of a mother to her son. Hekabe's pleas to Hektor to fight off Achilles from inside the walls is based in large part on her appeal to her role as his nurturer; the

---

39. See further 19.290–94, 22.431–36. On the women of the *Iliad* as unexpectedly authoritative commentators on the events of the poem, see Easterling 1991.

40. On the threat that women pose for the hero, see Monsacré 1984, 41–50, 78–94; note especially Paris' unheroic attitudes in book 3 (at, e.g., 448f.) and Helenos' advice to Aineias and Hektor to stop the army falling into the arms of their wives, to become a "delight" to the enemy (6.80–82).

only selfishness in her entreaty is her prayer for his pity on the grounds that if Achilles kills him outside the walls, she will not be able to bury her own child.[41] Thetis' response to Achilles' imminent death is subtly different. When she hears his lamentation over Patroklos, she muses on her "unhappiness as a mother of an outstanding child" (*dusaristotokeia*), dwelling on his healthy response to her nurture as a child, on his fate never to return home, and on his unhappiness while he is alive (18.54–64). Her acceptance that he will die soon after he has killed Hektor and her willingness to help him to new armor, recognizing that it is noble behavior to defend one's hard-pressed companions (95–96, 128–37), show that, despite her intense grief, she is prepared to suppress her mother's grief and further her son's only chance of "happiness," even when it means losing him.

The thought of a mother's self-denying love for her offspring is powerfully developed in the similes. The passage in book 12 depicting a widow handworker carefully making sure that she is paid with maximum fairness for her wool so that she can win a "shameful" payment to support her children (433–35) shows clearly that emotional promptings are sufficient to motivate a more or less disinterested concern for others. The parent-offspring similes drawn from the world of nature show this even more clearly, because in the animal world, things like self-oriented honor simply do not exist as motives for concerned behavior.[42] Two particularly interesting similes of this kind illustrate Achilles in various crucial states of emotion. First, he himself cites as an illustration of his selfless devotion to the cause of the Atreidai the case of a mother bird who gathers tidbits for her young, even though the search for morsels endangers her (9.323f.). As Achilles intends, the simile underlines Achilles' exemplary willingness to fight other men's battles (327). Less intentional is the way the simile underlines by means of contrast Achilles' self-confessed desire for reward (330–36). Second, in book 18, the comparison of Achilles with a lioness whose cubs have been stolen by hunters (318–22) emphasizes the purely affective side of Achilles' involvement with Patroklos. In each case, the crucial element for us

---

41. The thought is fiercely expanded by Hekabe at 24.208–16.
42. See above, p. 15f.

is the naturally other-regarding quality shown by a parent to its young, through which the poem seems to endorse the value of a relative altruism based on affection.

To return to the human women of the *Iliad*, their lot as figures on the periphery of the heroes' lives is a potent means of bringing out the true meaning of war for a community. With the exception of the mother-son relationship, women's relations with men are based (humanly and reasonably enough) on self-interest. But the women can highlight the claims of affection over and above those of *tîmê* as reasons for action in heroic life, as we saw happening with Andromache's unsuccessful plea to Hektor. The mother-son relationship, amplified by similes from the animal world, demonstrates again that the *Iliad* recognizes at least certain kinds of other-regarding virtues—a recognition reminiscent of the considerate mothers in Aristotle who sacrifice their relationship with the children that they have given away for adoption for the children's well-being.

Finally, we may attempt to calibrate the disinterested magnanimity of the gods of the *Iliad*. The obvious deity to watch is Zeus. Zeus often shows pity for particular mortals—for example, Sarpedon (16.431–61), Hektor (15.12–15, 17.200–208, 22.168–76), Patroklos (16.644ff.), Aias (17.648), Achilles in his grief (19.340–48), and the horses mourning over Patroklos (17.441–47)—and he expresses pity for mankind in general (17.446–47, 20.21).[43] His sympathy toward humans is particularly foregrounded in book 24, though Hermes displays the quality in an interesting way as he escorts Priam to Achilles' hut. The moral constraints on the gods to ensure the kindly treatment of Hektor's corpse and Priam are presented most forcefully by Apollo. He argues that Hektor's past record of sacrifices to the gods obliges them to make sure his corpse is returned to his family for proper cremation and last rites (33–38), and that Achilles' present behavior toward a "dumb piece of earth" is "murderous" (39), "immoderate" (40), relentlessly "implacable" (40f.), as wild as a lion's (41), so that the hero has lost pity and respect, *eleos* and *aidôs* (44f.). Further, when a human loses even a kinsman, he ultimately gets over his grief, while Achilles' treatment of Hektor's corpse is not befitting a person of his social dignity (52), and though he is of such a socially prestigious

---

43. See Edwards 1991, on 17.194–209, 441–42, 20.20–30.

rank, he should beware the gods' *nemesis*, lest they grow indignant at his unworthy behavior (53).

To these moral considerations, Hera opposes Achilles' superior *tîmê* as a goddess' son, whom Hera herself reared, and as the son of a mortal who was particularly dear to the gods (56–63). Zeus grants something to both sides. He yields to Hera on the matter of Achilles' superior *tîmê*, but like Apollo, he stresses Hektor's sacrifices to the gods, which they accepted for the *geras* that they were (65–76).[44] He yields to Apollo's moral arguments in his address to Thetis, whom he gives his order to tell Achilles that the gods, in particular Zeus, are angry at his irrationally violent treatment of Hektor's corpse (112–16). The suggestion of the other gods that Hermes should steal the corpse (23f.) is something he will not allow, because he wishes to preserve Achilles' *kûdos*, the glory, that is, of giving back the corpse of his own volition, to preserve Thetis' continuing *aidôs* and *philotês* (107–11).

The clear implication is that Achilles should accept Priam's ransom-gifts, "which will warm his heart" (76, 119). In all this, Zeus uses the honor-sanction to strengthen the claims of fair play and the emotion of pity, which he displays by sending Iris (174), the eagle portent (301, 314–21), and Hermes (332–38).[45] The resolution is clean and clear. It is also a reassertion of the ideal relationship between the ultimate and proximate drives to proper behavior. All parties agree that the gifts must be given and accepted before Hektor's body can be ransomed, and Achilles, Automedon, and Alkimos take them from the wagon (578f.). Related to the sanction of the gifts is that of the supplication ritual. Zeus informs Iris, and she informs Priam, that Achilles will not kill Priam, "for he is neither insensitive, nor thoughtlessly impulsive, nor a transgressor, but he will be careful to spare a suppliant" (157–58, 186–87). This is a sanction of whose force Achilles proves to be aware, though his patience is stretched to the limit: he warns Priam not to stir up his passions lest he attack the old man, though a suppliant, and transgress the behest of Zeus, as god

---

44. The theme of Hektor's piety is developed in book 24 at lines 422–23, 425–27.

45. The majority of the gods side with Zeus in this matter: 18–21 (Apollo), 23, 422f. (the gods in general); for the exceptions, Hera, Poseidon, and Athene (25f.), see above, p. 125 n. 24.

of suppliants (568–70).[46] Similarly, Hektor's body is washed and anointed out of Priam's sight, because Achilles recognizes that a display of grief might drive him to kill Priam and "transgress the behest of Zeus" (586). He "fears" and honors Zeus (116).

Apart from Zeus, only Hermes is presented as empathizing with Priam's human concern over his son and as showing the old king practical generosity. Revealingly, Zeus says that it is a particular pleasure (most *philos*) to Hermes to consort with humans (334f.). Hermes builds on Priam's earlier notion, advising him to supplicate Achilles in the name of his father, mother, and son (456–57). Priam does this in his speech to Achilles, concentrating naturally on Peleus, with whom he claims he has a special kinship (486ff., 503–6). The appeal stirs in Achilles a desire to lament his father (507, 511f.). The only deity equipped to direct his course by the altogether more affective set of coordinates is the mediator between man and god, who is pointedly marked out as such. Yet, as a god, not even he can match Achilles' magnanimity: both he and Zeus, who are never confronted by the reality of death, can literally never attain to the appreciation of fellow suffering that drives Achilles' magnanimity, however temporary that experience may be.

In the course of examining the magnanimity of the mortals and gods of the *Iliad*, we have located Achilles' magnanimity on the scale offered by the epic itself. We may conclude that it is unique in its intensity, in its sublimity, and in its centrality in the structure of the poem. To view Achilles' magnanimity in even deeper relief, we need to survey briefly the concept of magnanimity in other early epic, especially the *Odyssey* and the Hesiodic poems.

The section of the *Odyssey* most commonly presented as displaying generosity is the Phaiakians' entertainment of Odysseus and their conveying him home to Ithaka. One writer has called the Phaiakians' escort "the only example of purely disinterested behavior [he] can find in Homer."[47] On closer inspection, however, the motives for the beneficence of the Phaiakians turn out to be rather more complex. There is no lack of generous concern. Nausikaa's first words to Odysseus reveal something of the fellow feeling Achilles shows to Priam in the image of Zeus' jars: she says that Zeus dispenses prosperity

---

46. See above, p. 119 n.9.
47. Gagarin 1987, 288.

to the noble and the ignoble arbitrarily. She goes on to assure Odysseus that he will lack nothing that it is appropriate for a suppliant to be given (*Od.* 6.187–93), and she reminds her maidservants that all strangers are under the protection of Zeus (207–8). Nausikaa demonstrates a mixture of motives: fellow feeling that leads to her kindness, but also very much the sense that it is socially comme il faut in terms of *hiketeia* and *xenê*. Something of the same can be seen in the reaction of the Phaiakian elder Echeneos. On seeing the stranger on the hearth, he advises that he be raised up into a chair and that wine be brought so that a libation can be poured to Zeus, "who accompanies revered suppliants" (7.159–66); in this context, Alkinoös offers to convey Odysseus home (191ff.). More goodwill can be seen in Alkinoös' offer of Nausikaa's hand in marriage, cut short only by his considerate desire not to detain Odysseus if he does not want to remain, and by his willingness to transport Odysseus home, no matter what the distance (309–28). The guest-friendship gift of clothing and gold, and the tripods and cauldrons, are examples of Alkinoös' willingness to fulfill the guest-friendship rites, in the most generous measure (8.389–93, 13.13–15). Alkinoös can ultimately view the guest-friend/suppliant in terms of affection, as is clear when he says that a man in either situation is in the position of a brother (8.544–47). But at least pari passu with such generosity and affection is the sanction of the institutions of *xenê* and *hiketeia*, and at one point Alkinoös tells Odysseus that escorting strangers home is something the Phaiakians do as a matter of course (8.31–33). Poseidon may complain that, as a matter of objective fact (if not by active volition), the Phaiakians are dishonoring him by escorting the hateful Odysseus home (13.128–33), and Alkinoös may, as he assures Odysseus of a safe return, recall his father Nausithoös' advice that Poseidon would punish the Phaiakians for being escorts home to all and sundry (8.564–71), though it is far from clear why he mentions the prophecy at this point.[48] Yet there is no suggestion that Alkinoös is being so disinterestedly generous to Odysseus that he is prepared to chance the god's wrath by conveying him home.[49] It is closer to the mark to regard Alkinoös' treatment of Odysseus as an act of generosity and

---

48. See Hainsworth 1988, on 564–71.

49. There is, for example, no hint of such a thought at *Od.* 13.170–83, when Alkinoös remembers the prophecy as if for the first time.

a generous extension (from his own abundant resources) of the re-
quirements of *xeniê* and *hiketeia* than to view it as "purely disinter-
ested behavior."

There can be as great a number of motives leading to generosity
as to any other disposition. In the case of the Phaiakians we may
compare the motives that we might possibly feel when helping a
disadvantaged person in some action that he or she is unable to
perform. We may find ourselves prompted by the thought of what
onlookers might think or say if we do not do the "right" thing; but
this does not preclude the possibility that we may pity the disadvan-
taged person or feel it intrinsically right to help, and all three prompt-
ings may be operative. We have seen that we cannot call the
Phaiakians' behavior "purely" disinterested, but the text presents it
in a positive light. The word *purely* introduces the notion of degree,
and this is where I would distinguish the Phaiakians' generosity from
Achilles' toward Priam. The struggle is so much greater for Achilles;
his self-interest is minimal, his self-determination is more firmly as-
serted, and his obedience to divine ruling is accepted as an obliga-
tion—all may cause pain. For the Phaiakians, however, generosity
comes easily.[50]

When we turn to Hesiod, we find that concepts of kindliness and
cooperation involve much less disinterested concern than in the *Od-
yssey*. The *Theogony* couches all benevolence and cooperation in
terms of honor, whether they occur in relations between the gods or
between gods and mortals. The poem's chief concern is Zeus'
struggle for the "kingly honor" (462, 892; cf. 491, 881–85). To enlist

---

50. This is the case also with Nestor's kindly reception of Telemachos in
Od. 3 (see esp. 346–55). Eumaios and Eurykleia, for their part, are presented
as morally good, but on the aristocratic scheme of things, their coming to the
status of slaves limits their capacity for moral nobility within their role as
slaves to their master: to the memory of their former master, and to Odysseus
himself once he reveals his identity to them, they are faithful. See Auerbach
1953, 21; Rohdich 1980, esp. 36–41; Zanker 1986, 34; Zanker 1987, 147. Eu-
maios' humble reception of Odysseus disguised as a beggar in *Odyssey* 14 is,
within its own terms, another generous extension of the hospitality institu-
tion. Moreover, as Cairns 1993, 103–5 shows, it is clear enough that for the
Odyssey, *aidôs* can refer to "an altruistic concern for another's feelings"—for
example, when Telemachos asks Nestor and Menelaos not to spare him
unwelcome news of his father out of *aidôs* or pity (3.96, 4.326). But the
doctrine is writ incomparably large in *Iliad*. 24.

the support of the other deities against the Titans, he makes the promise that he will not deprive any helpers of the *gera* or *tîmê* they enjoyed among the immortals under Kronos, and that helpers who were "without *tîmê*" and "without *geras*" under Kronos will be granted *tîmê* and *gera* (392–96). An example of this thinking can be found in the way Zeus honors Hekate (411–52). He gives her gifts; she inherits a *tîmê* of heaven, is particularly honored among the immortals (411–15), retains all the *tîmê* she enjoyed since the first division under Kronos, and is especially honored on land and in heaven by her share of *tîmê* and *gera* (421–28). The *tîmai* of the gods, as can be seen in the example of Hekate, are embodied in the various provinces and portions of the universe with which they are honored, or have been, at one of the divisions, whether the original one (425) or Zeus' (73f., 112, 520, 885).[51] The honors bestowed on mortals are likewise tangibly embodied in their gifts, as when Hekate bestows prosperity as her *tîmê* on mortals who call on her, whether in the form of the king's dispensation of justice, the preeminence of an orator, the victory and glory of an army, the prizes and glory of an athlete, the good haul of a fisherman, or flourishing herds (429–47). Hekate's kindliness to mortals involves Zeus' allocation of the honors as her spheres of influence; mortals give Hekate *tîmê* in the form of honor and worship, and Hekate bestows on them *tîmê* as prosperity. Similarly, the honor of the Muses imparts to the king who promises fair judgment the ability to settle "even a big quarrel," for which men look on him as a god (80–93).[52] Thus, in the *Theogony*, competitive incentives and rewards can initiate cooperative behavior in human society; there is no indication that disinterested concern or a sense of fellow feeling are motives.

The same holds for Hesiod's poem on how the peasant farmer can best survive. The *Works and Days* seems to present a peasant community in which goods are limited and the ideal farmer must maximize his monopoly on them, a fact of life that apparently lies behind Hesiod's awareness that the social status of a household is subject to extreme flux. Zeus may exalt a household or cast it into obscurity (3–6, 244, 281, 284, 325–26),[53] which is a good reason for being pious,

---

51. Zanker 1988, 74–76.

52. On the relationship of this passage to *Od.* 8.169–73, see Zanker 1988, 77.

53. See further Zanker 1986, 29f.

so that you can buy up the property of others, rather than vice versa (336–41). The ultimate aim of the peasant farmer must be to achieve a high social position (which Hesiod seems to denote by the word *aretê*), based on material prosperity in the peasant community (286–92).[54] But this social rank must be won with sweat and after an uphill struggle (289–92): one must work to fill one's barn (298–302), self-sufficiency (30–34, 361–67, 383–404, 407f., 448–57, 477f., 493–503) and surplus (300f., 307, 308, 341, 379f.) being at a premium.[55] The rewards for one's efforts must be safeguarded by the proper processes of justice (213–319), which Hesiod is not prepared to take for granted in the present immoral age (174–212).[56] Small wonder, in the circumstances, that Hesiod commends the good spirit of rivalry that spurs potters, builders, beggars, and bards into productive competition (17–26). In such a world, acts of kindness are motivated by a finely tuned sense of self-interest, perhaps best summed up in the pronouncement "Have things measured out to you well from your neighbor, and give a good repayment, with the same measure and better, if you can, so that you will find something to rely on in the future too if you are in need" (349–51).[57] One gives parties preferably to one's neighbors, because they are the people most likely to give immediate help if one is in trouble (342–48). The overall picture of a hardnosed reciprocity is mercifully relieved, if only once, when Hesiod, while advising to give to givers and not to give to nongivers, suddenly announces that a man who gives willingly derives pleasure from giving, even if it is a big gift (one, that is, that Hesiod would find it hard to part with); however, anybody who, "trusting in his shamelessness," accepts a gift, even a little one, grows mean in spirit (357–60). The pleasure involved in giving is clearly only a by-product of the real purpose of the act, which is to oblige the beneficiary to reciprocate.

Given the uniqueness of the *Iliad* narrator's foregrounding of emotion and magnanimity, it is all the more impressive to realize just what depth of insight the epic achieves in this respect. And it is not emulated until Attic tragedy, my earlier discussion of Sophokles' *Aias*

---

54. Zanker 1986, 28–30.
55. Zanker 1986, 28.
56. Zanker 1986, 30–33.
57. Zanker 1988, 75f.

providing one example of the *Iliad*'s influence in this regard. If we take as the tragic moment the assertion of life in the face of death—for example, when Antigone faces death to do justice to her relationship, still alive, with Polyneikes—we have all the dynamics of the tragic moment in Achilles' acceptance of the paramount value of life's processes (whether grieving or allowing others to grieve, or showing fellow feeling and acting magnanimously on it) precisely when the hero experiences the deepest presentiment of his mortality. The positioning of the Priam and Achilles scene in the structure of the poem directs our attention to the weight of Achilles' personality, emotions, and preoccupations,[58] the special qualities of which are highlighted by the quarrel of the gods earlier in book 24.[59] In this cardinal matter, Homer processed the tragic moment so thoroughly that once tragedy assumed a form, it could quickly develop two and a half centuries later.

---

58. Macleod 1982, 8–35, esp. 26–28.

59. See Davies 1981. For Achilles as a tragic hero in book 18, see Rutherford 1982, 145–47, 149; for his knowledge of his death and his responsiveness to his "community of suffering" with Priam, see pp. 152–58; at pp. 158–60, moreover, Rutherford traces some of the influences of this attitude on, e.g., the *Aias* and the *O.K.*, with many fine observations on Achilles' sympathy for Priam.

Bibliography

The following abbreviations are used:

ABSA   *Annual of the British School at Athens*
AJP   *American Journal of Philology*
AuA   *Antike und Abendland*
BABesch   *Bulletin Antieke Beschaving*
BICS   *Bulletin of the Institute of Classical Studies*
CA   *Classical Antiquity*
CP   *Classical Philology*
CQ   *Classical Quarterly*
CW   *Classical World*
G&R   *Greece and Rome*
HSCP   *Harvard Studies in Classical Philology*
Ill Cl St   *Illinois Classical Studies*
JHS   *Journal of Hellenic Studies*
PLILS   *Papers of the Leeds International Latin Seminar*
RÉG   *Revue des études grecques*
SO   *Symbolae Osloenses*
TAPA   *Transactions of the American Philological Association*
WJb   *Würzburger Jahrbücher*
WS   *Wiener Studien*

Adkins, A.W.H. 1960a. "'Honour' and 'Punishment' in the Homeric Poems." *BICS* 7:23–32.
———. 1960b. *Merit and Responsibility*. Oxford.
———. 1963. "'Friendship' and 'Self-Sufficiency' in Homer and Aristotle." *CQ*, n.s., 13:30–45.
———. 1971. "Homeric Values and Homeric Society." *JHS* 91:1–14.
———. 1972. *Moral Values and Political Behaviour in Ancient Greece*. London.
———. 1987. "Gagarin and the 'Morality' of Homer." *CP* 82:311–22.
Annas, J. 1977. "Plato and Aristotle on Friendship and Altruism." *Mind* 86:532–54.
———. 1981. *An Introduction to Plato's Republic*. Oxford.
Argyle, M. 1991. *Cooperation: The Basis of Sociability*. London and New York.
Auerbach, E. 1953. *Mimesis: The Representation of Reality in Western Literature*. Trans. W.R. Trask. Princeton.

Beazley, J.D. 1954. "A Cup by Hieron and Makron." *BABesch* 29:12–15.

———. 1963. *Attic Red-Figure Vase-Painters*. 2d ed. New York.

Benitez, E. 1992. "Argument, Rhetoric, and Philosophic Method: Plato's *Protagoras*." *Philosophy and Rhetoric* 25:222–52.

Benveniste, E. 1973. *Indo-European Language and Society*. Trans. E. Palmer. London.

Bostock, D. 1986. *Plato's Phaedo*. Oxford.

Bothmer, D. von 1990. *Splendors of the Past: Ancient Art from the Shelby White and Leon Levy Collection*. New York.

Burkert, W. 1955. *Zum altgriechischen Mitleidsbegriff*. Ph.D. Diss., Erlangen.

Cairns, D.L. 1993. *Aidôs: The Psychology and Ethics of Honour and Shame in Ancient Greek Literature*. Oxford.

Caswell, C.P. 1990. *A Study of* Thumos *in Early Greek Epic*. Mnemosyne, suppl. 114. Leiden, New York, København, and Köln.

Claus, D.B. 1975. "*Aidôs* in the Language of Achilles." *TAPA* 105:13–28.

Crane, G. 1990. "Ajax, the Unexpected, and the Deception Speech." *CP* 85:89–101.

Crittenden, P.J. 1990. *Learning to be Moral: Philosophical Thoughts about Moral Development*. Atlantic Highlands, N.J.

Cunliffe, R.J. [1924] 1963. *A Lexicon of the Homeric Dialect*. London, Glasgow, and Bombay. Reprint. Norman and London.

Danek, G. 1988. *Studien zur Dolonie*. WS, Beih. 12. Vienna.

Davidson, J.F. 1988. "Homer and Sophocles' *Electra*." *BICS* 35:45–72.

Davies, M. 1981. "The Judgement of Paris and *Iliad* xxiv." *JHS* 101:56–62.

Dickie, M.W. 1978. "*Dike* as a Moral Term in Homer and Hesiod." *CP* 73:91–101.

Dodds, E.R. 1951. *The Greeks and the Irrational*. Berkeley, Los Angeles, and London.

Donlan, W. 1981–82. "Reciprocities in Homer." *CW* 75:137–75.

———. 1989. "The Unequal Exchange between Glaucus and Diomedes in the Light of the Homeric Gift-Economy." *Phoenix* 43:1–15.

Dover, K.J. 1983. "The Portrayal of Moral Evaluation in Greek Poetry." *JHS* 103:35–48.

Easterling, P.E. 1984. "The Tragic Homer." *BICS* 31:1–8.

———. 1987. "Notes on Tragedy and Epic." In L. Rodley, ed., *Papers Given at a Colloquium on Greek Drama in Honour of R.P. Winnington-Ingram*, 52–61. London.

———. 1990. "Constructing Character in Greek Tragedy." In C.B.R. Pelling, ed., *Characterization and Individuality in Greek Literature*, 83–99. Oxford.

———. 1991. "Men's κλέος and Women's γόος: Female Voices in the *Iliad*." *Journal of Modern Greek Studies* 9:145–51.

———. Forthcoming. "Holy Thebe." In *Festschrift Georgi Mihailov*, Sofia.

Edwards, M.W. 1987. *Homer, Poet of the Iliad*. Baltimore and London.

———. 1991. *The Iliad: A Commentary*. Vol. 5, *Books 17–20*. Cambridge.

Ellis, J. 1976. *Eye-Deep in Hell: Trench Warfare in World War I*. New York.

Erffa, C.E. von 1937. ΑΙΔΩΣ *und verwandte Begriffe in ihrer Entwicklung von Homer bis Demokrit. Philologus*, Suppl. 30, vol. 2. Leipzig.

Facey, A.B. 1981. *A Fortunate Life.* Ringwood.

Fehling, D. 1989. "Die ursprüngliche Troja-Geschichte, oder: Interpretationen zur Troja-Geschichte." *WJb* 15:7–16.

Finley, M.I. 1978. *The World of Odysseus.* 2d ed. Harmondsworth.

Fränkel, H. 1975. *Early Greek Poetry and Philosophy.* Trans. M. Hadas and J. Willis. Oxford.

Gagarin, M. 1986. *Early Greek Law.* Berkeley, Los Angeles, and London.

———. 1987. "Morality in Homer." *CP* 82:285–306.

Gill, C. 1990. "The Character-Personality Distinction." In C.B.R. Pelling, ed., *Characterization and Individuality in Greek Literature,* 1–31. Oxford.

Goldhill, S.D. 1986. *Reading Greek Tragedy.* Cambridge.

———. 1990."Supplication and Authorial Comment in the Iliad: Iliad Z 61–62." *Hermes* 118:373–76.

Gould, J.P. 1973. "Hiketeia." *JHS* 93:74–103.

———. 1983. "Homeric Epic and the Tragic Moment." In T. Winnifrith, P. Murray, and K.W. Gransden, eds., *Aspects of the Epic,* 32–45. London.

Griffin, J. 1980. *Homer on Life and Death.* Oxford.

———. 1986. "Heroic and Unheroic Ideas in Homer." In J. Boardman and C.E. Vaphopoulou-Richardson, eds., *Chios: A Conference at the Homereion in Chios 1984,* 3–13. Oxford.

Hainsworth, J.B. 1988. With A. Heubeck and S. West. *A Commentary on Homer's Odyssey.* Vol. 1, *Introduction and Books I–VIII.* Oxford.

———. 1993. *The Iliad: A Commentary.* Vol. 3, *Books 9–12.* Cambridge.

Halperin, D.M. 1990. *One Hundred Years of Homosexuality: And Other Essays on Greek Love.* New York and London.

Herman, G. 1987. *Ritualised Friendship and the Greek City.* Cambridge.

Heubeck, A. 1949. "Homerica: 1. Zur Stellung des Schiffskatalogs (B 484–779) in der Ilias; 2. N 345–360—Ein Interpretationsversuch; 3. Τιμή." *Gymnasium* 56:242–54 (Published in B. Forssman, S. Koster, E. Pöhlmann, eds., *Alfred Heubeck, Kleine Schriften zur griechischen Sprache und Literatur,* 115–27. Erlangen, 1984.)

Hoffmann, M. 1914. *Die ethische Terminologie bei Homer, Hesiod und den alten Elegikern und Jambographen.* Ph.D. Diss., Tübingen.

Hooker, J.T. 1987a. "Homeric φίλος." *Glotta* 65:44–65.

———. 1987b. "Homeric Society: A Shame-Culture?" *G&R*, 2d ser., 34:121–25.

Janko, R. 1992. *The Iliad: A Commentary.* Vol. 4, *Books 13–16.* Cambridge.

Jebb, R.C. 1898. *The Philoctetes.* Cambridge.

Jong, I.J.F. de 1987a. *Narrators and Focalizers: The Presentation of the Story in the Iliad.* Amsterdam.

———. 1987b. "The Voice of Anonymity: Tis-speeches in the *Iliad*." *Eranos* 85:69–84.

Kamerbeek, J.C. 1953. *The Plays of Sophocles.* Part 1; *The Ajax.* Leiden.

Kant, I. 1785. *Grundlegung zur Metaphysik der Sitten*. (Published in *Kants Werke: Akademie-Textausgabe*, 4:385–463. Berlin, 1968.)

Kirk, G.S. 1962. *The Songs of Homer*. Cambridge.

———. 1976. *Homer and the Oral Tradition*. Cambridge.

———. 1985. *The Iliad: A Commentary*. Vol. 1, Books 1–4. Cambridge.

———. 1990. *The Iliad: A Commentary*. Vol. 2, Books 5–8. Cambridge.

Knox, B.M.W. 1961. "The *Ajax* of Sophocles." *HSCP* 65:1–37.

Köhnken, A. 1975. "Die Rolle des Phoinix und die Duale im I der *Ilias*." *Glotta* 53:25–36.

———. 1978. "Noch einmal Phoinix und die Duale." *Glotta* 56:5–14.

Kraut, R. 1973. "Egoism, Love, and Political Office in Plato." *Philosophical Review* 82:330–44.

Leaf, W. 1886–88. *The Iliad*. 2 vols. London.

Lesky, A. 1961. *Göttliche und menschliche Motivation im homerischen Epos*. Sitzungsberichte der Heidelberger Akademie der Wissenschaften: Philosophisch-historische Klasse, Abh. 4. Heidelberg.

Lloyd-Jones, H. 1983. *The Justice of Zeus*. 2d ed. Berkeley, Los Angeles, and London.

———. 1987a. "Ehre und Schande in der griechischen Kultur." *AuA* 33:1–28.

———. 1987b. "A Note on Homeric Morality." *CP* 82:307–10.

Long, A.A. 1970. "Morals and Values in Homer." *JHS* 90:121–39.

Lynn-George, M. 1988. *Epos: Word, Narrative and the Iliad*. Atlantic Highlands, N.J.

MacIntyre, A. 1981. *After Virtue: A Study in Moral Theory*. London.

Mackenzie, M.M. 1981. *Plato on Punishment*. Berkeley, Los Angeles, and London.

Macleod, C.W. 1982. *Homer: Iliad, Book XXIV*. Cambridge.

Marg, W. 1973. "Zur Eigenart der Odyssee." *AuA* 18:1–14.

Merkelbach, R., and West, M.W. 1967. *Fragmenta Hesiodea*. Oxford.

Monsacré, H. 1984. *Les larmes d' Achille: Le héros, la femme et la souffrance dans la poésie d' Homère*. Paris.

Morris, I. 1986. "The Use and Abuse of Homer." *CA* 5:81–138.

Motzkus, D. 1964. *Untersuchungen zum 9. Buch der Ilias unter besonderer Berücksichtigung der Phoinixgestalt*. Ph.D. Diss., Hamburg.

Moulton, C. 1977. "Similes in the Homeric Poems." *Hypomnemata* 49.

Mueller, M. 1984. *The Iliad*. London, Boston, and Sydney.

Nagler, M.N. 1967. "Towards a Generative View of the Oral Formula." *TAPA* 98:269–311.

———. 1974. *Spontaneity and Tradition: A Study in the Oral Art of Homer*. Berkeley, Los Angeles, and London.

Nestle, W. 1942. "Odyssee-Interpretationen, I." *Hermes* 77:46–77.

Page, D.L. 1959. *History and the Homeric Iliad*. Berkeley, Los Angeles, and London.

Parry, A. 1956. "The Language of Achilles." *TAPA* 84:1–7. (Published in G.S. Kirk, ed., *The Language and Background of Homer*, 48–54. Cambridge, 1964.)

Pedrick, V. 1982. "Supplication in the *Iliad* and the *Odyssey*." *TAPA* 112:125–40.

Preisshofen, F. 1977. *Untersuchungen zur Darstellung des Greisenalters in der frühgriechischen Dichtung. Hermes*, Einzelschr. 34. Wiesbaden.

Qviller, B. 1981. "The Dynamics of the Homeric Society." *SO* 56:109–55.

Redfield, J.M. 1975. *Nature and Culture in the Iliad: The Tragedy of Hector.* Chicago and London.

Reeve, M.D. 1973. "The Language of Achilles." *CQ*, n.s., 23:193–95.

Reinhardt, K. 1961. *Die Ilias und ihr Dichter.* Göttingen.

Richardson, N.J. 1993. *The Iliad: A Commentary.* Vol. 6, *Books 21–24.* Cambridge.

Riedinger, J.-C. 1976. "Remarques sur la TIMH chez Homère." *RÉG* 89:244–64.

Robinson, D. 1990. "Homeric φίλος: Love of Life and Limbs, and Friendship with One's θυμός." In E.M. Craik, ed., *"Owls to Athens": Essays on Classical Subjects Presented to Sir Kenneth Dover*, 97–108. Oxford.

Rohdich, H. 1980. "Der Hund Argos und die Anfänge bürgerlichen Selbstbewusstseins." *AuA* 26:33–50.

Roisman, H. 1984. *Loyalty in Early Greek Epic and Tragedy. Beiträge zur klassischen Philologie* 155. Königstein/Ts.

Rosner, J.A. 1976. "The Speech of Phoenix: *Iliad* 9.434–605." *Phoenix* 30:314–27.

Rowe, C.J. 1983. "The Nature of Homeric Morality." In C.A. Rubino and C.W. Shelmerdine, eds., *Approaches to Homer*, 248–75. Austin, Tex.

Rutherford, R.B. 1982. "Tragic Form and Feeling in the *Iliad*." *JHS* 102:145–60.

Schadewaldt, W. 1966. *Iliasstudien.* Berlin.

Schein, S.L. 1984. *The Mortal Hero: An Introduction to Homer's Iliad.* Berkeley, Los Angeles, and London.

Schlunck, R.R. 1976. "The Theme of the Suppliant-Exile in the *Iliad*." *AJP* 97:199–209.

Schmidt, J.-U. 1986. *Adressat und Paraineseform: Zur Intention von Hesiods "Werken und Tagen." Hypomnemata* 86. Göttingen.

Schmitt, A. 1990. *Selbstständigkeit und Abhängigkeit menschlichen Handels bei Homer: Hermeneutische Untersuchungen zur Psychologie Homers.* Akademie der Wissenschaften und der Literatur, Mainz: Abhandlungen der geistes- und sozialwissenschaftlichen Klasse, Abh. 5. Stuttgart.

Schofield, M. 1986. "*Euboulia* in the *Iliad*." *CQ*, n.s., 36:6–31.

Segal, C. 1971. *The Theme of the Mutilation of the Corpse in the Iliad. Mnemosyne*, suppl. 17. Leiden.

Shapiro, H.A. Forthcoming. *Myth into Art: Poet and Painter in Classical Greece.* London.

Silk, M.S. 1987. *Homer: The Iliad.* Cambridge.

Snodgrass, A.M. 1974. "An Historical Homeric Society?" *JHS* 94:114–25.

Stagakis, G. 1975. *Studies in Homeric Society. Historia*, Einzelschr. 26. Wiesbaden.

Taillardat, J. 1982. "ΦΙΛΟΤΗΣ, ΠΙΣΤΙΣ ET *FOEDUS*." *RÉG* 95:1–14.

Taplin, O. 1992. *Homeric Soundings: The Shaping of the Iliad*. Oxford.

Thornton, A. 1984. *Homer's Iliad: Its Composition and the Motif of Supplication*. Hypomnemata 81. Göttingen.

Tredennick, H., and Tarrant, H.A.S., trans. 1993. *Plato: The Last Days of Socrates*. Harmondsworth.

Tsagarakis, O. 1979. *Phoenix's Social Status and the Achaean Embassy. Mnemosyne*, suppl. 32. Leiden.

Verdenius, W.J. 1985. *A Commentary on Hesiod: Works and Days, vv. 1–382. Mnemosyne*, suppl. 86. Leiden.

Weil, S. 1956. *The Iliad; or, The Poem of Force*. Trans. M. McCarthy. *Pendle Hill Pamphlet 91*. Wallingford, Pa.

Weintraub, S. 1985. *A Stillness Heard Round the World: The End of the Great War, November 1918*. London, Sydney, and Wellington.

West, M.L. 1978. *Hesiod: Works and Days*. Oxford.

Whitley, J. 1991. "Social Diversity in Dark Age Greece." *ABSA* 86:341–65.

Wilamowitz-Moellendorff, U. von [1928] 1962. *Hesiodos Erga*. Reprint. Berlin.

Willcock, M.M. 1976. *A Companion to the Iliad*. Chicago and London.

Williams, B. 1985. *Ethics and the Limits of Philosophy*. London.

———. 1993. *Shame and Necessity*. Berkeley, Los Angeles, and London.

Wilson, J.R. 1979. "Καί κε τις ὧδ' ἐρέει: An Homeric Device in Greek Literature." *Ill Cl St* 4:1–15.

Winnington-Ingram, R.P. 1980. *Sophocles: An Interpretation*. Cambridge.

Zanker, G. 1986. "The *Works and Days*: Hesiod's *Beggar's Opera*?" *BICS* 33:26–36.

———. 1987. *Realism in Alexandrian Poetry: A Literature and Its Audience*. London, Sydney, and Wolfsboro.

———. 1988. "τιμή in Hesiod's *Theogony*." *BICS* 35:73–78.

———. 1990. "Loyalty in the *Iliad*." *PLILS* 6:211–27.

———. 1992. "Sophocles's *Ajax* and the Heroic Values of the *Iliad*." *CQ*, n.s., 42:20–25.

Index

Achilles: and Achaian community, restored to, 109–13; and Achaian victory, 93; Adkins' neglect of, 3f.; and Briseis, 11, 16, 89; cursing *cholos* (wrath or anger) and *eris* (strife or conflict), 17, 59, 79, 101f.; and "double determination," 120f.; and Eëtion, 8f., 28, 41, 74, 91, 108, 118; early death, knowledge of, 8, 77–79, 81f., 96f., 100; accepting gods as arbitrators of fairness, 115, 118–21, 125; of Hektor as an *aristos*, 110; Hektor, ransoming of, 110–26; Hektor's corpse, preparation of, 17, 116, 119; Hektor's supplication for reciprocal respect in treatment of corpses, rejection of, 20, 106f; honor, reasserting role of, 115–17, 121–23, 125, 127f.; Isos and Antiphos, former kindness to, 74; Kalchas, defense of, 9, 57, 75; Lykaon as *philos*, 104f.; Lykaon's supplication, rejection of, 24, 74f., 103–6; magnanimity of, 4, 20, 28, 37, 41, 44, 113, 118, 120, 123–30, 135, 137f., 149, 151, 153f.; magnanimity of, unique in early Greek epic, 137–54; *nemesis* of, 10, 24, 31, 58, 88, 91; Phoinix on the Litai and Meleagros for, 34–36, 85, 88; pitilessness of, 23–25, 41; pity and respect, need for, rediscovered by, 115, 118–21, 125; supplication as an index of emotional and moral state of, 102; Tros' supplication, rejection of, 102; and the two jars of Zeus, 62, 122f., 130, 149f.; Zeus, respect for, 118–21, 128, 148f.; Zeus grants *kûdos* to, 12, 30, 121, 128, 148; Zeus orders acceptance of Priam's supplication, 30, 116, 118f.

—and Agamemnon: dispute with, 3f., 17, 30f., 37, 57, 75–79; former generosity to, 31, 36f., 39, 73–75, 146; insouciance over gifts of, 101; missing *charis* (gratitude) of, 37, 81–83

—and embassy: concessions to affective appeals of, 88–90; considered to be behaving wrongly after, 93f.; continues to talk in terms of *tîmê* after, 94–98; on "double destiny" to, 82f.; equation of honor and death in, 81–84; honor spurned in, 79–91; on *kêr* (doom) and *moira* (portion, death) to, 81–84; rejecting supplication of, 10f., 79–97; within rights till rejection of, 10f., 24, 31, 88, 91; thrown back on affective responses after, 92, 108; unmoved by appeal to *xeniê*, 34; unmoved by *philotês*-appeal of, 10, 13, 20f.

—and Hektor: as an *aristos*, 110; preparation of corpse of, 17, 116, 119; ransoming, 110–26; rejecting supplication for reciprocal respect in treatment of corpses, 20, 106f.

—and Patroklos: affective component in desire to avenge, 7f., 99f.; affective relationship with, 10f.,

161

Index of Passages

171